W9-AGH-802

The New York Times
Book of
Personal Finance

Also by the author:

The Great Merchants (with Tom Mahoney)
The Anatomy of the Floor

The New York Times
Book of
Personal Finance

by
Leonard Sloane

Times
BOOKS

For My Mother and Father

Library of Congress Cataloging in Publication Data

Sloane, Leonard
　　The New York Times book of personal finance.

　　Includes index.
　　1. Finance, Personal.　I. New York Times.
I. New York Times.　II. Title.
HG179.S53　1987　　　332.024　　　84-40426
ISBN 0-8129-1160-1

Manufactured in the United States of America

9 8 7 6 5 4 3

Acknowledgments

MANY MONTHS WERE SPENT CONDUCTING research and interviewing experts in the various subjects that are covered in this book. So many people provided help to me in this undertaking that I hesitate to list them all, but I would like to credit those who were of particular assistance.

My thanks first to Herbert Paul, a New York tax lawyer who read the entire book, chapter by chapter, and offered dozens of valuable recommendations and criticisms. In our discussions about personal finance, he always reached the heart of the question quickly and expertly, thereby allowing me to focus on the most significant and useful coverage of the field.

In addition, I owe a special debt of thanks to David S. Rhine, a partner in the certified public accounting firm of Seidman Seidman/BDO. After the passage of the Tax Reform Act of 1986, he suggested a number of changes in the book that would bring this edition up to date and made many helpful comments on the revised chapter on taxes.

Among the others to whom I wish to express my gratitude for reading portions of the manuscript are James Balog, Drexel Burnham Lambert; Julian Bush, Shea & Gould; Walter Bussewitz, American Council of Life Insurance; Peter T. Elinsky, Peat, Marwick, Mitchell & Company; Joel S. Isaacson, Weber, Lipshie & Company; Robert W. Johnston, Credit Research Center; Marvin Kaplan, Kaplan Company; John Maloney, Citibank; John

Marion, Sotheby's; Sam Schiff, Insurance Information Institute; Alice Shabecoff, National Urban Coalition's Community Information Exchange; David Shechet, Shechet, Haskin & Company; and Michael Sumichrast, National Association of Home Builders.

I am deeply indebted to John M. Lee, an assistant managing editor, and Fred Andrews, the financial-business editor, of *The New York Times*, for their encouragement, advice, and suggestions concerning personal finance. Jonathan B. Segal, vice president and editorial director of Times Books, was also extremely helpful in the development and execution of the ideas in this book.

Special thanks also go to Kenneth P. Norwick, of the law firm of Norwick & Schod, for his assistance when the book was conceived. In addition, I am grateful to Carol Guttman for her outstanding editorial services.

No words can adequately express my appreciation to my family: my wife, Annette, and my sons, Elliot and Steven. Their love and support during the long months that this book was in progress were of inestimable help in bringing the process to a conclusion. Without them to prod and motivate me when my energies lagged, and to counsel me during both research and writing, there would have been no book. In effect, they share the authorship with me.

Of course, there can be no sharing of the blame in the event that problems later arise. Any errors, misinterpretations, and shortcomings are mine alone.

Leonard Sloane

Preface

THIS BOOK BRINGS TOGETHER IN one accessible volume the basic elements of personal finance for individuals and families. As such, it can serve as a guide through the tricky economic rapids that Americans must maneuver in their continuing efforts to do a better job of earning, saving, and investing.

Never before have people faced as many choices. Deregulation, which recently has affected so many industries in the United States, has swept through financial services as well. Whether in banking, insurance, securities, real estate, or other aspects of money management, the opportunities for selectivity have spread to such an extent that people everywhere are confused and uncertain.

The New York Times Book of Personal Finance presents these various alternatives in a concise, direct format. The emphasis is on providing enough information so that you can make your own well-informed selections in the financial marketplace. Financial counselors may advise you, and salespeople of various financial products may attempt to sell them to you, but the final decision must, and should, be yours. And with a better understanding of the concepts and vocabulary of personal finance, your chances of making the right decision at the right time will be very much improved.

This updated edition was researched and revised after the enactment of the landmark Tax Reform Act of 1986. Many vital changes affecting the personal financial lives of millions of Americans were made by this overhaul legislation—and its effect on virtually all aspects of financial planning has been, and will continue to be, enormous.

An entirely new Chapter 3, on taxes, was therefore prepared to highlight the key elements of the law and its implications for individuals and small businesses. Other sections of the book were also revamped in keeping with other modifications of the Internal Revenue Code.

If this book has any predilection, it is to talk *up*, rather than *down*, to the reader. The assumption here is that readers are intelligent men and women, knowledgeable in many different fields and probably aware of many of the aspects of personal finance that are discussed. The hope is that when you read the following chapters, or refer specifically to one or more of them, you will find enough data and interpretation to serve as a solid basis upon which to understand the points that are presented. If you find it necessary to investigate a matter further, the groundwork will have been laid and the initial knowledge obtained may lead you to the additional sources.

Personal financial planning means, moreover, that you are dealing with a moving target. Your goals may vary as the years go by, while the laws, regulations, and procedures governing your planning will certainly change, if they have not already done so. But the essential precepts of taking control of your own financial affairs will not alter, nor will the strategies and tactics that govern the planning which should be undertaken by everyone.

In order to simplify the sentence structure of the book, the words "he" and "his" have been generally used throughout, instead of "he or she" and "his or hers." This selection of words was made for ease of reading only and is not meant to slight women—whose desire to learn more about personal finance is often as great, if not greater, than that of men.

Contents

IV.   Real Estate

V.   Planning for the Future

Part One

Money Basics

Chapter One

Your Net Worth

PERSONAL FINANCIAL MANAGEMENT BEGINS WITH an accounting of where you have been, where you are now, and where you would like to be in the future. Until you create a written record of your current and anticipated future levels of financial activity, you cannot realistically expect to move forward with an intelligent and sustained program of saving, investing, borrowing, earning, and spending money.

Thus a sensible approach toward managing your personal or family funds should start with a determination of your net worth—the excess of your assets over your liabilities. Although all too few men or women are willing to sit down with pencil, paper, and calculator to work out the numbers, such a personal computation is well worth the effort. Just as a Wall Street securities analyst can scan the balance sheet and profit-and-loss statement of a corporation to find out what it has accomplished and where it is headed, so can an individual get a handle on his financial well-being by studying his own personal financial dossier. Without such a tabulation, moreover, it is difficult to properly establish a family budget and plan ahead with authority and confidence.

1

There are other reasons for wanting to know, at least once a year, how much you are worth. Knowledge of your net worth can help you make adjustments now to minimize, if not eliminate, certain taxes. Knowing how you stand financially is also of value in figuring out what you can afford to do or buy, both as a worker and as a retiree. In short, your net worth is a benchmark of your financial success, a numerical indicator of your position in life, and a symbol of what you have accumulated during your working years.

THE PERSONAL BALANCE SHEET

To calculate net worth, an individual, like a corporation, must draw up a balance sheet. Although the procedures in developing a personal balance sheet may not be as sophisticated as they are in the corporate world, the techniques are nevertheless the same—a presentation of your assets on one side and a list of your liabilities on the other. The former, of course, should exceed the latter, or else you are in financial difficulties.

One caveat before starting: Don't be concerned if your calculations are not always precise. If you cannot come up with exact numbers in each category, plunge on with this exercise nevertheless. Approximate the figures as best you can when tallying your assets and liabilities. The very fact that you are taking the time and trouble to undergo this annual personal inventory makes it all the more probable that you intend to exercise self-discipline against overspending, to maintain good financial habits, and to do whatever is necessary to wind up with a higher rate of savings and investment.

The essence of a balance sheet is that both assets and liabilities are presented as of a specific date. It is a "still picture" of finances that can and do fluctuate from day to day but are assumed to be in balance when this document is prepared. Therefore it is best to select a convenient date—such as the last day of a month or the end of the year—as the target for bringing together your personal financial data.

To get the process under way, assemble the principal records of your present financial circumstances. Banks or other institutions may provide printed forms, but you can use any type of ruled paper for the listings. Simply draw a line down the center and list your assets on the left side and your liabilities on the right side.

Cash and Cash Equivalents

The first category in the asset column should be cash and cash equivalents. This listing would include, of course, the money in your checking and savings accounts. A subcategory might also take note of the cash surrender value of your life insurance and your present equity, or vested interest, in a corporate pension or profit-sharing plan.

Securities and Investments

Next comes the total market value of your securities and investments, as of the date that the balance sheet is compiled. You can locate many of these prices in your local newspaper's financial section, while the others can probably be obtained from a stockbroker. This section of the balance sheet encompasses such assets as mutual fund shares, Treasury issues, and money market investments, as well as the conventional common and preferred stocks and corporate and municipal bonds. Real estate acquired solely as an investment, like commercial property or undeveloped land, should also be included here.

Real Estate

Owner-occupied real estate is another major classification covering your ownership of a home or homes, whether it is a house, condominium, cooperative apartment, or vacation cottage. List only the actual market value of all your real estate assets—a real estate broker, current newspaper ads, and recent sales by neighbors may be useful in helping you come up with the right amount—even if the purchase price may have been lower or if there are outstanding mortgages on the property.

Personal Possessions

The most difficult category to assess on the asset side of the ledger is the market value of those personal possessions that have significant resale value. It makes sense to evaluate these items as conservatively as possible, since the amount that you would realize from a forced sale would in all likelihood be much less than the purchase price. Check the local classified advertisements to get an idea of the fair depreciated value of such items as automobiles, jewelry, antiques, furniture, and furs—and you will probably come up with a realistic figure.

Other

Finally, place all of your remaining assets in a catchall category and add it to the list. Among them might be such items as trade or professional tools and equipment, a loan receivable, or a closely held business investment.

Mortgages Outstanding

At the top of the liability column for most American families is the amount still outstanding on the primary residence mortgage. This category is designated as mortgages payable and would also incorporate money owed on any other real property in your possession.

Installment Loans

A second broad classification of liability is installment loans due for big-ticket items, such as a car, an appliance, furniture, or a contractor's services. To compute the overall amount, multiply your total monthly payments by the remaining number of months before the various contracts are repaid.

Accounts Payable

Accounts payable to companies and individuals for any reason are still another liability. This category would include current payments owed to department stores, utilities, oil and credit card companies, as well as to doctors, dentists, and other professionals with whom you deal. Here, too, the balances outstanding should be totaled to arrive at the composite amount payable.

Other

The last section of the liabilities column is usually a wrap-up of miscellaneous personal debts. In this category are past due accounts, pledges to charities, and loans outstanding on insurance policies. Federal, state, and local taxes due, if not an unusually high figure, may also be lumped together under miscellaneous.

Now it becomes a relatively simple task to figure out your net worth, by adding all of your assets and all of your liabilities separately and then subtracting liabilities from assets. And when a net worth statement is compiled every year, you can easily determine if you are progressing, retrogressing, or standing still financially. Naturally you won't be able to get your hands on the overall amount of your net worth immediately, since so much of it is in the form of physical, or fixed, assets. But you can go on from this realistic bottom-line number to develop other measures to quantify your family's financial well-being.

THE MONTHLY BUDGET

One financial record that every family ought to prepare is a monthly budget, listing planned income and spending, as well as highlighting the areas where alterations can effectively be made. This budget, which can be consolidated easily on a quarterly and annual basis to avoid distortions, ought not to clamp a set of restrictions on family spending. Instead it should be as simple as possible in order to avoid arguments over insignificant sums and constrictions on your personal lifestyle. Remember that the type of budget that works for the family next door may not work for yours.

Nevertheless, a budget is a money management system by which you can detail your various fixed expenses, outline which variable expenses are available for pruning, and demonstrate statistically how discretionary dollars may be utilized for more worthwhile purposes. A budget also gives you an occasion to closely examine every substantial family expense to learn whether contractions or expansions are necessary.

It is easy to think of reasons for not bothering with a budget. Some might say that this form of financial planning takes too much effort and energy. Others might claim that budgeting is a useful technique for corporations, governments, and wealthy individuals, but of little value to the average family. But these rationalizations do not address themselves to the primary advantage of budgeting—minimizing or eradicating financial surprises. With a properly prepared budget, your anticipated income and obligations are brought into balance in advance, thereby avoiding financial crises stemming from an imbalance. So it is important not to be put off by the idea of budgeting. A good budget is a means of identifying goals and establishing a step-by-step program for reaching them. A budget can also help you explore new financial dimensions and reduce taxes. By dividing your spending into major categories and channeling your available funds into them as appropriate, a budget provides the guidelines within which you can choose to operate for optimum results.

A good way to get started is to find out where your money is going now. You can then determine where the fat is in your present spending and how it can be turned into fiscal muscle. Doing so is not as hard as it may seem at the outset, since the proper listings can be made on the basis of records that you probably already have. Moreover, your budget need not be divided into highly restrictive compartments, nor need it attempt to be any more strictly defined than to the nearest $100.

To draw up your monthly budget chart, or income-and-expense statement, you can use two sheets of paper—one for income and the other for outgo. On the right side of each page, make three columns, headed last month, next month's target, and next month's actual spending.

Income

The categories under income are few and for most families would embrace regular take-home pay from the salaries of husband and wife, other earnings from whatever sources, and additional income from such items as interest, dividends, and capital gains. Pay stubs, bankbooks, and confirmation slips usually provide the basic information covering last month's portion of the income sheet. If there are any questions, it makes sense to underestimate the numbers, rather than overestimate them.

Outgo

Outgo requires more complicated figuring and is likely to have a half-dozen or more categories—many of which have subcategories listed below. First are fixed obligations, like mortgage or rent payments, insurance premiums, installment loan payments, and tuition costs. Then every family has a large number of monthly variable obligations, with food, clothing, entertainment, and laundry among the most prominent. Transportation expense is a category all its own, as are medical and dental costs, and a monthly allocation for expected savings and investment. There are also a variety of household operating expenses—gas and electricity, home heating, telephone, repairs, and improvements. And finally you should leave some room for discretionary expenses that would cover such things as recreation, alcohol and tobacco, newspapers and magazines, contributions, and vacations.

Once the pages are ready for the actual numbers to be inserted, take out your canceled checks and check stubs for the last month. Also dig up other spending records that you may have, including credit card receipts, bills, and store register tapes. Divide all of these checks and records into piles corresponding to one of the outgo categories. Then by adding the amounts in each pile, or estimating where there is no documentation, you have a fairly accurate profile of last month's spending pattern.

Budget Analysis

Now the moment has arrived when your judgment comes into play. Are you pleased with this spending pattern? Are your expenses for entertainment so high that you are not putting as much money as you would like into savings or investment? Are you able to reduce your household expenses to allocate more for a vacation fund? What other changes could be made that would help you meet your short- and long-range goals?

Every family must decide for itself how much money, or what percentage of its income, to allocate to each category. The rules of thumb that guided spending in the past have been overturned by the current changes in lifestyles. For example, the belief that the cost of carrying a home, whether by a rental check or a mortgage payment, should not exceed 25 percent of take-home pay is no longer as widespread as it once was because of the increasing cost and scarcity of housing. And the "typical" family of four for which these rules were made—the working father, the stay-at-home mother, and the two school-age children—is no longer typical in this era of two-paycheck families, frequent divorce, and modern living relationships.

Your budget analysis involves an estimation of how you intend to spend your money next month and for the rest of the year. Using the chart detailing last month's spending as a model, and taking into account the desired changes, project your finances for the forthcoming month.

Fixed obligations are difficult to change even slightly, since the consequences of missing a mortgage payment or letting your life insurance lapse are usually too severe even to contemplate. Obviously it is possible to reduce your fixed obligations by, say, moving to a less expensive apartment or converting your life insurance from whole life to term and thereby paying lower premiums. But the greatest opportunities by far to make the changes in your spending pattern lie in your variable expenses.

If you are serious about wanting to save or invest more, the money will probably have to come from one or more of these categories. Can you postpone or even forget about that vacation? Can you substitute other food for steak on your dinner table? Can you cut out your weekly movie or your monthly weekend in the country? Can you manage with one car instead of two?

Be realistic about your projected cutbacks or else you may find yourself with such a strict budget that you cannot, or will not, live with it. If you set spending limits that are impossible to meet, you are only kidding yourself. And don't forget that lots of small expenses may not show up as a separate category or subcategory but could still add up to a large enough sum to throw your budget out of whack.

Miscellaneous expenses for telephone calls, snacks, and impulse purchases should not be overlooked. Provide for personal allowances in your plan and let all the family members, children included, decide how to handle their own allotments. Nor should the possibility of a personal emergency or property damage be neglected. Perhaps an additional category in your budget for the unplanned and the unexpected ought to be included with a definite amount set aside each month.

Once the new month is over, compare your actual expenditures with the targeted spending. It is unlikely that your projections worked out to the dollar, and the comparisons between the planned and actual spending columns will show the degree of difference. Fine-tune your budget as the months go by according to your experiences. Your figures are not cast in bronze, and they can and should change with circumstances. Don't let these alterations get you down, even if you have to modify your targets regularly throughout the year. Your budget is a guide to spending as you would like to spend—and nothing will serve you better in preparing and sticking to a budget than your innate common sense.

ORGANIZING FAMILY RECORDS

The personal balance sheet and personal budget are valuable tools in planning an individualized financial strategy. But you should also organize and maintain the records and other important papers on which your strategic decisions are based. Such documents include stock and bond certificates, mortgage records, personal papers, tax returns, and receipts for major purchases. And these records should be accessible not only for your perusal but also to a spouse or to an executor in the event of an emergency.

Organizing these key records so that others can work with them, moreover, gives you a better grasp of your own personal finances. As you assemble your papers and list your most meaningful documents, you may find holes in your financial planning program that should be plugged. As soon as you come across such missing links in the program, try to obtain the necessary records and put the required information in its proper place.

Many important papers should be stored in a safe deposit box at a bank. Stocks and bonds, whether registered in an individual's name or in bearer form, are best kept there, as are home mortgage papers, trust agreements, contracts, and automobile titles. Birth and marriage certificates, citizenship and naturalization papers, divorce and adoption agreements, and military service papers, while not directly involved in financial planning, are often of use in verifying information that affects your financial status and should also be retained in a safe deposit box. Photocopies for your files at home should be made of any documents that are used often.

Current financial records, however, should be stored in your home. A steel filing cabinet with manila folders, a strongbox, large metal or cardboard boxes, or even cigar boxes are potential storage areas for this type of information. Whatever you use, the storage place should be convenient to where you handle your personal bookkeeping. These records can be filed either alphabetically or by category, although the latter is usually faster to work with at income tax time.

Receipts for medical, dental, and drug bills ought to be kept in the current file at least until the end of the year for which you complete your tax return. Other receipts—for items like automobiles, furniture, and appliances—should also be retained, both as proof of the value of these items and as evidence if you take an unusually large sales tax deduction on your income tax. Retention of charge account and credit card statements, with the proper receipts attached, could also be useful, since the interest payments indicated on the statements are tax-deductible.

Another section of your current file should include a record of monthly mortgage or rental payments. If you owe money to an individual or an individual owes money to you, a record of the appropriate payments, as they are made, should be on file as well. Also essential to this file are all of your bank records for the current year, including statements, passbooks, deposit slips, and canceled checks. The backup data on securities transactions, ranging from confirmation slips to monthly or quarterly statements, also ought to be included.

When you complete your tax forms, the receipts and other information used to compile the final figures should be removed from the current file and stored separately with your tax-return copies. Then the same folders can be used as you repeat the procedure, collecting the appropriate receipts for the following year.

It is also advisable to prepare two special compilations. One is an inventory noting where all your major personal and financial documents are located: in your safe deposit box, in your file at home, or elsewhere. This reference sheet or sheets should include the names, addresses, and telephone numbers of your key advisors—lawyer, accountant, stockbroker, insurance broker, and anyone else who is to be contacted in connection with your finances when you are unable to handle your own affairs.

The other compilation is of all the vital numbers in your family's financial life. Starting with Social Security numbers and including the numbers of your insurance policies, your securities, your bank accounts, and your credit, charge, and other cards, this list can prove to be invaluable in case the actual records are lost or destroyed. Copies of both lists should be placed in your safe deposit box and in your file at home—and also given to your executor as a further precaution.

UNDERSTANDING INFLATION

Balance sheets, budgets, record-keeping, and compilations are essentially contrivances for personal financial management. But without an understanding of how inflation—an increase in the general price level—erodes your present and future buying power, these tools are little more than mechanical devices.

Economists define two basic types of inflation: demand-pull and cost-push. Demand-pull inflation refers to a condition in which consumer and industrial prices keep rising, triggered by a continuing high demand for bank loans or a sharp rise in exports. Cost-push inflation, the most common kind in recent years, describes a situation in which consumer and industrial prices keep increasing to meet the costs of a continuing demand for higher wages.

Whichever type of inflation is stronger at any particular moment, one of the greatest difficulties it creates is the pervasive attitude among consumers that prices will always rise, which then tends to become a self-fulfilling prophecy. As you and your neighbors accept spiraling prices as a way of life, there are widespread knee-jerk demands for higher wages, higher prices, and automatic cost-of-living adjustments. The automatic fuel adjustment on gas and electric utility bills is just one example of how inflation permeates everyday life in the United States.

In the late 1970s, the annual inflation rate was in double digits. When economists later talked about an inflation rate of "only" 8 or 9 percent, many families thought they were much better off. Yet at 8 percent inflation, the price of goods and services will more than double in about nine years. Individuals rush to seek out investments that will "beat" inflation, frequently rejecting yields of 8 percent as too low because that rate is no higher than the inflation rate.

What inflation does to the typical family, then, is create unrealistic expectations that they attempt to fulfill for their self-content. As millions of Americans see it, salaries must rise more quickly than inflation, expenses must not increase any faster—and any deviation from this desired end is disastrous. One reason for the recent large upsurge in personal bankruptcies has been an overwhelming impetus for many consumers to spend their disposable income to beat the inflation rate—leaving them without a financial cushion for unplanned expenses or emergencies.

Your family's goal should be financial security. It comes when you have developed and sustained a workable money management plan for both the short and the long term. And this plan will be most personally rewarding when you see results from your own efforts.

You work for your money in order to spend it, but spending can be in the form of a mortgage payment, a dinner at a fine restaurant, a vacation, or ten shares of common stock. If you can arrive at the objective of having more discretionary income after taking care of your basic requirements, you will, at the very least, enjoy the realization that you have more control over your earnings than your earnings do over you.

The remainder of this book will be devoted to ways and means of helping you make the most of the myriad money management decisions that you face throughout your life. To shape the best decisions, you must be familiar with the possibilities available, you must be comfortable with the language used by salespeople and others in the field of personal services, and you must be aware of the underlying concepts upon which well-founded judgments are based. An understanding of personal finance is as important to you as an understanding of corporate finance is to Wall Street. And there is no better time than the present to begin.

Chapter Two

Banking

IT USED TO BE SO very simple. There were clear-cut distinctions between the various kinds of financial institutions. On one side were commercial banks and on the other stood thrift institutions. Thrift institutions consisted of savings and loan associations, mutual savings banks, and credit unions, and each had its special niche in the banking world.

Today the lines have become so blurred that they scarcely exist. Checking accounts, once the sole province of commercial banks, are now offered by institutions under other names as well. Interest-bearing checking accounts, once unheard of, are now common in all kinds of banking establishments. All institutions offer variations of long-term certificates of deposit, under such names as money market certificates or small-saver certificates.

Yet even now there are distinctions. In many instances, the interest paid to savers and charged to borrowers differs, depending on the institution. Charges for services offered are not the same everywhere, and some bankers may even offer a particular service free in order to attract business. A good example are the MasterCard and Visa credit cards issued by banks, with some charging a fee for the card, others charging no fee under certain circumstances, and a variety of different rates of interest for bills unpaid after the specified grace period existing throughout the industry.

In deciding which bank or banks to choose, therefore, it pays to shop around to find the one or ones that best fit your needs. Among the considerations that might go into this decision are: Is the bank conveniently located? How do its charges stack up against its competitors'? Does the branch have a twenty-four-hour automatic teller machine for obtaining cash and handling other transactions at odd hours? What is the general attitude of the tellers and officers? Is the bank's policy on loans to a depositor more favorable than to a non-depositor? And, of course, are accounts at the institution insured—as the overwhelming majority are—up to $100,000 per account by an agency of the federal government, such as the Federal Deposit Insurance Corporation, the Federal Savings and Loan Insurance Corporation, or the National Credit Union Administration?

Here are the major categories of financial institutions, along with their basic characteristics:

COMMERCIAL BANKS

Commercial banks call themselves full-service banks to denote that they offer a full spectrum of services to savers and borrowers. There are approximately 15,000 commercial banks in the United States, ranging from the giants, Bank of America in California and Citibank in New York, to much smaller institutions in towns across America. Commercial banks, most of which are members of the Federal Deposit Insurance Corporation, are sometimes known as trust companies because of the fiduciary, or trustee, services to corporations and individuals that they also provide.

A bank's basic financial structure is divided into two broad classifications: assets and liabilities. Assets include the loans and mortgages on which the banks receive interest. Liabilities are primarily the deposits by the public on which the banks pay interest. Bank profitability is largely determined by the difference, or spread, between the interest rates a bank charges for loans and mortgages and the interest rates it pays for deposits.

On the asset side, commercial banks have in their arsenal virtually every type of loan imaginable. Business loans represent the largest portion, but there are also all kinds of consumer loans—either secured by a borrower's property or unsecured. If you need an installment loan, a guaranteed student loan, or a personal loan, a bank is one of the first places to go on your comparison shopping tour. Commercial banks are also increasingly offering mortgages, although many of them are in the form of loans on business and industrial properties, as opposed to loans on houses, condominiums, and cooperative apartments.

On the liability side at commercial banks, checking accounts are the major type of deposit account held by customers. In addition, most of these banks offer a variety of savings accounts and certificates, with an often confusing miscellany of names and levels of interest rates. The offerings range from passbook savings accounts to a collection of long-term certificates, with higher interest rates pegged to formulas often related to Treasury bill rates.

THRIFT INSTITUTIONS

Thrift institutions, encompassing savings and loan associations and mutual savings banks, were originally created to encourage savings and promote home ownership. But they have since diversified into a broad range of other services. Today many savings and loans, which have their greatest concentration in the Far West, and savings banks, which are strongest in the Northeast, are often barely distinguishable from commercial banks.

Savings and loans are also known as building and loan associations, savings associations, and cooperative banks. Approximately 5,000 units are now functioning under charters from either the federal government or one of the states. The bulk of the savings and loans are members of the Federal Savings and Loan Insurance Corporation.

With fewer than 500 operating, savings banks are far less numerous. In most instances, savings banks provide insurance to their depositors through the Federal Deposit Insurance Corporation.

Home mortgages traditionally constitute the bulk of the thrift institutions' loans outstanding. In recent years, many savings and loans and savings banks have been plagued by the enormous number of long-term, low-interest mortgages outstanding, while interest rates paid to depositors on shorter-term certificates have risen. This negative spread has been responsible for the surge of government-assisted acquisitions of many weaker thrifts by stronger banks and savings and loan associations.

As for deposits, thrift institutions concentrate on savings accounts and both short- and long-term certificates of deposit. Most of them also offer, however, a variety of checking accounts widely referred to under the acronyms of NOW accounts and Super NOW accounts.

CREDIT UNIONS

Credit unions are a special kind of thrift institution—cooperative ventures for saving and lending created by individuals with a common bond. This common bond might be employment in the same company or industry, membership in the same union or professional association, or residence in the same area. Whatever the connection, a credit union brings together people with something in common in order to establish a nonprofit institution and, theoretically at least, to offer financial services at lower cost. There are approximately 12,000 federally chartered credit unions and another 8,700 state-chartered credit unions.

Members of a credit union are technically shareholders, rather than depositors, but their shares, in most cases, are insured by the National Credit Union Administration, one of the federal deposit insurance programs. The typical credit union offers a slightly higher interest rate on regular savings accounts than savings and loan associations and savings banks, plus free life insurance up to a relatively small limit on each account. A modest premium is also the norm when it comes to longer-term certificates issued by credit unions.

In recent years, more and more credit unions have begun to offer share draft accounts—interest-paying transaction accounts that are their version of the checking-like instruments offered by other thrift institutions. Share drafts are the equivalent of a check on your credit union account, with the money in the account continuing to earn interest until the draft clears.

Loans issued by credit unions are usually for automobiles, home improvements, and other general purchases, but some unions have expanded their programs and also offer larger loans for homes and other major purchases. Collateral requirements are often not as stringent as at more impersonal financial institutions, especially in/the case of credit unions for workers at a particular corporation. In addition, employees can repay their credit union loans—and make deposits into their accounts—through the relatively painless method of a payroll deduction plan. Such automatic deductions are an aid to those who are unable or unwilling to budget a regular fixed percentage of their wages for savings.

CHECKING ACCOUNTS

The two basic types of deposits are checking accounts and savings accounts. Although different names may be used for such accounts, depending on the institution, and each of the two broad categories has a number of varieties, your bank accounts probably fit into one or both of these primary purposes.

Checking accounts have become popular because checks offer a convenient alternative to cash kept around the house or separately purchased money orders for bill-paying purposes. They also give an accurate running record of how most of your money is being spent and provide an excellent proof of payment as well. Although there have been, and will undoubtedly continue to be, moves to create a checkless society through automatic or telephone-generated withdrawals from bank accounts or the increasing use of bank cards, checks are still the most important device for transferring money from one person to another. Automatic, preauthorized electronic payments may be the wave of the future, but right now they are by no means as widely used a method of moving dollars as checks.

Checking accounts can be opened in the name of an individual, more than one individual, a company, a trust, or an organization. Signatures must be on file with the bank authorizing the proper persons to write checks against a particular account. Not only must there be sufficient funds in an account for a check written against it to clear, but deposits made by check cannot be drawn upon until the bank receiving the deposit is satisfied that it will obtain these funds from the bank on which it was drawn. In cases where the second bank is in a distant state, you may be forced to wait as long as three weeks or more before being able to use the deposited funds. Some states, however, have set limits on clearance delays and federal legislation has been proposed to do the same thing.

Monthly Statements

Banks normally issue their checking account customers monthly statements itemizing all deposits and withdrawals during the period. You can reconcile the statement with your checkbook by using a form usually included in the monthly enclosure. When discrepancies arise between the bank's figures and your own, you should rectify them as soon as possible by recomputing your figures. If you still cannot find the error, contact the bank for assistance in determining how to reconcile your bankbook balance and the statement balance. A service charge for stopping payment on a check, overdrawing an account, or providing a duplicate statement—which are among the fees that some banks levy—could account for the disparity.

Checking accounts—which banks call demand deposits, since withdrawals can be made at any time simply by writing checks—come in two traditional forms: regular and special. However, an ever-expanding number of variations now exist in keeping with greater competition and the breakdown of barriers separating commercial banks and thrift institutions.

Regular Checking Accounts

With a regular checking account, a minimum balance is required at all times, typically an average of between $100 and $500. With such a balance, there are usually no fees for writing checks, making deposits, or maintaining the account. If the balance falls below the minimum amount, though, monthly maintenance, per check, or penalty charges may be imposed. If you can maintain the minimum balance—thereby losing the interest on whatever amount would not otherwise be in this account—and you write a lot of checks every month, a regular checking account is your best bet.

Special Checking Accounts

Special checking accounts do not have minimum balance requirements. Instead there is generally a monthly fee of, say, $2 or $3, plus a charge per check of 10 or 15 cents. Some banks even charge special checking account holders a fee for making a deposit or for each individual item on their deposit slips. A special account makes sense if you write relatively few checks, so that the per check charges and monthly maintenance fee add up to less than the interest lost on the extra funds kept in a regular account to maintain the minimum balance.

Other versions of checking accounts being marketed and advertised by banks include overdrafts, whereby automatic lines of credit up to a certain limit are added to your regular or special checking account so that you can write checks for more money than you have in the account; electronic transfers, whereby funds can be deposited, withdrawn, or moved among accounts in the same bank through twenty-four-hour automatic teller machines; and bill-payer services, whereby money is transferred monthly or on another schedule to regular creditors.

NOW and Super NOW Accounts

Many thrift institutions—and commercial banks as well—use a device that looks like a checking account but is called a negotiable order of withdrawal, or NOW, account. With such accounts, which have no interest rate ceiling, your funds continue to earn interest until the "check" that you have written goes through the clearing process. Super NOW accounts, or money market checking accounts, are ceiling-free transaction accounts that operate the same way but require higher minimum deposits than NOW accounts.

SAVINGS ACCOUNTS

Savings accounts are offered by financial institutions in many different formats, such as passbook accounts, money market deposit accounts, and a variety of certificates of deposit. Passbook accounts offer the flexibility of withdrawing or depositing money at any time without penalties, while certificates commit you to maintain the deposit for a specific period to obtain the higher interest rates offered. If you have, or want, to make an early withdrawal with a certificate, a penalty and loss of interest are usually imposed.

Basic day-to-day passbook, or statement, savings accounts no longer have an interest rate ceiling and require no minimum deposit. With a passbook account—still called by that name although many financial institutions have changed their formats to monthly statements—savings are completely liquid. Depending on the institution, interest is compounded daily, monthly, semiannually, or annually. This can make a difference in the amount of interest earned, regardless of the type of account, as seen in this example:

Savings Growth

What a Weekly Series of $1 Deposits Will Grow to in the Future at 10 Percent Interest

	Daily Compounding		Monthly Compounding		Quarterly Compounding		Semiannual Compounding		Annual Compounding
Year		Year		Year		Year		Year	
1	$ 54.78	1	$ 54.73	1	$ 54.70	1	$ 54.68	1	$ 54.65
2	115.42	2	115.19	2	115.09	2	114.97	2	114.76
3	182.52	3	181.99	3	181.75	3	181.44	3	180.89
4	256.78	4	255.78	4	255.33	4	254.72	4	253.63
5	338.96	5	337.29	5	336.55	5	335.51	5	333.64
6	429.92	6	427.34	6	426.19	6	424.58	6	421.65
7	530.57	7	526.83	7	525.15	7	522.79	7	518.47
8	641.97	8	636.72	8	634.37	8	631.06	8	624.97
9	765.25	9	758.13	9	754.94	9	750.43	9	742.11
10	901.68	10	892.25	10	888.02	10	882.03	10	870.98
15	1835.86	15	1805.33	15	1791.69	15	1772.26	15	1736.37
20	3386.67	20	3307.63	20	3272.44	20	3222.33	20	3130.08
25	5961.15	25	5779.37	25	5698.83	25	5584.36	25	5374.67
30	10235.04	30	9846.15	30	9674.74	30	9431.85	30	8989.60

Source: Thorndike Encyclopedia of Banking and Financial Tables

Banks figure savings account interest in a number of different ways. Calculating by the day-of-deposit to day-of-withdrawal method, interest is based on the actual number of days that the funds are in the account. With the last in–first out method, the yield is calculated from the day of deposit to the end of the interest period, and withdrawals are subtracted from the last deposit, so that earlier deposits accrue interest longer. Using the first in–first out calculation, the yield is also figured from the day of deposit to the end of the interest period, but withdrawals are charged against either the first deposit in that period or its beginning balance. And computing by the low balance method, the yield is calculated only on the lowest amount in the account during the interest period. Day-of-deposit to day-of-withdrawal accounts usually pay the highest interest.

If your savings account has the "deposit grace days" feature, it means that you can make a deposit by the tenth day of a month, yet earn interest from the first day of that month. "Withdrawal grace days" let you take out funds a few days before the end of an interest period without losing interest. Some banks insist that you keep at least a small amount of money in your account until the end of the interest period in order to earn any interest for that period at all.

MONEY MARKET DEPOSIT ACCOUNTS

Money market deposit accounts with no rate ceiling were created by commercial banks and thrift institutions to compete with the money market funds offered by mutual fund organizations. The accounts are especially designed for individuals who want to earn money market rates of interest but do not want to tie up their funds in certificates of deposit or who expect interest rates to rise.

The interest rate on money market deposit accounts is adjusted upward or downward periodically, usually every week in keeping with changes in the overall money market. You can make unlimited deposits into and withdrawals from such accounts at the bank but are permitted to write only three checks every month.

The minimum balance required for these accounts was $2,500 in 1984. But the Depository Institutions Deregulation Committee—the federal interagency group established to phase out restrictions on interest rates and balances at financial institutions—made changes that reduced this requirement to $1,000 at the beginning of 1985 and eliminated minimum balances entirely at the beginning of 1986.

CERTIFICATES OF DEPOSIT

Certificates of deposit, also known as savings certificates or term accounts, are advantageous when you are willing and able to keep money in an account for a specified time. CDs pay a higher rate of interest than the passbook rate because of the requirement that the funds be kept in the account for a fixed period. Since 1983, minimum deposit requirements and all interest-rate ceilings were removed from fixed-term accounts maturing in more than 31 days. And, depending on the bank, there is a certain amount of flexibility in the purchase of CDs.

For example, with some accounts, you can withdraw the interest as earned, although the principal cannot usually be touched. With others, you are permitted to deposit additional funds to the principal amount. In the instances where you are permitted to withdraw money prior to maturity—the option allowing you to do so is the bank's, as stipulated in the agreement signed when you opened the account—advance notice is often required and penalties are imposed. Most banks, however, have penalties of one month's interest if the original maturity of the CD is a year or less and three months' interest for certificates with longer maturities.

Maturities of CDs generally range from three months to ten years, with the interest rate typically rising as the term of the certificate increases. Until recent years, maximum interest rates were set by law, but virtually all interest-rate controls on CDs have since been removed. The most popular CDs with the public have proven to be those with six-month maturities.

Although most bank term certificates have fixed rates, there are some variable-rate CDs on the market as well with

rates indexed to, say, Treasury securities or the prime lending rate. Furthermore, certain banks have established a procedure whereby the interest rate available on a CD is tied to the
amount invested—the bigger the deposit, the greater the rate.
Other banks offer extra interest on CDs to individuals who
maintain checking or other accounts there. And still others design
the exact maturity of a CD to meet a customer's needs—the so-
called Gucci CD.

Seven- to Thirty-One-Day CDs

Even shorter-term certificates entered the banking picture
when seven- to thirty-one-day accounts paying current market
interest rates were authorized late in 1982. When they were created, these accounts paid interest at the three-month Treasury
bill rate at thrift institutions and one quarter of a percentage
point less at commercial banks. But now there are no rate ceilings
at all, just as with the longer-maturity CDs.

Deposit Insurance

Whether you have a checking or a savings account and whether
you prefer passbook savings, a money market account, or a certificate of deposit, it makes sense to keep your funds in an institution where accounts are insured by an agency of the federal
government. Accounts are insured for a maximum of $100,000
by each of the three federal agencies that do so. You can, however, obtain insurance for larger amounts by establishing accounts
in different banks or by setting up other accounts in the same
bank according to what bankers term a separate "right and ca-
pacity." This could mean a joint account, an account in the name
of a spouse or child, or a trust account. The rules governing
deposit insurance are quite specific, so when in doubt ask a bank
officer or inquire at the appropriate insuring agency.

SAFE DEPOSIT BOXES

Another important service of depository institutions is a vault
containing safe deposit boxes that are rented to the public. These

lockboxes—which typically range upward in size from 1½ by 5 by 22 inches and cost from about $15 to more than $300 a year—are places to store items that you want to be better protected from theft or fire than would be the case in your own home. Although laws governing safe deposit boxes vary from state to state, experts say that the things to keep in a safe deposit box are generally articles of intrinsic value. The things not to keep there are documents that are needed in a hurry when the owner dies.

Articles to Be Kept in a Safe Deposit Box

Among the articles that fit into the intrinsic value category are securities, mortgages, titles and deeds, court decrees, and important personal documents, such as birth and marriage certificates, military service records, adoption agreements, and citizenship papers. Valuables—such as jewelry, rare coins and stamps, and family heirlooms—are also best stored in a safe deposit box.

In addition, it is worth preparing and placing in your box an inventory of the property in your home, including the purchase dates and prices. If you have photographs of these items, serial numbers of your electronic and electrical equipment, and details about heirlooms and collectibles, so much the better.

Articles to Be Kept Out of a Safe Deposit Box

It is usually not advisable to keep an original will in a safe deposit box because a time-consuming legal procedure must be followed in many states to allow someone else to "enter" after the death of the boxholder. In those states, banks immediately seal a safe deposit box once the boxholder dies and will not permit anyone—even a family member or an executor who has the key—to open it until authorized to do so by a court or a state taxing authority. Therefore the original will, along with such documents as cemetery deeds and burial instructions, might be better held by your lawyer, executor, or accountant, with a duplicate put in a safe place at home.

Large amounts of cash represent another category of items that do not belong in a lockbox. Some financial advisors believe that such holdings are an unacceptable moral hazard. The presence of a substantial amount of cash in a safe deposit box could be construed as an indication of criminal activity or intent to evade income taxes.

Finally, unregistered property belonging to others has no business being in your box. Jewelry or negotiable bearer bonds that are unregistered by name, even though the property of another person, may be presumed instead to be owned by the boxholder. After the death of the owner of the box, it becomes the burden of his estate to prove otherwise—a burden that can be difficult, if not impossible, to overcome.

Individual Versus Joint Ownership

Many families rent safe deposit boxes under the joint ownership of the husband and the wife. This may be convenient when both parties are alive, but a number of disadvantages of joint ownership in many states make individual ownership a better idea.

For example, joint ownership of the box generally does not mean that the contents are jointly owned. Unidentified items, such as jewelry and silver, will be deemed to belong to the first owner to die. Moreover, in the case of a husband and wife, this property will not come under the provision of the 1981 tax law that only half of the value will be taxed to the estate of the first joint owner to die. Furthermore, the box will be sealed following the death of the first joint owner to die, just as in the case of a single-owner box.

Access rights can be assured to both parties just as easily as joint ownership by having a single owner, with the other spouse signing a bank access power form allowing entry. Be careful about using a printed general power of attorney form, since it may run into resistance from some banks that prefer—or insist—on their own forms.

Safe Deposit Box Insurance

Although a safe deposit box, as its name indicates, is designated as a place of safekeeping and is certainly a more secure storage location than a mattress, drawer, or strongbox at home, the possibility nevertheless exists that the items in the box may be stolen or destroyed by fire. The odds are slim, however, given the elaborate security and protection systems that most banks have in their vaults, but thefts amounting to an aggregate of millions of dollars' worth of property have occurred.

State laws vary as to the rights of those who rent boxes and those who use them. There is therefore no clear-cut answer to the question of which party is liable when a safe deposit box is burglarized. And banks are sure to assert that as long as they exercise reasonable care and diligence in safeguarding the contents of a box, they are relieved of any further liability to the user.

Despite the disclaimers that many banks make on their application cards and elsewhere, some victims of a lockbox burglary have sued their banks to recover their losses—and at times have been successful in obtaining partial or full reimbursement. A number of banks, in fact, have purchased safe deposit insurance to provide for claims of this kind. But banks that are so protected rarely mention the fact, since some safe deposit officials feel this type of advertising could be construed as admitting to customers and potential customers that their vaults are not safe.

As a result, many renters have purchased special insurance policies for the contents of their boxes, in addition to their personal floater policies and homeowner policies. You can purchase burglary and robbery coverage tailored specifically for safe deposit box owners, including most valuables but excluding cash. Such coverage eliminates the necessity of suing a bank and proving its negligence through expensive and time-consuming litigation before receiving reimbursement for losses.

At the very least, you should know the precise contents of your safe deposit box in the event of any emergency. An inventory can be made on a plain sheet of paper or on a checklist form provided by insurance companies. But remember to keep this record at home—and not in the box whose contents are described.

Chapter Three

Taxes

THE UNITED STATES HAS A a rigid tax structure and no one has the legal right to evade taxes. But all of us have the right to avoid paying one penny more than we are required to pay.

Judge Learned Hand, the distinguished American jurist, expressed it well in his dissent from a 1947 decision by the United States Court of Appeals for the Second Circuit: "Over and over, courts have said that there is nothing sinister in so arranging one's affairs as to keep taxes as low as possible. Everybody does so, rich or poor; and all do right, for nobody owes any public duty to pay more than the law demands: Taxes are enforced exactions, not voluntary contributions. To demand more in the name of morals is mere cant."

The taxes faced by the average family are often overwhelming. Taxes are paid not only to the federal goverment, but also to many states, cities and counties. The types of taxes include sales taxes, real estate taxes, estate taxes, gift taxes, and of course, the most pervasive category of them all: income taxes.

The Internal Revenue Code, the compilation of federal laws detailing the imposition and collection of income taxes, was completely revamped in 1986 by the most sweeping overhaul of the nation's tax structure in the 73-year history of the federal income tax. The revisions in the code achieved by the Tax Reform Act (TRA) of 1986 were so extensive that most individuals will have to develop an entirely new frame of reference when calculating their taxes.

TRA was initially billed as a measure to foster greater fairness and simplicity in tax preparation and collection. The question of fairness in the new law will probably be argued for many years. But there's little doubt that its simplicity at this point raises more questions than it resolves. Numerous complications have been added to the already problematic routine of determining how much tax is due to Uncle Sam.

No summary therefore can do justice to the treacherous waters of this landmark legislation. Nevertheless, it is important to understand at least the basics of the law in order to file your tax returns as accurately as possible and to plan for the future in an organized manner.

THE TAX REFORM ACT OF 1986

The following is an outline of some of the most important elements of TRA that affect individuals and small businesses. The general effective date of most provisions is January 1, 1987, although there are many exceptions:

Individual Tax Rates

This, the most publicized aspect of the law, creates just two basic tax brackets, 15 percent and 28 percent, instead of the 15 brackets ranging from 11 percent to 50 percent that had been used previously. In addition, there is also a marginal tax rate of 33 percent for married people filing jointly with taxable incomes between $71,900 and $149,250, and for single filers with taxable incomes between $43,150 and $89,560. But because these individual rate cuts do not become effective until March 15, 1987, the two-bracket system will not be fully in place until 1988— after which annual adjustments will still be necessary to offset inflation.

This means that in 1987 a blended structure will be in effect, encompassing both the old and the new rates. In that year, there will be five brackets: 11 percent, 15 percent, 28 percent, 35 percent and 38½ percent.

Tax Brackets for a Married Couple Filing Jointly

1986

Taxable Income	Rate
$0–$3,670	0%
$3,671–$5,940	11%
$5,941–$8,200	12%
$8,201–$12,840	14%
$12,841–$17,270	16%
$17,271–$21,800	18%
$21,801–$26,550	22%
$26,551–$32,270	25%
$32,271–$37,980	28%
$37,981–$49,420	33%
$49,421–$64,750	38%
$64,751–$92,370	42%
$92,371–$118,050	45%
$118,051–$175,250	49%
Above $175,250	50%

Source: Joint Committee on Taxation

1987

Taxable Income	Rate
$0–$3,000	11%
$3,001–$28,000	15%
$28,001–$45,000	28%
$45,001–90,000	35%
Above $90,000	38.5%

1988

Taxable Income	Rate
$0–$29,750	15%
Above $29,750	28%*

*There is, in effect, a higher rate for joint taxpayers with income above $71,900.

Filing Levels

Taxpayers must generally file an income tax return, according to TRA, if their gross income equals or exceeds certain levels. Among the largest classes of taxpayers, those income levels for 1987 and 1988, respectively, are: single people under age 65, $4,440 and $6,350; married couples filing jointly with both under age 65, $7,560 and $8,900; and married couples filing jointly with both age 65 or over, $10,000 and $10,100.

In some instances, taxpayers do not have to file at all if their gross income does not equal or exceed the amount of their personal exemption. An exception to this rule are taxpayers with unearned income over $500 claimed as a dependent by another and taxpayers that cannot claim any standard deduction.

Personal Exemptions

The personal exemption, the equivalent of a deduction, has

been sharply increased for every individual, spouse and dependent. Compared with an exemption of $1,080 (indexed for inflation) in 1986, the amount was changed to $1,900 in 1987, $1,950 in 1988, and $2,000 thereafter, after which it will again be indexed for inflation. There are no longer extra exemptions for men and women who are blind or who are at least 65, though they have been given an additional standard deduction.

However, the benefit of a personal exemption—including those for a spouse or dependents on the same tax return—will be phased out beginning in 1988 for upper-income taxpayers. The phase-out is accomplished by adding a 5 percent surcharge to the 28 percent rate, with the amount of income subject to this 33 percent rate depending on the number of exemptions that are claimed.

A dependent claimed on another tax return cannot take a personal exemption on his own return. Until TRA, many dependents received a double tax break, since they could claim an exemption on their returns and still be claimed as a dependent by a family member providing more than half of the dependent's support.

If you do claim a dependent who is more than four years old, that dependent must have a Social Security number, which must be included on your return. This requirement was inserted to make it easier for the Internal Revenue Service to determine when the same dependent is being claimed illegally by two different taxpayers, primarily divorced or separated parents.

Standard Deduction

The standard deduction, which in recent years had been called the zero bracket amount, returned in 1987 with an increase, giving nonitemizers an opportunity to pay lower taxes. This flat deduction rose in 1987 to $3,760 for married couples filing jointly and $2,540 for single filers—and will advance further in 1988 to $5,000 for joint filers and $3,000 for single taxpayers. Afterwards, this deduction will be adjusted each year for inflation.

A standard deduction for blind taxpayers and those 65 and over has been added to the one that everyone else receives. The amount is $600 for each blind or elderly person and $750 if the blind or elderly person is single.

Five classifications of taxpayers are not eligible for the standard deduction. They are: married taxpayers filing separately if either spouse itemizes, nonresident aliens, American citizens with excludabe income from United States possessions, individuals who file for periods of less than a year because of accounting changes, and estates, trusts or partnerships.

Itemized Personal Deductions

A number of familiar personal deductions and other tax preferences were eliminated by TRA, and others were restricted. For example, state and local sales taxes are no longer deductible, while the floor on deducting unreimbursed medical expenses rose to 7½ percent from 5 percent of adjusted gross income. What's more, the deduction for a two-income married couple filing jointly has been repealed and the deduction for contributions to charitable, educational and religious institutions has been retained only for those who itemize.

Job-related moving expenses can also be claimed only by employees and self-employed persons who itemize their deductions. A new floor of 2 percent of adjusted gross income has been created to limit write-offs for miscellaneous expenses, such as safe deposit box rentals, job-related education costs, legal, accounting and investment counseling fees, professional and union dues, subscriptions to investment, advisory or professional publications, and most unreimbursed employee business expenses.

A big change affecting millions of taxpayers constrains the deductibility of personal interest on consumer debt for items like car loans, credit card finance charges and Internal Revenue Service interest charges, which will be abolished over a five-year period beginning in 1987. Interest on debt for investment purposes can in general be deducted only up to the amount of an individual's investment income, a cutback that also has a five-year phase-in. Thus the real cost of many loans can double for some taxpayers.

As for mortgage interest deductibility, it has been limited to that on a principal or a second residence. Deductions can be made only to the extent that the amount of the loan does not exceed the purchase price plus home improvements, along with medical and educational loan costs. In no case can the loan be larger than the fair market value of the home, minus any outstanding mortgage. Under a grandfather clause, interest on debt incurred before August 17, 1966, however, is deductible even if it is larger than the cost of the residence.

Deduction for the Self-Employed

A self-employed individual can deduct 25 percent of the amount he pays for himself under an insured or self-insured health or accident plan, up to that person's earned income. But the deduction—available to both itemizers and nonitemizers—cannot be claimed by anyone eligible for participation in another plan provided by his or his wife's employer.

If the health plan covering the self-employed person also covers his employees' dependents, it may also be used to cover his own dependents. Whatever is not deducted under this classification, however, is deductible under the medical expense classification and subject to its 7½ percent floor.

Income Averaging and Earned Income Credit

The law repealed income averaging, which had been a useful technique for those whose income in one year was substantially higher than it had been in recent years. No longer can taxpayers save money this way when their income in the averaging year is $3,000 higher than 140 percent of their average taxable income in the three prior years.

In contrast, the earned income credit, which provides a subsidy for low-income workers who maintain a household and have dependent children, has been increased. This credit is now 14 percent of the first $5,714 of earned income, for a maximum of $800. There are also annual inflation adjustments and phaseouts of the credit above certain levels of adjusted gross income.

Additional Reportable Income

Among the items that have become taxable as a result of TRA are the portions of college or university scholarships and fellowships won by degree candidates that are utilized for room, board, equipment and travel. All of the scholarship and fellowship funds received by nondegree candidates are taxable, as are certain federal grant funds for which the recipient has to perform future services as a federal employee.

In order for prizes for scientific, literary or artistic merit to be considered tax-exempt, the winners must designate a tax-deductible charity to which the award will be given. The maximum annual exclusion from taxation of income earned abroad by United States citizens has been reduced to $80,000 in 1987, $85,000 in 1988, $90,000 in 1989, and $95,000 in 1990. And unemployment compensation benefits paid to most taxpayers are now fully taxable too.

Fringe Benefits

Certain frequently used fringe benefits were reinstated by TRA. The tax-free status of group legal services plans was extended so that employees will not be taxed for employer payments for legal services. Similar treatment was provided to educational assistance plans, with the annual tax-free benefit raised to $5,250 for each employee.

Most employee benefit plans, moreover, now fall under comprehensive nondiscrimination rules regarding eligibility and benefits. Among the categories of plans covered by these rules are health plans, group-term life insurance plans and dependent care assistance plans.

Capital Gains

Another major tax change is the elimination of the long-standing special tax treatment of long-term capital gains, which most recently has been defined as profit on assets held for more than six months. With the removal of the favorable 60 percent exclusion from income for long-term gains—which placed a ceiling of 20 percent on such gains, based on the former maximum tax bracket of 50 percent—all capital gains are now taxed at the same rate as ordinary income. The one difference is that in the transition year of 1987, the top long-term capital gains rate is 28 percent, even though the maximum rate for ordinary income and short-term capital gains is 38½ percent.

Furthermore, both long-term and short-term capital losses now offset ordinary income on a dollar-for-dollar basis. When capital losses cannot be deducted against ordinary income in one year—the maximum allowed is $3,000 annually—they can be carried forward to future years.

Gains on sales of securities sold on securities exchanges must be recognized on the actual trade date, rather than the settlement date. In the past, those who realized such gains on securities sold during the last few days of one year and did not receive payment until the following year also had the alternative of utilizing installment reporting and being taxed in the payment year.

Home-Office and Hobby Deductions

Before passage of the law, some individuals avoided the strict requirements on deducting home-office expenses—which include regular and exclusive usage of the office as a principal place of business or to meet customers—by renting a portion of their home to their employer. But this may no longer be done, even if the individual is an independent contractor to a company rather than an employee.

The home-office deduction, moreover, has been limited to the net income connected with the office in the home, not to the net income of the entire business. So when deducting rent, depreciation, utilities and insurance related to the home-office, the overall amount cannot be used to create or increase a loss from the business as a whole, although deductions can be carried forward into subsequent years.

Deductible hobby expenses are lumped together with other miscellaneous itemized expenses and subject to a 2 percent floor. In order to take this deduction, you must demonstrate that this activity is a business, which can be accomplished by showing profits in three out of five consecutive years. Horse breeding or racing requires two-out-of-seven-year profitability to be considered a business.

Individual Retirement Accounts

TRA cuts back sharply on the little guy's shelter by restricting the tax-deductible contribution to individual retirement accounts for many taxpayers. It does so by limiting the full deduction of $2,000 annually of earned income, or $2,250 for a spousal I.R.A., when individuals are active participants in a company-funded retirement plan and have an adjusted gross income above a certain level. Of course, taxes on the earnings of an I.R.A. continue to be sheltered for all workers, so that a tax incentive still exists to some extent for retirement savings to be made this way.

Participants in corporate pension and profit-sharing plans, as well as members of Keogh plans, can deduct their full payment into an I.R.A. if their income is no more than $40,000 when married or $25,000 when single. Such participants lose a proportional part of the deduction if their income is between $40,000 and $50,000 when married and between $25,000 and $35,000 when single. For plan members with income above $50,000 when married and $35,000 when single, there is no deduction for an I.R.A. contribution.

401(k) Plans

The popular 401(k) plans, also known as salary reduction plans or cash-or-deferred accounts, were restricted by TRA. The maximum amount that employees can earmark for deferral via these plans each year was lowered from $30,000 to $7,000, with adjustments to be made beginning in 1988 in keeping with increases in the Consumer Price Index. No more than 25 percent of annual compensation can be deferred in such a plan, though.

The law tightened the rules established to forbid discrimination in 401(k) plans in favor of highly compensated employees, thereby limiting the percentage of individuals in this category at a company who may participate. Matching employer contributions must also be made on a nondiscriminatory basis.

Other limitations imposed on 401(k) plans include restricting hardship withdrawals for such situations as medical emergencies to an employee's actual elective deferrals, prohibiting new plans by state and local governments or tax-exempt employers and requiring all loans from a plan, except for a principal residence, to be repaid within five years. On the other hand, plan sponsors may no longer require more than one year of service for participation and cannot make 401(k) deferrals a condition for receiving other benefits, except for matching contributions.

Withdrawals From Retirement Plans

Under TRA, there is a general 10 percent penalty on early withdrawals from qualified retirement plans by everyone, not just owners of 5 percent or more of a business. An early withdrawal is one made before age fifty-nine-and-a-half, death or disability.

A number of exceptions were provided to escape this 10 percent penalty tax. You can roll over a withdrawal into an I.R.A. or other retirement plan or you can take it as a life annuity without paying a penalty. Another exemption from the penalty is distributions to most employees for unforeseen hardship, a category covering medical expenses. Most workers who are age fifty-five or older and take early retirement are also not affected by the penalty.

When a withdrawal is made from most plans, it is treated on a pro-rata basis. Only part is tax-free as a return of the employee's contribution, while the remainder is taxable. And a 15 percent penalty will be imposed on annual payouts from a plan to the extent they are more than 125 percent of the defined benefit dollar limit. That limit is five times greater for lump-sum distributions.

Life Insurance

Although the inherently tax-advantaged nature of life insurance has been retained, the law made some significant changes. The exclusion allowing a beneficiary who is also a spouse and who selects the alternative of collecting the proceeds in installments to get $1,000 worth of interest tax-free every year has been repealed. A penalty of 10 percent has been imposed on withdrawals from any annuity prior to age fifty-nine-and-a-half. And the tax-favored treatment of insurance to cover pre-arranged funeral expenses has been limited to $25,000.

The I.R.S. position on nondeductibility of interest on certain policyholder indebtedness was also reaffirmed by TRA. Any consumer loan incurred to purchase or carry single-premium life insurance is not tax-deductible.

Family Tax Planning

Not only is the differential between the highest and lowest income tax brackets much less than it was pre-TRA, but it has also become much more difficult to shift income among family members. Thus two techniques that had formerly been frequently used to transfer income from a higher-taxed member to a lower-taxed member are not as effective as they once were.

One way that family income-splitting is stifled is a measure that taxes all unearned income of a child under age 14 in excess of $1,000 at the top tax rate of his parents, regardless of who provided the assets. This "kiddie tax" affects custodian accounts at banks and securities firms under the Uniform Gift to Minors Act, as well as other accounts set up in the name of a young child. When the child reaches 14, all investment earnings, as well as wages, are generally taxed at his rate.

The other casualty of the law is grantor trusts—led by the well-known Clifford trusts, but also including spousal remainder trusts—through which assets are shifted to a child or other person for a specified period before being returned to the grantor. Since the income from these assets is now taxed to the grantor, instead of to the beneficiary as before, such trusts have lost their tax advantage. Even some older trusts in which the beneficiary is a child of the grantor and under 14 have lost their effectiveness as an income-shifting device.

Employee Achievement Awards

Certain employee achievement awards for length of service or safety are excludable from reportable income. However, these honors must be tangible personal property awarded during a significant presentation, in an effort to prevent them from being used as disguised compensation. If the awards are in the form of cash, gift certificates or similar items, they have to be reported as income.

To exclude length of service awards from taxable income, they must be received after the first five years of employment and the award winner must not have received such an honor during the previous five years. Similarly, to exclude safety awards from taxable income, they must not be given to managers, administrators or other professional employees who are not normally responsible for meaningful safety work.

The maximum that a recipient of these awards may exclude is $400 annually for each award and $1,600 annually for all awards. Furthermore, the fair market value of these awards must be used in calculating this amount, instead of the wholesale value at which they may have been purchased.

Alternative Minimum Tax

The rate of the alternative minimum tax, which applies to upper-income taxpayers with many so-called preference items that reduce their regular taxes, has been increased to 21 percent from 20 percent. At the same time, the preferences that are added to an individual's regular income in computing this tax has been expanded to encompass many new items, among them deferred gains from certain installment sales. Missing from this list are two exclusions that have been eliminated from the code: the dividend exclusion of $100 for single filers and $200 for married filers, along with the 60 percent net long-term capital gain exclusion. Of course, when the alternative minimum tax exceeds your regular tax, you pay the alternative tax.

Also new in TRA is the phasing out of the exemptions applying to the alternative minimum tax, which amount to $40,000 for joint filers and $30,000 for single filers. The phase-out begins with alternative minimum taxable income of more than $150,000 if married or $112,500 if single. These exemptions are cut by 25 percent of the amount of that income exceeding these levels.

When a charitable contribution of appreciated property is made and the untaxed appreciation is allowed as a regular tax deduction, this appreciation now becomes a preference item. And net operating losses are deductible against minimum taxable income only to the extent of 90 percent of that income.

Municipal Bonds

Municipal bonds have historically enjoyed exemption from federal income taxes, based on the constitutional provision that the federal government may not tax obligations of state and local governments. But the law takes a step towards breaking down this wall of tax separation by subjecting some municipals to the alternative minimum tax.

The municipal bonds that fall under the minimum tax are new issues above specified amounts deemed to be in the private activity category and issued for nonessential functions. Such private activity bonds—so named because they provide benefits to private parties—are issued for broadly defined purposes like airports, hazardous waste disposal facilities, student loans, mass commuting facilities and single- or multi-family mortgages.

A further change affecting municipals is that all tax-exempt interest has to be reported on individual returns, despite the fact that no tax may be due. This requirement goes into effect with returns filed in 1988.

Travel and Entertainment Expenses

The rules for deducting travel and entertainment expenses have been toughened by TRA. Most noticeable is the provision limiting the deduction for business entertainment expenses to 80 percent of the cost, except for certain business banquets in 1987 and 1988.

The same 20 percent reduction was made in the deduction for business meals on overnight travel. Meals for which the business purpose is obtaining investment advice from a professional are no longer deductible at all. For any meal to be deductible as an entertainment expense, it must be directly related to or associated with the business—and business must be discussed before, during or after the meal. The "quiet business meal" for goodwill purposes, at which business is not actually talked about, is not deductible anymore. The meal or entertainment cannot be "lavish or extravagant" under the circumstances if deductibility is the objective, and the taxpayer or his representative must be present at the meal or entertainment.

No deductions for tickets to an entertainment event can generally exceed the stated ticket price, except when the purpose of the event is to benefit a charitable organization, the entire proceeds go to this charity and the event uses volunteers for most of the work. The deductions for leasing private luxury sports boxes, known as skyboxes and sold at a higher price than other seating, are being phased out over a three-year period.

Whatever part of employee unreimbursed travel and enter-tainment costs is deductible now must be aggregated with other miscellaneous itemized deductions. Employer reimbursements for these costs are not subject to the same 2 percent floor of adjusted gross income that affects this category of miscellaneous deductions.

Travel

In an effort to stem the perceived excesses by some taxpayers in expense account living, the law restricts deductions by business travelers on cruise ships, ocean liners and similar luxury water transportation. With relatively few exceptions, anyone choosing this method of transportation instead of faster and cheaper air-plane travel is limited to a deduction equivalent to twice the highest federal employee per diem travel allowance rate muli-tipled by the number of days in transit.

This restriction, however, is not applicable to conventions held on cruise ships. The existing rules permitting up to $2,000 worth of deductions for conventions on American-flag cruise ships traveling between ports in the United States remain unchanged.

Deductions are also barred for travel expenses by teachers and others for whom travel is a form of education. The deductibility of vacations disguised as charitable trips is ended, with allowances made only when there is "no significant element" of personal pleasure involved. And writeoffs are disallowed for the costs of attending seminars for investment purposes that are unrelated to actually carrying on a business.

Tax Shelters

Tax shelters—primarily units in limited partnerships in such fields as real estate, oil and gas, and equipment leasing—were for many years bought by taxpayers who sought immediate de-ductions against other income and the hope of capital gains when the shelter terminated. Under TRA, though, pure tax shelters have been largely abolished.

That's because write-offs are now more difficult to take, since all income received by individuals is divided into three categories:

active (salary and business profits), portfolio (interest, dividends, royalties and capital gains) and passive (a business in which the taxpayer does not materially participate). And losses from such passive activities, of which limited partnerships are the prime example, can be deducted only against income from these activities each year, although unusable losses may be carried forward to apply against passive income in future years.

These passive loss limitations, moreover, are retroactive, covering partnership investments that were made before January 1, 1987, as well as new shelters. But there is a four-year phaseout for such deductions held on the law's enactment date, with 35 percent subject to the new rule in 1987, 60 percent in 1988, 90 percent in 1990 and 100 percent in 1991 and beyond.

Among the exceptions are deductions for rental real estate, which, even though falling under the passive activity rule, permit those with an adjusted gross income of $100,000 or less to offset nonpassive income with up to $25,000 in losses. A further exception allows the use of up to $25,000 in losses against nonpassive income for investors with an adjusted gross income of $200,000 or less in low-income housing and real estate rehabilitation projects. And working interests in oil and gas drilling operations, which typically require greater involvement than the purchase of limited partnership units, continue to be fully deductible against all kinds of income.

Small Business Taxes

The maximum corporate income tax rate was lowered to 34 percent from 46 percent, effective July 1, 1987. But at the same time, the number of corporate tax brackets was cut to five from seven.

Bad debt deductions must now be made in the year that the debt actually becomes totally or partially worthless—a change that forces businesses to use the direct charge-off method. Formerly, they had the option of also utilizing the reserve method, whereby a bookkeeping reserve was created for bad debts and a deduction was made for each year's addition to that reserve.

Companies that sell under a revolving credit plan are not allowed to use the installment method for sales, paying tax on the profits of those sales as payments are received. Instead, the law requires them to report their net income in the year that the sale is made.

There are now also uniform rules affecting most small businessmen that apply to the deductibility of all costs incurred in manufacturing or construction. Interest costs will generally be capitalized where the interest is allocated to the construction of real property or the production of long-lived personal property.

Investment Tax Credit

The investment tax credit—representing the equivalent of a cash discount from the federal government for investments in business equipment, including a car used for business purposes—was abolished on a retroactive basis for any business property placed in service effective January 1, 1986. This action eliminated a desirable 10 percent credit for assets with a recovery period of five or more years and 6 percent for assets with a recovery period of three years.

To ameliorate the severe effects of the loss of the investment tax credit, transitional rules were created so that the changes are being phased in, rather than applied immediately. Those rules cover machinery that was acquired earlier than the date this provision went into effect but not actually placed into service until afterwards.

What's more, the amount of equipment that can be expensed, or deducted currently, by most small businesses is now $10,000 a year. But you cannot claim depreciation deductions on any portion of equipment purchases that has been expensed.

Business Vehicle Deductions

Automobiles used for business reasons and placed in service after 1986 are to be written off over five years, compared with three years in the pre-TRA years, thereby raising the cost of ownership. Moreover, the depreciation deduction cannot exceed $2,560 in the first year of ownership and $4,040 in subsequent years—a schedule that is slightly less favorable than the former depreciable amounts.

On the other hand, the rate at which expenses can be deducted has been accelerated in the early years of the writeoff. Thus business car owners can now deduct 63 percent of their expenses in the first two years of driving, compared with 52 percent under the previous procedure.

Real Estate Depreciation

For owners of real estate, not only was the depreciation period lengthened, but the rate at which property can be written off was also changed. Depreciation is an annual deduction that allows writeoffs of capital investments in property or equipment used for business purposes.

In the past, all real estate was depreciated over a nineteen-year period. But with TRA, residential rental property has to be written off over twenty-seven-and-a-half years and commercial property has to be written off over thirty-one-and-a-half years. Both kinds of property, moreover, must be written off using straight-line depreciation, which gives equal deductions during the entire period of depreciation. (In the past, accelerated depreciation, whereby a larger percentage of the cost is recovered in the earlier years of the investment, was also permitted.)

A related change places real estate under the limitations of the "at risk rules" for all property put into service after 1986. Those rules restrict writeoffs for losses on investments to the actual cash invested and borrowings for which the investor is personally liable. Previously, real estate was exempted from such restrictions.

Also limited is the depreciation deduction of owners of co-op apartments—legally referred to as tenant-stockholders who own shares of stock entitling them to occupy a particular apartment in the building—although such a deduction may be carried forward to future years. There is no longer any deduction for payments that should be charged to the capital account of the co-op.

Business Credits

The law extended a number of key business credits. The credit for research and development won an extension until 1988, although the percentage was cut to 20 from 25. The targeted jobs credit, created to encourage employment of the hard-to-hire and based on a percentage of wages, was continued. And the energy credits for solar energy, geothermal, ocean thermal and biomass were extended as well. But the individual residential energy credit was allowed to expire.

Choosing a Fiscal Year

Partnerships, personal services corporations formed by professionals, and S corporations—the kind in which taxes are usually imposed on the shareholders, rather than the corporations—must now use a taxable year that conforms to that of their majority owners. Before this rule was put into place, the owners of these closely held businesses could defer taxes for many months.

An exception to this rule is when the closely held business convinces the I.R.S. that it has a legitimate business purpose for the different fiscal years and that the tax deferral will be for no more than three months. Another is that a partnership does not have to adopt the tax year of its majority interest partners unless those partners have owned this interest for the three preceeding years.

Gift and Estate Taxes

The transfer tax on generation-skipping trusts—through which assets are given to someone in the generation below that of the person making the transfer—was tightened by TRA to plug a loophole. That loophole allowed grantors to avoid the transfer tax by establishing such a trust directly for the benefit of a grandchild, without an intervening interest in the trust by the parents of that grandchild. Now that kind of trust will be taxed, although, because of exemptions, it affects only the very wealthy.

Another modification is the establishment of a special tax rate schedule for nongrantor trusts and estates. In 1987, that rate starts at 11 percent on the first $500 of taxable income and rises to 38½ percent on taxable income of more than $15,150. Starting in 1988, it is 15 percent of the first $5,000 of taxable income, with the remainder taxed at 28 percent. When the taxable income of the trust or estate is between $13,000 and $26,000, the advantage of the 15 percent bracket is phased out.

Filing Requirements

To avoid a penalty for underpayment of taxes, you must file estimated returns when withholding does not satisfy your tax liability and the estimated tax is $500 or more. Quarterly estimated tax payments now have to total 90 percent of the current year's liability, up from the previous percentage of 80, or 100 percent of the former year's tax bill. Whatever is withheld from wages or salary is considered part of these estimated tax payments.

Trusts and estates are also required to make estimated tax payments. Estates, though, do not have to make such payments in the first two years.

The rate of interest paid on tax underpayments and overpayments has been changed, with different rates set for each and the prime rate eliminated as the benchmark. The tax underpayment rate is three percentage points higher than the federal short-term rate, while the tax overpayment rate is two percentage points above the federal short-term rate. But tax shelter deficiencies and sham transactions are penalized at the rate of 120 percent over the regular rate.

Substantial underpayments—defined as more than $5,000 or 10 percent of the correct tax, whichever is larger—are penalized with a tax of 20 percent. The penalty for failing to pay tax is 1 percent per month, regardless of when this failure occured, to a maximum of 25 percent. Negligence, or intentional disregard of I.R.S. rules, now is applicable to the entire Internal Revenue Code. And the fraud penalty is 75 percent of the amount of the underpayment attributable to fraud.

The I.R.S. may abate any interest charges that are generated due to certain governmental errors or delays, as long as the taxpayer is not partially responsible. But interest will be abated only for the time related to the failure of the revenue service to perform its routine administrative acts.

Chapter Four

Use of Credit

BORROWING HAS LONG BEEN PART of the American way of life. Polonius's aphorism in *Hamlet*—"Neither a borrower nor a lender be"—has given way to an enormous system of borrowing and lending that has enveloped the entire economy. Without credit, government, business, and individual spending would grind to a halt within a short period of time.

Consumer installment credit has particularly exploded since the end of World War II, when pent-up demand for durable goods helped to fuel the first of the postwar booms. In the 1970s alone, this form of debt increased by 68 percent. Not only did many more consumers use debt during the last decade, but the median amount of credit incurred soared as well.

Consumers have taken out loans to buy homes, automobiles, furniture, clothing, vacations, medical and dental care, and just about every other possible product and service available. Many have borrowed wisely and well, while many others have borrowed at the wrong time, the wrong place, or the wrong price. Your ability to be in the first category of borrower, rather than the second, has a lot to do with your ability to achieve financial fitness—both in real terms and as a state of mind.

Meaning of Credit

The word "credit" is derived from the Latin word *credo*, which means "I believe." A person who is credible is one who is believable. When you ask a bank, department store, or other source for credit, you are asking that source to believe in you.

Throughout history, credit has been one way of transferring resources from the haves to the have-nots. Early moral and legal codes often recognized two distinct types of loans. The first kind was of food, clothing, and other necessities—and interest was not allowed to be charged on these items. The second, of animals and seeds, was loaned to increase the numbers of what was borrowed. A portion of that increase, whether the firstborn young animal or the first crop harvested, was given as interest to the provider.

Now, of course, these distinctions have been eliminated and all borrowers are expected to pay interest on whatever loans they undertake, unless there are special circumstances like a loan from a family member or close friend. When people borrow today, out of necessity or for convenience, they rent a certain amount of money (the principal) for a certain length of time (the term) by paying interest (the finance charge).

Purposes of Credit

When you are considering the use of credit, there are a number of key factors to keep in mind. Is the purpose for which you are borrowing important enough to go into debt? Do you want to start consuming now, rather than later, badly enough to pay a hefty interest charge? Is the interest rate as low as possible for this purpose? Is there another source or sources of credit that might be better for you? And is there any potential danger from this debt that could cause you problems later?

Shopping for credit is as important, if not more important, than any other shopping you may do. And when you shop for anything, it is never smart to buy on impulse. With impulse buying, you often spend more than necessary and frequently wind up with a product or service that makes you unhappy.

Such is the case when you shop for credit. So many companies "sell" credit, and so many terms and interest rates are available, that it is easy to make the wrong decision if you rush. That wrong decision could cost you hundreds, if not thousands, of dollars. Take your time and shop carefully before going into debt.

THE COST OF USING CREDIT

Never, never sign your name on the dotted line before reading the truth-in-lending statement that the creditor is required to give you with the credit contract. But even before reaching this stage, you should satisfy yourself as to the real cost of the loan.

Annual Percentage Rate

The first consideration is to determine the annual percentage rate, or APR. This is the real finance charge and the best benchmark for measuring and comparing the cost of credit from different sources. Other interest rates do not give you the true picture of that finance charge and should always be converted into the annual percentage rate, which relates the cost of the loan to the amount of time you have the funds. If you borrow $100 and repay it in installments of $9 over twelve months, your total finance charge is $8. But that does not mean your annual percentage rate is 8 percent.

The reason is that you are paying back the debt in installments and have the use of the full $100 for only the first month. There is less principal available to you in each succeeding month. So when the annual percentage rate is calculated, it works out to 14.5 percent.

The next consideration is the overall finance charge in dollars. This is the amount of all of the financing expenses and should be made available to you both as a total and as monthly payments for a specified period.

For example, the interest cost per $1,000 for a loan with an annual percentage rate of 15 percent is $83 for one year, $163.52 for two years, $247.76 for three years, $335.84 for four years, and $426.80 for five years. Here is how those amounts compare with the interest cost per $1,000 for other selected annual percentage rates:

Total Interest Cost Per $1,000 of Credit If Repaid in Equal Monthly Installments over Various Periods of Time

Annual Percentage Rate (APR)	One Year	Two Years	Three Years	Four Years	Five Years
12%	$ 66.08	$129.68	$195.56	$263.84	$334.40
15%	83.00	163.52	247.76	335.84	426.80
18%	100.04	198.08	301.40	409.76	523.40
21%	117.32	233.12	356.12	486.08	623.00

Source: Household International

Finally, watch out for the additional charges that may be tacked on to the cost of the loan. These costs, such as service charges, do not have to be included in the quotation given by the lender as the annual percentage rate.

With all of this information at hand, you can make the various comparisons of available lending sources and select the creditor that is most appropriate. It may be that a prospective creditor charges a slightly higher annual percentage rate but requires a lower down payment or monthly payments. As a result, you may find this lender a more convenient source of the funds you need, even though the cost is greater. Whatever lending source you select, take the time to learn the facts about costs, terms, and other charges.

COMPUTING THE FINANCE CHARGE ON OPEN-END CREDIT

As you compute the cost of borrowing, it is important to understand how creditors calculate finance charges. There are three basic methods of computing open-end, or revolving, credit charges: the adjusted balance, the previous balance, and the average daily balance.

Under the adjusted balance method, the monthly finance charge is computed upon the balance remaining after giving credit for payments received during the billing period. With the previous balance method, no allowance is made for payments during the billing period, so the finance charge is levied on the entire amount outstanding at the beginning of the month. And under the average daily balance method, your balance for each day in the billing period is totaled and then divided by the number of days in the period.

Of the three computations, the adjusted balance method usually costs you less than the others. Let's say the outstanding balance at the beginning of the month is $1,000, the annual percentage rate is 18 percent (1½ percent a month), and a $100 payment is made on the fifteenth of the month. Your finance charge that month would be $13.50 with the adjusted balance method, $15 with the previous balance method, and $14.25 with the average daily balance method.

DETERMINING CREDITWORTHINESS

Credit is not available to everyone. Before any creditor will make credit available to you, certain standards must usually be met:

Ability to Pay

At the top of most creditors' lists in deciding whether they want to extend credit is your ability to repay the debt. Creditors look at your sources of income, which for most people are the regular wages earned on the job. Your income may also be derived, wholly or in part, from investments, alimony, or public welfare assistance. A lender must take these sources into account, as well as the stability of your earnings and, at your request, your credit record.

Collateral

In addition to earning power, creditors often also want collateral before granting credit. Collateral is something that a creditor has the legal right to take from you if you fail to repay the loan. When you buy a home, the house itself is collateral for the mortgage. Similarly, when you finance a car, the automobile is collateral. Other assets frequently used as collateral are stocks, bonds, savings accounts, and insurance policies.

Credit References

Lenders usually demand to see credit references, especially for large amounts of money. These references are others who have extended credit in the past—a bank, department store, utility, oil company—and can report on your performance. You can begin accumulating good credit references by applying for a retail or oil company credit card and paying your bills systematically. A favorable rating will be in your credit file the next time you need to borrow and will be a plus if you apply for a home mortgage, auto loan, or other major loan in the future.

TYPES OF CONSUMER CREDIT

Credit comes in different sizes and shapes. One way of differentiating it is by the method of payment, with the breakdown in two parts: single-payment credit and installment credit.

Single-Payment Loans

Single-payment loans are those paid back in one lump sum at maturity. Some are time loans, with a fixed maturity date for repayment, while others are demand loans, which are repayable whenever the lender makes a request for payment. Although some single-payment loans require interest to be paid monthly or quarterly, the key point is that the entire principal is due in one payment. Such loans are frequently renewable at the interest rate that is current at the time of renewal.

Installment Loans

In contrast, both interest and principal of installment loans are repaid in specific amounts at specific times. Such loans, which may be for a car or an appliance, are normally paid back monthly, with the most widely used schedules calling for paybacks over twelve to sixty months. Even if your monthly payments are equal during the payback period, you are paying more interest and less principal during the payments at the start of the loan than those at the end. Late charges are typically assessed for missed payments.

Secured Loans

Loans can also be divided into the secured and unsecured variety. Secured personal loans are those for which a specified item serves as security or collateral for repayment. For most secured loans, involving the purchase of a home or an automobile, the security is the product that has been purchased on credit. Passbook loans are secured by your savings account and require that you always retain the amount of the loan in your account. However, for other loans, the collateral is an item of value that is unrelated to the purpose for which credit was undertaken. For instance, jewelry or furs can be pledged as collateral with certain lenders who hold the property in return for granting a loan.

Unsecured Loans

Unsecured loans require no collateral and are granted on the basis of a person's credit rating and references. One of the most common kinds is signature loans issued primarily on the basis of a signed agreement to repay. For example, student loans issued under the Guaranteed Student Loan Program are signature loans, but with the important addition of a federal guarantee.

Similar to signature loans are line-of-credit loans that do not require a separate application every time you want an advance. Instead your credit is checked at the outset and a dollar maximum, or line of credit, is established for you. With such loans, you may borrow up to your limit at any time or, if the lender so specifies, for a certain period, such as a year or two.

A variation on line-of-credit loans are overdraft loans, which let you write your own loan up to your limit—in effect, an extension of your checking account. After a maximum amount has been established by a bank or other financial institution, you can use your regular checks even when there are not enough funds to cover them in the account. Such an overdraft automatically becomes a loan to you at an agreed-upon rate of interest and typically in multiples of $50 or $100. With overdrafts, the interest charge for the service generally begins when you use the line of credit and ends when you repay the amount owed.

Automobile Loans

Still another way of classifying loans is by the use to which they are put. For example, automobile loans are offered by a wide variety of lenders. At one time, such loans were restricted by creditors to three years, then they were extended to four years and now they have maturities of as long as five years—longer than the life of some cars. As the maturity increases, the monthly payment decreases, but the dollar finance charge rises. Most finance rates on used-car purchases are higher than those for buying a new car.

Debt Consolidation Loans

Many lenders also offer debt consolidation loans—large loans designed to give you enough money to repay all of your small ones. The result is lower monthly payments, since you have put all your debts into one basket and stretched out the payback over a longer period. At the same time, though, the interest rate on the new loan is probably higher than on the smaller debts, so that your total finance charge will be greater in the long run. Debt consolidation loans may make sense when you cannot keep up with your current payout schedule. But such a loan should not be undertaken without the realization that you will be paying more for the privilege of relieving some of the time pressures of repayment.

WHERE TO GET CREDIT

There is a wide variety of places from which to obtain credit, each with its advantages and disadvantages. Most depository institutions and other financial services companies are in business to make a profit—and lending funds at a higher interest rate than their own cost of money is a primary way for them to do so. Other concerns, like retailers and oil companies, whose principal businesses are in other industries, also extend credit to the public as a sideline to their primary activities. And sometimes private loans are available on a formal or informal basis from family, friends, or employers. But the major sources of funds for individuals are the companies in the financial community that are organized for the purpose of making loans.

Commercial Banks

Commercial banks are the best-known and most widely used institutions for borrowing. Although more of their lending is to business and industry than to the consumer, they represent a vital portion of the expanding consumer credit universe. In addition to personal and automobile loans, banks issue credit in such ways as mortgages, home improvement loans, and guaranteed student loans. Most commercial banks also issue the Visa and MasterCard credit cards through which they both extend credit on purchases and make cash advances.

Employed persons with an adequate income and a good credit history can generally borrow from commercial banks without cosigners. But some banks, especially in times of tight money, may give preference in lending to their regular depositors. Attempting to borrow from the same bank in which you have a checking or savings account, therefore, could be not only convenient, but also a means of insuring that your application will be looked upon with favor.

Thrift Institutions

Savings and loan associations and savings banks, known as thrift institutions, have historically concentrated their lending on home mortgages. In recent years, however, they have increased their other consumer lending to compete more with most other sources of credit.

These savings institutions, moreover, typically charge lower interest rates than other lenders for passbook loans and home improvement loans. Nevertheless, there are limitations in some states as to the number and degree of services that they are permitted to supply to their customers.

Credit Unions

Credit unions, which are thrift institutions that lend only to members, specialize in consumer loans and make very few loans to business. Most of them make personal, automobile, and home improvement loans. Some others with substantial memberships and resources make mortgage loans as well.

Because credit unions have the tax benefits of a cooperative, and often have low overhead and operating costs when they are located on the premises of the members' company, their finance charges on loans are normally lower than at other institutions. Many credit unions, run by fellow workers or club members, also provide free or inexpensive credit life insurance, a service that other lenders offer—if not insist upon—at a much larger fee. Remember that if you have a loan outstanding at a credit union restricted to employees and you change jobs, you may be required to immediately repay the entire amount outstanding.

Consumer Finance Companies

Consumer finance companies, also known as personal finance, small loan, or industrial loan companies, do not usually obtain their funds from customer deposits, like commercial banks, savings institutions, and credit unions. Instead they borrow from other sources and then relend to the public. In many states, they will lend in amounts as small as $100. Customers usually go to finance companies for personal loans, both secured and unsecured.

Some of these companies have storefront offices that are less forbidding to the public than the more imposing banking institutions. But because they are more willing to assume greater credit risks than some other lenders—an activity that involves substantial investigation and collection costs—finance companies generally charge considerably higher interest rates than the more traditional credit sources. As a rule, finance companies use a graduated interest scale, with the highest rates charged for the smallest loans.

Insurance Companies

Insurance companies allow their policyholders to borrow against the cash surrender value of their whole life and certain other life insurance policies. This is, in effect, a loan of your own money, since the cash value is the amount that you could receive if you cashed in the policy.

The biggest advantage of borrowing from your insurer is the substantially lower interest rates, which could be far less than half the rates from other sources, depending on the age of the policy and the state in which it was purchased. You usually have the option of repaying the interest and/or the principal whenever you desire—although the interest will compound until paid. But don't forget that if the loan is outstanding at your death, that amount will be deducted from the face value of the policy before the insurance is paid to your beneficiary.

Pawnbrokers

For individuals who need funds quickly and want privacy, pawnbrokers may be the only people to whom they can turn for credit. Operating in most cases from street-level stores, pawnbrokers lend about one third of the value of the personal property that they accept as security. When repayment of the loan is not made at the maturity of the loan—which may range from one month to six months—the unredeemed property held by the pawnbroker is sold to others.

If you cannot obtain a loan somewhere else, pawnbrokers may therefore meet a need by allowing you to pledge certain property and turn it into cash. If you don't redeem the collateral, you have lost the item but have no further obligation. The disadvantages of using pawnbrokers, however, are not just receiving a small percentage of the item's worth, but also the extraordinarily high interest rates charged, which could be more than three times the level at banks and savings institutions for personal loans.

USING CREDIT CARDS

When you charge goods and services on a credit card, you are obtaining unsecured, open-end credit. Such arrangements have become enormously popular throughout the United States, and it is the rare family in the 1980s that does not have one or more credit or charge cards issued by a bank, financial services corporation, oil company, or other organization.

Historically, individual merchants have used credit as a selling tool, usually billing their customers on a monthly basis. The first credit cards were issued by retailers in the early 1900s in the form of metal plates. Somewhere around two decades later, the giant oil companies created their own cards to stimulate the sale of gasoline. In 1951 the multipurpose bank cards appeared on the scene for use in particular communities.

Today these plastic identification cards, which can be used for virtually everything from traffic fines to college tuition, offer many advantages to the consumer. They minimize the need to carry large amounts of cash, foster telephone and mail ordering, reduce check writing, and serve as a crutch in emergencies, at home or abroad. They allow you to pay for a multitude of purchases with a single check and let you take advantage of sales even when cash is unavailable.

But credit cards also stimulate impulse purchases and sometimes encourage you to buy merchandise that is not really needed. If you cannot meet your current obligations, an additional credit card could be one more burden to prevent you from living within your income. With credit cards, there is also the possibility of errors on the monthly statement—errors that can be corrected, but sometimes only after a lengthy and frustrating effort. Then there is the matter of paying the finance charge.

Different credit card issuers have different policies regarding due dates of payments and finance charges. When using credit cards as a convenience and paying bills within the allowable twenty- or twenty-five-day period, no interest is charged and you have the use of your money longer than otherwise. But many individuals take advantage of an extended payment schedule, which normally means an installment loan with rates of 1½ percent a month, equivalent to 18 percent a year or more on the unpaid balance. Thus the effect of paying off an outstanding credit card account over many months is an extra finance charge for the credit.

Single-Purpose Cards

There are three basic kinds of credit cards. The first is the single-purpose card that is used for charging purchases from one specific company, such as a retailer or oil company. Stores, telephone companies, gas stations, hotel and motel chains, and automobile rental companies offer free cards to those who meet their credit specifications. Some require full payment within a month or so after receipt of the bill, others allow partial payment with finance charges on the balance each month, and still others have revolving accounts where the monthly payments drop as the outstanding amount declines. In recent years, the use of single-purpose cards has been broadened to include charges at related companies, such as stores in different cities under the same ownership.

Bank Cards

Probably the most ubiquitous of all credit cards is the bank credit card bearing the name Visa or MasterCard. Each bank issues its own cards, but the credit system is linked to a national and international organization, allowing customers to charge goods and services in thousands of places. The cards were initially free at most banks, but the pendulum has been swinging toward an annual fee in addition to the interest charge for balances outstanding more than about a month.

Travel and Entertainment Cards

Finally there are the travel and entertainment, or T&E, cards issued by such national organizations as American Express, Diners Club, and Carte Blanche. They were first designed solely for business people but are now utilized by the average consumer as well. These companies charge their cardholders an annual fee and usually call for full payment of the outstanding amount each month. Major purchases like airline tickets are often an exception to this full-payment rule. Although some leniency is possible, late payers may be charged interest, assessed an additional charge, or refused renewal when their membership expires at the end of a year. Other services available to holders of travel and entertainment cards include travel insurance on trips charged to the card, volume discounts, and group life insurance.

Whatever type of credit card you may have, don't lose it—because you may be responsible for whatever purchases have been charged to it, with a ceiling of $50 per card. Make sure that you keep a list of all your credit card numbers, along with the addresses and telephone numbers of the issuers. If a card is lost or stolen, call each issuer immediately and follow up with a letter. Insurance is available to cover the $50 liability on credit cards either as a rider to homeowner policies or as a separate policy. Some companies also charge a fee to notify card issuers of a loss.

CREDIT BUREAUS

Of the about 2,000 credit bureaus in the United States, one of them probably has a file on you. This information is used by subscribers to the credit bureau to assist them in granting credit to the public. But you should also be aware of what is in your record, even if not applying for credit at the moment.

Furthermore, the knowledge as to what is in your credit file is a right, rather than a privilege bestowed at the option of the credit bureau. The law is specific in stating that everyone can find out about the information in his file at any time.

As one specialist in consumer credit puts it: "First you should get a medical checkup, then a dental checkup, and then a checkup on your reputation. I think everyone should check on their reputation every two years."

Making a Credit Checkup

If you are willing to take the time and trouble to follow through, a credit checkup is easy to get. It all starts with a visit or written request to your local credit bureau—an organization that serves as a clearinghouse of credit information. You can usually find the nearest one by looking in the yellow pages under "Credit Rating or Reporting Agencies" or by inquiring at a nearby Better Business Bureau, bank, or department store.

Credit bureaus, technically known as consumer reporting agencies, collate and sell credit data on consumers to credit grantors, insurers, and other businesses. They do not assign credit ratings to anyone; such decisions are the role only of the actual credit grantors. Some credit bureaus are cooperatives run by the retailers in a city or region; others are independent businesses, and still others are branches of large national chains like the Trans Union Credit Information Company, TRW, Inc., and Credit Bureau, Inc.

Credit bureaus are not allowed to collect information about a person's lifestyle, religion, or politics. Such information may be gathered by another type of consumer reporting agency, called an investigative agency. But even investigative agencies are not allowed to interview third parties or collect personal data on subjects like lifestyle, religion, or politics without informing you first, except when the report is made in connection with employment. Thus the proper role of a credit bureau is to gather facts about a person's credit history and provide this material to its subscribers. These subscribers, in turn, may request that information only when considering the person for credit, insurance, or employment.

Credit bureaus, which are increasingly important in our credit-oriented society, cooperate with each other in many different ways. Primarily this cooperation takes the form of exchanging files—and computer tapes, in keeping with the growing trend toward the use of electronic data processing—when people move to a new area and apply for credit.

When you inquire about your file at a credit bureau, it will probably demand proper identification. Once you supply this identification, the information must be supplied. Federal law requires a credit bureau to disclose the "nature and substance" of the data in your file. All of the information in your file and the sources of that information should therefore be disclosed to you. Although written disclosure is not required by federal law, many credit bureaus provide it anyway. In some states—such as New York and California—written disclosure is required by state law.

If you have been denied credit on the basis of information in a credit report within the last month, the credit bureau must supply the reason at your request and at no cost. Otherwise, there is a small charge, usually not exceeding $10, for the information from your file.

Categories of Information

In a typical credit report, there are four principal categories of information on which the extension of credit is based by grantors who receive the report. One is the basic disclosure data such as name, current and former addresses, spouse's name, and both Social Security numbers. Secondly, there is a category encompassing past and present employment information on the husband and the wife, including the number of years employed and their salaries. The third category consists of public record notations that may be related to a person's credit history and potential, such as litigation, judgments, and bankruptcies.

Finally, there is an actual credit profile of accounts outstanding, typically summarized in coded form with each account's opening date, last purchase, amount owed, and amount past due. The terms of sale—open, revolving, or installment account—are listed, along with the normal manner of payment.

After examining your credit file, you can question any item believed to be erroneous, vague, or misleading. The credit bureau must then reinvestigate and delete whatever data it cannot substantiate.

Examining Your Records

If, for any reason, the credit bureau does not change a disputed item, you have the opportunity to make a hundred-word explanatory statement that must be entered into the same file. Furthermore, when an adverse item is removed by the bureau or a favorable explanatory statement added, you can ask that all credit grantors who received reports on you during the last six months be notified.

Besides correcting errors, examining these records has another potential advantage. Sometimes a credit bureau's information may be incomplete, thereby preventing a person with an excellent credit history from having that history fully disseminated to credit grantors. If you notice such omissions, you can give the credit bureau the names of the missing accounts and ask that they be contacted for inclusion in your file. Many bureaus charge a fee of about $1.50 a name for this service, though none of them guarantees that the missing companies will respond to a request for information.

But it is well worth the effort to assure yourself as much as possible that your records are accurate and up-to-date. The wrong information in your file now or the omission of favorable information could prevent you from getting credit later when you need it. Exercise your right to check up on the credit checkers.

PREPAYMENT PENALTIES

When you repay a self-amortizing installment loan of five years or less before the final payment is due, you will probably be charged a penalty that increases your actual cost of the funds. Many lenders use a method called the Rule of 78s to determine this additional amount for certain short-term consumer loans.

The Rule of 78s is a mathematical technique to calculate the interest portion of debt service payments. It allocates a slightly larger share of the early loan payments to interest, rather than principal, than would be allocated under the actuarial method. The difference increases with the length of the contract. As a result, when you pay off, say, a one-year loan in six months, your effective interest rate is higher than it would have been if it had been repaid in a year.

Take the case of a one-year loan that calls for twelve equal monthly payments. Under the Rule of 78s, $^{12}/_{78}$ of the interest is due in the first month, $^{11}/_{78}$ in the second month, and so on, until the final month when $^{1}/_{78}$ of the interest is paid. However, if you pay off the loan in six months, you will have paid $^{57}/_{78}$, or 73 percent, of the interest.

The rationale for the Rule of 78s is that since you have the use of the full amount from your creditor only in the first month, you should pay the largest interest in that period. In the second month, you have a little less of the creditor's funds and the interest is a little less. This steady reduction of the principal means that you have the effective use of about half of the loan for its duration. By the last month, you have the least amount of the creditor's money and your interest payment is the least.

The Rule of 78s comes into play only if you prepay your loan, and if so the creditor benefits at your expense. There isn't much a consumer can do about the Rule of 78s except to ask, when borrowing, if the actuarial method could be used instead. If the lender says no, your choices are to try to get the loan elsewhere, accept the Rule of 78s, or avoid borrowing the money.

CREDIT LIFE INSURANCE

Credit life insurance is frequently offered and in some instances required by lenders, providing funds for the full payment of a loan in case the borrower dies. Some insurance plans also provide for continuing the monthly payments if the borrower becomes disabled. Such insurance is available when credit is used for major purchases, such as a house, mobile home, or automobile.

This insurance, however, is usually very expensive. Although some creditors—credit unions being the most obvious example—offer credit life insurance for relatively small amounts with their loans, most charge a stiff price for this service.

Not only is the price of credit life insurance high, but there is also a tendency among some retailers, who receive a high commission on the insurance sale, to high-pressure customers into buying it along with the product. Sometimes you may be told that everyone who buys the item also buys insurance.

Families should structure their existing life insurance to be sufficient to cover the repayment of a loan in the event of the breadwinner's death. When it is not, then more regular life insurance is probably called for. If you decide to buy credit life insurance, keep the documents related to the purchase with your important personal papers. That may be the only way for your family to know that such benefits are due after your death. And in many states, it may also be a stimulus for your family to receive a refund of that portion of the insurance premium covering interest on the loan that was not paid.

PITFALLS OF CREDIT

Credit has its dangers, as some consumers have discovered to their regret. Many Americans know how to use credit wisely, but many others do not. And the latter group often becomes mired in financial difficulties from which escape is extremely laborious.

How can you determine when you are overextended? Credit counselors have developed certain rules of thumb to guide them in pointing to potential trouble spots in a family's credit picture. Among them are: Do your debts, excluding your home mortgage, exceed 15 percent of your take-home pay? Are you being hounded by creditors for slow payment or nonpayment? Are you taking a cash advance from one credit card to pay current charges on another? Have you completely depleted your cash reserve?

In addition to these warning signals, there are a number of other problem areas in the credit field. An awareness of these problems may not be enough to avoid these pitfalls, but it can help you understand how you are affected by them.

Holder-in-Due-Course

For example, the holder-in-due-course doctrine refers to the intricacies involved when the seller of a product or service on credit sells your credit contract in good faith to a third party, often a financial institution. The third party might insist that you continue making payments—even if the product or service was faulty or inadequate—claiming that it bought the credit contract in good faith and is not responsible for defects or difficulties. In recent years, though, federal regulations and some state legislation have minimized this abuse.

Debt Pooling

Debt pooling, whereby private companies act as your bill payer for a fee that could be as high as 35 percent of the amount outstanding, is another consumer credit abuse. These poolers take all or part of your income and use it to pay your creditors, after taking a big chunk of the money for their own services and without providing any financial or budgeting advice. Pooling is illegal in most states, but poolers operate nationally by sending letters to creditors who find themselves in debt over their heads.

Repossession

Still another credit pitfall is repossession, through which a creditor can remove his collateral and sue you for any difference between his receipts from the repossessed item and the amount owed—plus expenses, lawyers' fees, and court costs. Certain repossession tactics that violate constitutional guarantees have been ruled illegal and buyers must be notified when their case is coming to court. Nevertheless, repossession is a possible threat to everyone who has purchased merchandise such as automobiles, furniture, or appliances on credit and has used that merchandise as collateral. If you contact a creditor when in financial difficulties and make a good-faith effort to reschedule payments, however, you may be able to avoid repossession.

PERSONAL BANKRUPTCY

The Federal Bankruptcy Code was rewritten in 1978—the first complete overhaul of the federal bankruptcy laws in eighty years—and the substantially more liberal rules took effect the following year. Its enactment has focused public attention on two extremes of credit usage: the debtor over his head making a good-faith effort to repay what he can, and the debtor who uses bankruptcy to avoid payment.

In the first full year that the new code was in effect, the fiscal year ending September 30, 1980, more than 380,000 individuals filed for bankruptcy. This number was a whopping 82 percent increase over the previous year. In more recent years, the number of filings for personal bankruptcy has been even larger.

The bankruptcy law was designed to offer rehabilitation for debtors and a fresh start for men and women overburdened by their bills. It provides for two primary ways of filing for personal bankruptcy: Chapter 7, which allows the individual to liquidate most of his debts by the sale of property that has not been exempted; and Chapter 13, a repayment plan for debtors with a steady income who can pay off at least part of the debts that have been incurred. In both cases, debtors do not have to be insolvent and generally get to keep more assets than they did under the old law.

A number of amendments to the Bankruptcy Code were enacted in 1984, however, designed to prevent the abusive bankruptcy filings that had, according to many creditors, proliferated following the new law. Among them were provisions giving bankruptcy judges discretion to summarily dismiss such abusive filings and, under certain conditions, barring the same individual from filing a bankruptcy case within six months after dismissal of another case.

Chapter 7, or voluntary straight bankruptcy, established a comprehensive federal standard under which real and personal property is exempted from seizure by the courts. Included in this uniform list of exemptions per person are $7,500 in a residence or other assets, $1,200 in a car, $500 in jewelry, and $750 in books or tools of the trade. Also exempted is any item of personal property—a chair, bicycle, suit—with a market value of less than $200, with a maximum aggregate of $4,000. And unless a state specifically denies its residents the option of taking these federal exemptions, individuals can choose either the federal list of exemptions or their own state's list of exemptions.

Once judged bankrupt, a person cannot file for straight bankruptcy again for six years. For those who choose Chapter 7, this information remains in their records at the local credit bureau for ten years. Those who have gone through Chapter 13 will find this notation in their files for seven years.

Before filing for bankruptcy, it might be worth consulting your nearest consumer credit counseling service, one of the hundreds of affiliates of the nonprofit National Foundation for Consumer Credit in Washington, D.C. These organizations—financed by local banks, merchants, and other businesses—not only give general budgeting advice, but also help families in financial difficulty by working out payment plans with their creditors. The counselors examine your income and expenses, determine your living costs, and allocate the remainder to the individuals and companies to whom money is owed. Lenders will often allow debt extensions when they know that you are being assisted by a credit counseling service.

CONSUMER PROTECTION LEGISLATION

Five major federal laws protect consumers who purchase on credit. Each covers a particular aspect of credit that affects millions of Americans in their day-to-day activities.

Truth in Lending Act

The Truth in Lending Act, formally called the Consumer Credit Protection Act, is the forerunner of most credit protection laws and was designed to rectify many serious abuses in consumer credit practices. For loans of specific amounts, known as closed-end loans, the law requires that creditors explain before the contract is signed exactly what the cost will be in such ways as the annual percentage rate to be charged and the total amount of the finance charge until maturity. For open-end, or revolving, credit, which is not for a specific amount, creditors must disclose the annual percentage rate, the monthly rate of interest, and the manner in which the finance charge will be calculated.

Equal Credit Opportunity Act

The Equal Credit Opportunity Act prohibits discrimination in the granting of credit on nine different bases, including age, marital status, sex, race, national origin, and religion. It was enacted principally to prevent credit discrimination against women and therefore prohibits lenders from denying credit on the basis of gender. The law also states that lenders cannot insist that a woman's husband cosign her loan, and it guarantees that women can have their own separate credit histories.

Fair Credit Reporting Act

The Fair Credit Reporting Act lets you find out about your credit record to learn when a negative credit decision is based on a credit report. It also allows you to be informed about the "nature and substance" of the information kept in your file by a credit reporting agency, and gives you the right to correct and amend erroneous information.

Fair Credit Billing Act

The Fair Credit Billing Act permits you to challenge and correct billing information. It prohibits creditors from sending, or threatening to send, adverse reports to a credit agency until the specific rules covering disputes have been followed. In some instances, it lets you withhold payment from a credit card company if you have tried unsuccessfully to resolve a problem with a merchant. And it requires creditors to resolve billing disputes within a specified time period.

Fair Debt Collection Practices Act

The Fair Debt Collection Practices Act protects you from abusive, deceptive, and unfair debt collection practices by collection agencies. It outlaws the use of threat and obscenity, prohibits false and misleading statements, and restricts the time and frequency of collection practices. Under the law, debt collectors are also required to verify the accuracy of the bill and to give the consumer an opportunity to dispute the charges.

Chapter Five

Rights as a Consumer

FOR DECADES, AMERICAN CONSUMERS HAVE sought to better assert and protect their rights in the marketplace. Yet despite years of educational activity, court cases, legislation, and regulations on both the federal and state levels, many consumers are either unaware of their rights or unable or unwilling to pursue them. Consumerism still has a long way to go before accomplishing its goal of alleviating many problems that individuals continually face as buyers of goods and services from a wide variety of businesses. Consumer groups have been sluggish in developing and implementing new strategies at the same time that conservative public interest groups have multiplied to promote their views opposing government interference with private business.

As a practical matter, every individual bears the ultimate responsibility for protecting his own rights. Whatever consumer protection has been enacted into law or voluntarily made available by business, consumers—individually and collectively—must in the final analysis determine for themselves what information is needed and how such information is to be used.

Consumers are constantly seeking out data concerning the quality, price, and proper usage of the items they buy. They read, hear, and view advertising for goods and services, and visit the stores where the products are sold in an effort to obtain the best value for their money.

But consumerism goes beyond the concept of wise buying habits. It is an undertaking for economic equity that attempts to gain for consumers equal weight with producers. And these efforts to achieve economic justice are an integral part of this movement in which all consumers participate, to one degree or another.

However, in many ways consumers have to depend on both government and business for protection and information. Consumers cannot control the manufacture and distribution of the products they buy, and in many ways must rely on their elected officials to enact or enforce desirable legislation concerning their rights as buyers. The consumer movement grew over the years as a response to consumer problems and dissatisfactions that were not being addressed by government or business.

Because of an ongoing tension between consumer and corporate interests, government frequently serves as the judge, mediator, or referee. In many communities, local government activities benefit the consumer in addition to the national and statewide consumer protection programs. But even with these programs, personal consumer education is still required so that individuals can determine the proper sources of information, define their own interests, and take steps to remedy wrongs.

President John F. Kennedy, in his 1962 consumer message to Congress, listed four basic consumer rights—the right to be informed, the right to be protected from dangerous products, the right to choose goods and services freely, and the right to be heard. President Gerald R. Ford added a fifth: the right to consumer education. Since then, an intense debate has raged as to the appropriate role of government in encouraging these rights.

THE CONSUMER MOVEMENT

While the consumer movement, with its emphasis on consumer rights, is generally regarded as a recent development, its origins date back to the nineteenth century. In the 1890s, local and state consumers leagues were established in order to use consumer pressures as a weapon for improving working conditions in manufacturing and retailing. Consumers leagues were early supporters of the then-novel concepts of minimum wages and social insurance.

During the next decade, these organizations and their national umbrella, the National Consumers League, founded in 1898, became more involved with other issues such as health and sanitation. By the late 1920s, there was a burgeoning consumer concern over the influence of advertising and the paucity of useful product data. This led to the formation of Consumer's Research in 1929 and its offshoot, Consumers Union of the United States, in 1936, both independent, consumer-supported, product-testing organizations. They each publish magazines that disseminate their test results, and offer commentary on various products and manufacturer marketing practices.

Consumers Union, a nonprofit organization that is the largest product-testing group in the country, publishes *Consumer Reports*, an impartial assessment of brands in various categories. It also educates consumers about their relationship with the marketplace, and has pushed into such areas as consumer advocacy, the cost of credit, and social activism. Yet even though the organization and the magazine reach a large audience, they play a smaller role than their counterparts in many Western European nations. These groups are frequently supported by government subsidies, and their publications have relatively larger circulations.

Beginning in the 1960s, consumer protection, one form of government regulation of economic activities, had a renaissance. Some trace its revitalization to court actions that spurred legislation to benefit the consumer. Others cite President Lyndon B. Johnson's appointment of Esther Peterson to the new post of Special Assistant to the President for Consumer Affairs. Since then, two of the strongest voices for national consumer interests have been the Consumer Federation of America and the groups associated with the country's best-known consumerist, Ralph Nader.

The Consumer Federation, founded in 1967 with headquarters in Washington, D.C., is the largest national consumer advocacy organization and now includes the National Consumers League. It is a coalition of more than 200 organizations, including state, regional and local consumer associations, labor unions, consumer cooperatives, associations of retired people, and special-interest groups.

Ralph Nader Organizations

Ralph Nader, who has become a personal symbol of the drive for a consumer protection policy, burst into public view in 1965 with his best-selling indictment of the Detroit automobile industry, *Unsafe at Any Speed*. He later assembled groups of student activists, known as Nader's Raiders, and created the first public-interest law firm. Afterward, he formed a consortium of many consumer organizations, under the umbrella of Public Citizen, Inc., to pursue his consumer interests.

These interests have expanded from the initial campaign for improved vehicle design as a means to achieve traffic safety to proposals for safe gas pipelines and more wholesome meat-packing standards. These organizations work in such areas as law reform, health, safety, taxes, and energy. Their roles are to investigate consumer problems, publicize research results, propose corrective measures, lobby for appropriate legislation or regulations, and monitor their implementation. But each Nader group, to one degree or another, is an institutionalization of the man and depends largely on Ralph Nader himself for its existence and success.

Federal Consumer Organizations

One failure of the consumer movement has been its inability to secure passage of legislation establishing an agency at the federal level to represent the interests of consumers. Although there have been presidential consumer advisors and consumer offices in existing federal departments and agencies, enactment of a separate agency for consumer protection or office of consumer representation has eluded the pro-consumer forces. Such an office, proposed since 1961, would not only act as a clearinghouse for consumer complaints, but would also represent the interests of consumers before federal agencies and courts, suggest consumer legislation to Congress, publish consumer materials, and work with state and local governments to promote and protect consumer activities. But although legislation creating such an office has been approved at different times by the Senate or the House of Representatives, it has never been enacted into law.

Consumerists were more successful in backing the authorization of the Consumer Product Safety Commission. This independent five-member agency was created in 1973 and charged with curbing fatalities and illnesses associated with consumer products. It has had a wide-ranging impact because of its ability to make judgments about the safety of some 15,000 items and issue safety standards that products must meet for sale in the marketplace. For instance, its regulations and standards have resulted in the banning of hair dryers with asbestos and the requirement that toys may not have small parts which can be swallowed by children. Despite the claims by some business critics that the commission does not understand manufacturing and product use—and thereby promulgates overly burdensome rules while attempting to protect consumers—the C.P.S.C. has been regularly reauthorized in one form or another by Congress.

WARRANTIES

A warranty is the promise that comes with the product—and to many consumers it is as important, or more important, than price in deciding whether the product is a good buy. Moreover, federal and state laws protect the public against false and misleading warranties from manufacturers.

Warranties are written guarantees to the purchaser of the integrity of a product and the good faith of the maker. Often referred to as guarantees, warranties generally specify that the manufacturer will, for a period of time, be responsible for the repair or replacement of defective parts and will also sometimes provide periodic servicing. In other words, with a warranty the seller stands behind his products.

The federal consumer product warranty law calls for disclosures—not only of limitations and disclaimers but also of actual guarantees—that consumers can understand when purchasing products costing more than $15. It is designed to stimulate greater understanding of written warranties by detailing in clear, unmistakable language what is and what is not being offered.

Neither manufacturers nor retailers are required to offer warranties, but if they do, they must follow certain conditions. Even if they don't, products are generally subject to the doctrine of implied warranties—in effect, promising that the product will perform the function it is designed to perform. Thus a reclining chair must recline and an alarm clock must have a working alarm.

The law also distinguishes between two types of warranties: full and limited. It states that whichever kind the manufacturer has selected must be shown to consumers prior to the purchase.

Full Warranties

With full warranties, manufacturers must correct defects by repairing or replacing the product at no charge within a "reasonable time," regardless of who owns the product during the warranty period. Furthermore, you cannot be required to do anything unreasonable to obtain warranty service, like shipping a piano to a customer service center.

Limited Warranties

Any deviation from this unconditional assurance must be specifically designated as a limited warranty. According to the Federal Trade Commission, "limited means 'be careful—something's missing.' " For example, a limited warranty could cover parts or labor, but not both. It could allow only a partial refund or credit. It could be warranted only for use in the home. It could require you to return the product to the store for service and to pay for handling. Or it could cover only the original owner of the product. Moreover, one product might have two warranties—a full warranty on one part and a limited warranty on the others. So don't just look for the word "full" on the warranty and stop reading.

Retailers must give consumers complete and understandable explanations of any written warranty before purchases are made. All of the warranties being offered by a retailer can be kept in a binder at a central location or copies of individual warranties can be displayed near or on the product they cover.

Warranty Guidelines

Shoppers will obviously be better off selecting products with full warranties, if possible. When making a purchase, especially of a big-ticket item, comparison shopping for warranties should be undertaken, along with comparison shopping for prices, product availability, workmanship, serviceability, and style. Here are some of the guidelines to check out concerning warranties:

- Find out where the service will be provided. Is there a nearby retailer or repair center where the item will be serviced, or must it be returned to the manufacturer at the customer's expense? Will service calls or home pickups be made for appliances, pianos, and furniture while the warranty is in effect?

- Determine the length and terms of the warranty period. Some companies warrant the entire product for the entire period, whereas others warrant parts of the product for different times. Ask if use of the product affects the length of the warranty.

- Make certain whether all of the parts of the product are covered by the warranty. And check whether labor is also included or whether it is performed at the expense of the customer.

- What will the warrantor do when the product fails— replace it, repair it, or offer a refund? Is there a time limit for replacement, and are there provisions for "loaner" units?

- Determine exactly what assurances the warranty provides and what it does not. And make a note of the

identity and location of the warrantor, so that if the
product is unsatisfactory, you will know what company
is ultimately responsible for product failure and where
it is located.

In disputes between the consumer and the manufacturer or
retailer over a product warranty, private settlement mechanisms,
such as arbitration tribunals, are often used. Unpaid qualified
volunteers acceptable to both parties are used as arbitrators, and
their findings in most states are considered final and binding.
As an alternative to a costly trial and in situations where informal
procedures may suffice, such a method of settlement could be
the answer for individuals with a complaint against the maker
or seller of products that they purchased.

BETTER BUSINESS BUREAUS

Consumer-business arbitration tribunals are one of the many
services offered by Better Business Bureaus. In addition, these
bureaus provide a central location where consumers can check
the record of a merchant or manufacturer before they buy, as
well as a place to register a complaint after they have bought
neither wisely nor well.

Better Business Bureaus are private voluntary organizations
supported by business with no connections to any governmental
body. As such, they cannot pass judgment on prices or quality
and have no power to force companies, whether reputable or
disreputable, to make an equitable settlement. However, member
companies of these bureaus subscribe to codes calling for prompt
responses to consumer inquiries, honest advertising, and fair adjustments to justified complaints. And many bureaus are effective
in obtaining redress for aggrieved customers who have been unable to come to an agreement with the seller of a product that
does not work or perform as expected.

The first Better Business Bureau was started in New York in
1912 as the Vigilance Committee—established to eliminate advertising abuses and create advertising standards. Later that year,
a national vigilance committee was formed to extend this effort

on a regional and national level. That organization became the National Better Business Bureau, which merged in 1970 with the Association of Better Business Bureaus to form the present umbrella organization called the Council of Better Business Bureaus.

Today more than 150 Better Business Bureaus in the United States operate in both large and small cities, as well as in four foreign countries. They receive financial support from 100,000 businesses around the country concerned with truth in advertising and the vitality of the free enterprise system. On the national level, the Council of Better Business Bureaus develops and maintains numerous voluntary, self-regulatory programs designed to enhance public confidence in business.

One program is designed to reassure the public about the accuracy of national advertising in all media. The National Advertising Division and its appeals body, the National Advertising Review Board, review challenges to particular ads, determine the issues, collect and evaluate data, and negotiate agreements with the advertisers involved. All reports about closed cases are made public every month.

Consumer arbitration consistent with state law, which local bureaus offer free to buyers and sellers willing to accept the results, has become an important part of the Better Business Bureau operation. The Better Business Bureau pays all administrative costs of the arbitration. Representation by a lawyer is not required, nor are rigid rules of evidence used. Thousands of disputes, especially in the automotive and construction fields, are handled annually by panels of trained community volunteers through fact-finding hearings, which more and more consumers recognize as a fast, fair, and flexible process—and through which they often find redress that would not have been obtained otherwise.

SMALL CLAIMS COURT

Your local small claims court is probably the best-known place for you to bring legal action when you have an unresolved complaint against another party involving a relatively small loss. In some states, suits against individuals and businesses in small claims courts can be brought for as much as $5,000, although in most states the limit is no more than $1,500.

Also known as conciliation courts or magistrate's courts, small claims courts are usually conducted informally so that you do not need a lawyer. In addition to saving on legal fees, you also save on court costs, which are normally only about $10. You argue your own case in front of a judge or arbitrator and the entire process is concluded in a short period of time.

Filing a Claim

Before filing a claim, determine at the outset whether you have a solid case. Mere anger at another party is not sufficient grounds for an action. Ask yourself whether the other party has caused you to suffer monetary damages through either negligence, intentional behavior, or breach of contract. This contract can be oral or implied as well as written. Thus you could sue over clothing lost by a dry cleaner, an unreturned deposit from a retailer, or a contract battle with a personal service business. The other party, however, must be located in the jurisdiction of the court where the suit is brought.

Once you decide to go forward, you can usually find the nearest small claims court in the telephone book under the listing of the appropriate city or township. When complaining about a business, your claim should be against the actual owner, either an individual or a corporation, rather than an employee or the business name of the company printed on a sign in the front of the building. Pinpointing the proper name and address is sometimes tricky and could involve searching through business directories at the county clerk's office, writing to the secretary of state of your state, or simply taking a good look at the company's license.

You then insert this name on the claims form at the filing office of the court, along with your name and address, the amount in dispute, and the reasons for your suit. At that time, you will be given a date for a court appearance and a summons will be issued to the other party. If the mailed summons is not accepted, you may have to arrange for personal delivery by a third party, such as a marshal or a friend who will sign a notarized statement saying that the notice was served.

Under the small claims system in most states, you cannot sue for mental anguish, nor can you claim compensation for time off from work while you are contesting the matter in court or filing the suit. In addition, you cannot claim the full replacement cost of a lost or damaged item unless it is brand new.

Appearing in Court

When you get to court, the best strategy is to be very specific about the damage that you have suffered. In the brief time you have available, start with a one-sentence summary of your case and then recite the events in chronological order. Be prepared to document actual dollar losses with canceled checks, receipts, and estimates from reliable sources. Learn the local court procedures, so that you will feel more confident during the course of the trial. Present the physical evidence of damage to the court, along with letters, photographs, and related data. You can also bring witnesses with you for backup and you can subpoena others.

Shortly after the trial, the court's decision is normally mailed to you. But even if you win the judgment, the losing party may not be in any hurry to send you a check. If a letter or two requesting payment has no effect, you might have to pay a sheriff or marshal a small fee for trying to collect the money or, when necessary, seize some of the other party's assets.

If the losing party is an individual, you can attempt to have his wages garnisheed. When it is a company, the task could become more difficult, since you might have to locate its assets before collecting your due. Locating those bank accounts, business properties, or other assets, though, is frequently a task that involves the additional expense of a lawyer, because public officials are usually too burdened to do that kind of research. So it does not make sense to bring a small claims action just to teach the other party a lesson. If you don't feel that you have both a good chance of winning the case and a good chance of collecting the judgment, don't waste your time.

CREDIT DISCRIMINATION AGAINST WOMEN

Women often have special difficulties in obtaining credit, despite their right to equal treatment with men. It requires special vigilance, plus an understanding of the laws designed to prevent credit discrimination, for women to ensure that they will be able to achieve credit equality. Unfortunately, women often have a particular need to obtain credit at times of major trauma, such as divorce, illness, or death of a family member, when they may be less desirable credit risks.

Credit discrimination against women dates back to the days when relatively few women worked outside the home. It continued into the modern era, with lenders offering such reasons as "a woman's working life may not be continuous" or "a woman may stop working after she becomes pregnant or has children." But the Equal Credit Opportunity Act of 1975 put an end to any legal basis for such arguments and made credit more available to women than ever before.

Under this law, all women have the right to get credit in their own names. Single women cannot lose their credit standing when they marry, nor can married women lose it when they become widowed or divorced. Alimony, child support, and separate maintenance must be considered in the same light as any other income. Mortgage grantors must consider a wife's full- or part-time income when evaluating a family's creditworthiness. Creditors cannot ask any questions regarding childbearing or child rearing and they must give the reason if they deny credit.

In addition, for all joint credit accounts that have been opened since mid-1977, lenders are required to recognize the "participation" of a married woman, even though she has not cosigned the agreement opening the account and is not legally obligated to pay the bills. Under this provision, the names of both husband and wife will be on file at the local credit bureau and—as the account is used and the debt is repaid—the wife will be building up her own separate credit history. Credit accounts established before mid-1977 can be changed to reflect the participation of both husband and wife.

Credit Guidelines for Women

Despite these built-in protections, some women still have problems when they apply for a loan. In many instances, these problems arise because a large number of women do not have a separate financial identity. Among the ways to ensure such a separate identity are:

- Open a checking account in your own name, even if you are married and have a joint account with your husband.

- Apply for a credit card from a local specialty store, department store, or oil company, also in your own name. Don't be discouraged if the first establishment rejects your application; keep applying to one lender at a time. If the card issuer insists that you have a cosigner at the outset, change the account to your name as soon as you have established a solid pattern of repayment.

- Borrow a small sum from a bank, thrift institution, or credit union. If you don't need these funds for a worthy purpose, put them in a savings account or a certificate of deposit and use the interest earned to help pay the interest due on the loan. After paying off the loan, you will find it easier to get credit the next time you have, or want, to borrow.

- Make a major purchase—such as an automobile, furniture, or an appliance—on the installment plan at a retail outlet. A prompt repayment record every month will go into your personal file at the nearest credit bureau and mark you as a good credit risk.

All of these steps will prove to creditors that payments are being made directly by the woman herself, rather than by her husband or anyone else. Don't forget that a credit card issued to Mrs. John Doe may not be sufficient when claiming that the payments on this card were made independently by the wife, since that name is a social title and could be held by a succession of women. But such a card in the name of Mary Doe, with a different account number than John Doe, means that records of the repayment will go into Mary's credit file rather than John's.

If you suspect that you are being discouraged either overtly or subtly by a lender from applying for a loan because you are a woman, let him know that you are aware of your rights. Explain that it is illegal to dissuade someone from applying for credit because of sex or marital status. Perhaps a question to the lending officer, or his boss if necessary, asking which government agencies regulate the institution, or a simple statement that you intend to file a complaint will be enough to change his attitude.

COMPLAINING TO GOVERNMENT AND INDUSTRY

Your right to complain is basic. If the item you buy does not perform as promised, if the service you receive is inadequate, or if the bills you get are continually in error, you can, and should, complain. In doing so, you should follow certain rules that are likely to lessen your aggravation and increase your odds of succeeding in obtaining a refund, repair, correction, or whatever you are seeking.

Although you can complain in person or by telephone to the offending party—many companies have installed toll-free 800 numbers—you stand a better chance of getting your message across with a letter. Otherwise you could be venting your anger on a clerk, teller, or salesperson who has no authority to solve your problem. The complaint letter should be as short and polite as possible, while still including the basic facts of the situation, as you see them. Of course, give your name, address, and telephone number. Include a precise statement of the problem, noting what went wrong along with dates, places, and serial numbers. And provide applicable evidence to support your case; a specific request for a refund, replacement, apology, etc.; a deadline for action; and a threat that you intend to carry out if no action is taken.

Never say that you will act illegally or defame the character or motivation of others. But if you have charged a purchase, you can threaten not to pay for it until a satisfactory adjustment has been made. You can also state that you will stop your patronage of that merchant or manufacturer or tell others how you have been treated. There is probably no threat that a customer relations manager or consumer affairs director has not heard before. But if you can combine one with a direct or indirect appeal for sympathy and the facts back up your contention, you may get what you want.

Never send the original sales slip, canceled check, or other evidence with your complaint letter. Include a photocopy instead. Address the letter to the chairman or president of the organization, whose name usually can be found through a telephone call to the company or in the business directories at your local library. He may never see your letter, but if it is routed to the proper person at the company with an attached note from the office of the president, you may obtain better results.

For maximum effectiveness, copies of this complaint letter should also be sent to your state and local consumer protection departments, to the local Better Business Bureau, and to the appropriate federal agency. It may take weeks and months to get replies to these letters, but at least you will have the satisfaction of using the leverage of these agencies to force the store or manufacturer to investigate your case and possibly to make amends.

Federal Enforcement Agencies

Among the major federal enforcement agencies in credit-connected matters are:

National Banks

Comptroller of the Currency
490 L'Enfant Plaza East, S.W.
Washington, D. C. 20219

State-Chartered Banks Belonging to Federal Reserve System

Federal Reserve Board
20th and C Streets, N.W.
Washington, D. C. 20551

Banks Insured by Federal Deposit Insurance Corporation

Federal Deposit Insurance Corporation
550 17th Street, N.W.
Washington, D.C. 20429

Federally Chartered Savings and Loan Associations

Federal Home Loan Bank Board
1700 G Street, N.W.
Washington, D.C. 20552

Federal Credit Unions

National Credit Union Administration
1776 G Street, N.W.
Washington, D.C. 20456

Stores, Finance Companies, and Non-Bank Credit-Card Issuers

Federal Trade Commission
Pennsylvania Avenue at 6th Street, N.W.
Washington, D.C. 20580

Major Industry Groups

If your letter to the store or manufacturer does not result in action to your satisfaction, another alternative is to send a letter to one of the organizations that certain industries have established to hear consumer complaints. As these panels are supported by

business, they are not necessarily the most neutral source in set-
tling disagreements between businesses and the public. Nevertheless, many of them make a sincere effort to establish the facts
of a particular situation and serve as mediators between the concerned parties.

Some of the major industry groups that you can contact are:

Advertising

National Advertising Division
Council of Better Business Bureaus
845 Third Avenue
New York, NY 10022

Appliances

Major Appliance Consumer Action Panel
20 North Wacker Drive
Chicago, IL 60606

Automobiles

Automotive Consumer Action Program
National Automobile Dealers Association
8400 Westpark Drive
McLean, VA 22101

Automotive Repairs

Automotive Service Council
118 Industrial Drive
Elmhurst, IL 60126

Carpets

Carpet and Rug Institute
P.O. Box 2048
Dalton, GA 30720

Contractors

National Association of the Remodeling Industry
1901 North Moore Street
Arlington, VA 22209

Correspondence Schools

National Home Study Council
1601 18th Street, N.W.
Washington, D.C. 20009

Credit

Associated Credit Bureaus
P.O. Box 218300
Houston, TX 77218

Door-to-Door Sales

Direct Selling Association
1730 M Street, N.W.
Washington, D.C. 20036

Electronic Equipment

Electronic Industries Association
2001 I Street, N.W.
Washington, D.C. 20006

Funerals

Thana CAP
135 W. Wells Street
Milwaukee, WI 53203

Furniture

Furniture Industry Consumer Advisory Panel
Box 951
High Point, NC 27261

Homes

National Association of Home Builders
15th and M Streets, N.W.
Washington, D.C. 20005

Mail Order

Direct Mail Marketing Association
6 East 43rd Street
New York, NY 10017

Mobile Homes

Manufactured Homes Institute
P.O. Box 35
Chantilly, VA 22021

Moving Companies

American Movers Conference
1117 North 19th Street
Arlington, VA 22209

Travel

American Society of Travel Agents
4400 MacArthur Blvd.
Washington, D.C. 20007

With complaints against a professional person—such as a doctor, dentist, or lawyer—it is usually harder to obtain satisfaction when you think that you have been wronged. Nevertheless, many of the appropriate professional associations in your county have peer review panels that listen to consumer grievances. These complaint panels have a built-in bias in favor of the members of their associations, but your filing of a grievance could lead to a settlement if the professional in question does not want the trouble and possible damage to his reputation of a hearing.

Part Two

Insurance

Chapter Six

Life Insurance

MOST AMERICAN FAMILIES NEED LIFE insurance and most have it. Nevertheless, too many families do not understand the concept of this insurance, how much to buy, and which options are most applicable to their individual needs.

The result is that most insurance purchased in this country is bought largely on the basis of a salesperson's recommendations. Yet as qualified and as concerned with your personal financial objectives as any life insurance agent may be, his recommendations will more than likely be colored by the products and services that he sells.

In addition, insurance is frequently wrapped in an almost incomprehensible jargon. It is confusing and complex, and as many people see it, a depressing subject that relatively few outside the business want to think or talk about.

You should, however, have at least a basic knowledge of insurance. The more you know about the types of life insurance available, the guidelines for selecting the appropriate coverage, the best methods of cost comparisons, and the other principal considerations in choosing a policy, the more you will be able to ask the right questions and get the right insurance coverage. No one knows your personal situation as well as you do—and no one should be able to sell you insurance unless you are firmly convinced of its value. That decision ought to be yours and should be based on your understanding of how insurance works and how your needs can best be satisfied.

HISTORY OF LIFE INSURANCE

Some form of life insurance has been in existence from virtually the earliest civilizations. The Babylonian Code of Hammurabi, which dates back to 1800 B.C., states that if a life has been lost, "the city or district governor shall pay one mina of silver to the deceased's relatives." Ancient Greece and Rome also had their own particular versions of insurance.

In more modern times, there is a record of a policy issued in London in 1583 to a man who paid 32 pounds for a year of insurance protection. He died within that year and his beneficiaries received 400 pounds.

The first general life insurance company in the United States was established in 1794, but it went out of business after selling only six policies in five years. In the mid-1800s, hundreds of burial societies were created by ethnic groups that had emigrated to this country. But many of these societies were short-lived, which left a lot of their policyholders without coverage at their deaths. It was also in that era that the first American mortality table was published.

Insurance in the United States has historically been regulated by each of the fifty states. State insurance departments are a good source of information about coverage available in their jurisdictions.

POOLING RISKS

The concept of insurance is that of pooling of risk. A group of people share the risks that all of them experience, with each person in the pool contributing an equitable amount. The entire group of insureds supports the pool through the payment of a sum of money called a premium that makes the payment of all claims possible.

What happens under this concept is that most of the insured will not need to tap the fund created by the group most of the time. But when one member of the pool dies, his heirs can make a withdrawal from the fund based on the face amount, or the amount stated in his policy. Insurance companies cannot predict any individual's death, but because they know at what rates men and women at each age level have died in the recent past, they can generally estimate how many members of the pool will die every year in the future. They therefore base their mortality tables and annual premiums on these estimates.

Such predictions utilize the law of large numbers, which says that the larger the number of exposures, the more closely the actual losses will equal the underlying probability of loss. The premiums that insurers institute reflect this predictability.

Until the funds received by insurance companies are paid out as claims, they are invested in a variety of assets, including bonds, mortgages, real estate, and stocks. Earnings on these assets, combined with the amounts derived from policyholder premiums, are used to cover the costs that the insurance companies incur in providing their services and to make a profit as well.

Every policyholder has the right to name a beneficiary or beneficiaries. Besides the primary beneficiary, you can select a contingent beneficiary, who would receive the proceeds if the primary beneficiary died before you. Another possibility is leaving a life interest in the proceeds to a primary beneficiary, with any remainder going to the secondary beneficiary. As long as you have reserved a right to do so, you can change your beneficiary arrangements at any time.

Not everybody can purchase a life insurance policy from every insurance company. Some insurers restrict availability in various ways. For example, certain policies are sold only to those whom the industry calls preferred risks, while others are available to people living in certain areas or belonging to certain religious or social groups. Some of the lowest-cost policies are of one or more of these restricted types.

PURPOSES OF LIFE INSURANCE

The most common purpose of life insurance is to cushion a family financially if the primary wage earner dies prematurely. In short, life insurance is a security blanket—something to replace your paycheck and to wrap around your dependents when you die. The funds from an insurance death benefit payable to a specified beneficiary are immediately and automatically available, while other funds may be held up in probate.

Ideally, the death benefit that you buy with insurance should be substantial enough so that when added to your other assets it lets your family retain its way of life and cover anticipated educational and medical expenses. Therefore, the more dependents you have and the younger you are, the more insurance you need. Single people with no dependents generally do not need insurance, nor do working couples without children, unless they want to provide the surviving spouse with enough money to live as though their two salaries were continuing.

There are other purposes for life insurance. You can use it to pay off a home mortgage or other debts existing at the time of death; to provide a life income starting at retirement; and to establish a fund for death expenses and estate and inheritance taxes. You can use it, in some cases, for forced savings or to make charitable bequests after your death. Life insurance benefits can be tailored to virtually any of your requirements or those of your beneficiaries.

Life insurance death benefits are usually not subject to income taxes. They are included in a deceased person's estate, unless the beneficiary was the policyholder, but if this estate is large enough, estate or inheritance taxes may be due. If the proceeds are taken by the beneficiary in installments, rather than as a lump sum, the interest portion of each payment received is taxable.

HOW MUCH IS ENOUGH?

The commonly accepted rules of thumb for calculating proper life insurance coverage once stated that the breadwinner should have between three and six times his annual income in insurance, or that he should put aside 5 percent of his salary for insurance premiums. However, these rules have long since become outdated. With the growing recognition that different families have different protection needs, insurance advisors now structure individualized answers to the question of how much life insurance is enough.

You should consider first how many dependents you have, how long they will remain dependents, how well you would like them to be provided for, and what other assets and income they will have. Then comes a listing of the family's requirements that includes immediate cash for final expenses and readjustment, as well as future income during the pre- and post-retirement years of the surviving spouse. Finally comes the calculation of the amount of insurance that must be added to the anticipated assets and income to meet these needs.

With such an analysis, it becomes evident that financial circumstances and lifestyle requirements are really the determining factors for how much is enough. Whereas a young family with children may need 60 to 75 percent of its current after-tax income if the principal wage earner should die, a wife with grown children who lives alone might be able to get by with 40 percent of her husband's after-tax earnings. Whatever figures you come up with, your life insurance program should be periodically reassessed in keeping with the changes that occur in your life.

INSURANCE ACCEPTABILITY

Insurance companies select the risks that they wish to insure and classify them based on degrees of insurability so that premium rates can be developed. As a result of this process, which is called underwriting, the overwhelming majority of all life insurance applicants are accepted by insurers at the standard premium. But a small percentage is given a rated policy, or accepted at extra-risk rates, and an even smaller group of applicants is denied insurance altogether.

Among the major considerations in this underwriting process are age, sex, physical condition, financial status, occupation, smoking habits, and hobbies or avocations. For instance, when you have a health problem or are overweight, you may find it difficult to buy insurance at the standard rate. Some companies use a numerical rating system, whereby every factor gets a positive or negative point value. If your point value is acceptable to the insurance company—with lower scores more desirable than higher scores—then you qualify for a standard policy at standard rates. If not, you may be "rated" and thereby required to pay higher premiums for the same amount of insurance.

When one person wants to insure the life of another, the purchaser of the policy must have what is called an insurable interest in the other party. The definition of an insurable interest normally means a financial interest in the continued life of the insured, but love and affection are also considered to be in that classification.

MAJOR TYPES OF LIFE INSURANCE

The two major categories into which the bulk of all policies fall are term insurance and whole life insurance.

Term Insurance

Term insurance is pure insurance, the simplest available, providing financial protection only for a limited, specified period of time. Since it is temporary protection and does not generate any savings or investment, term insurance is the least expensive kind of protection. If death occurs within the time limits of the policy, the face value is paid. But the coverage ends and nothing is paid if the insured survives beyond the term of the policy.

Term insurance can be sold for, say, one, five, ten, or twenty years and is typically unavailable for purchase after age sixty-five or seventy. If you stop paying premiums, all benefits cease because term policies do not contain cash values or paid-up insurance benefits.

Many term insurance policies have renewal or conversion options. Renewable term allows you to automatically extend the policy length for another specific period until a maximum age, without a physical examination. But every time you renew, your premiums—all of which are stated in the contract—will increase because you are older. For example, a thirty-year-old man buying $30,000 worth of annually renewable term insurance coverage might pay a premium of $85 in the first years of the policy. At age forty, however, the premium might be $98; at fifty, $220; and at sixty, $497.

A conversion option lets you exchange your term policy for a permanent plan of insurance in the same rating class, usually based on your age at the conversion date. Here, too, the conversion can be made regardless of the insured's health or occupation.

Besides the basic level term insurance policy providing a constant amount of insurance and annual premiums for a fixed time period, there are two major variations. One is decreasing term insurance, widely used in connection with home mortgages, in which coverage declines in value from year to year or from month to month. The second is increasing term insurance, where the value goes up periodically and which is frequently sold in a package along with other policies.

Whole Life Insurance

Whole life insurance—also referred to as cash-value, ordinary life, or straight life insurance—offers protection up to an agreed-upon amount for a person's lifetime, plus a savings program. Part of each premium pays for immediate insurance protection and part is used to pay in advance for future protection, thereby providing a strong incentive to save money. In contrast to the temporary nature of term insurance, moreover, whole life is permanent as long as you keep paying the premium.

Premium payments are spread over your entire life or, in the case of limited payment life policies, for a specified number of years or until a certain age. Generally these premiums do not fluctuate, thereby making whole life insurance cost more than term insurance in the early years of the policy and less than term insurance in the later years.

A distinctive characteristic of whole life insurance is that its cash value accrues according to a predetermined annual schedule on a tax-deferred basis. Thus in addition to the protection of the policy manifested in the death benefit, there is an investment aspect with a number of useful features for insurance buyers. The cash value builds up slowly during the period that the policy is in force, so that there may be little during the initial years but a substantial amount at retirement. If you keep the insurance in force and live to be a hundred, the cash value equals the face value and you would receive that amount as the policy is terminated.

Take the case of a $30,000 policy purchased by a thirty-year-old man for an annual premium of $435. The cash value would grow in the following way:

Cash Value of a $30,000 Policy Purchased by a 30-Year-Old Man for an Annual Premium of $435	
Age 35	$1,830
Age 40	$4,260
Age 45	$6,990
Age 50	$9,960

Source: American Council of Life Insurance

With whole life, you can borrow from the insurance company up to the current cash value and repay it whenever you want, however you want, and if ever you want. Furthermore, the interest paid on such loans is generally tax-deductible. But if the insured dies before the loan is repaid, this amount is deducted from the death benefit.

Many older policies have low interest rates of between 5 and 8 percent. Accordingly, if you want, or have, to borrow money, those policies may very well be a better source of funds than most other credit sources. The money borrowed at such a low rate can also be used for investment at a higher rate.

Some whole life policies are sold as minimum deposit plans, under which a number of the premiums can be paid with money borrowed against the cash surrender value that the policy has accrued. Designed to be cost-competitive with term insurance, minimum deposit insurance has tax advantages—primarily for those in high tax brackets—because the interest on the loans may be tax-deductible.

Another feature of the cash value in whole life insurance is that you can authorize the insurer to automatically draw from that amount to keep the insurance in force if a premium is missed either accidentally or intentionally. Or if you want to stop paying premiums at retirement, you can use the cash value to retain the insurance for as long as it will last. Other possibilities are using cash value to buy an annuity or to purchase paid-up insurance with a lesser face value that will last the rest of your life, or taking cash value as a lump sum when giving up the policy. When you die, of course, the cash value becomes part of the death benefit and reduces the actual cost to the insurance company.

OTHER KINDS OF INSURANCE

Besides the basic term and whole life insurance, many other types of policies are sold to the public. These include:

Endowment Insurance

Endowment insurance offers protection for a specific period of time, like ten or twenty years, or to age sixty-five. It allows you to accumulate funds, with the face value paid at the maturity date—either in a lump sum or in installments. If the insured dies before the maturity date, that face amount is paid to the beneficiary. The premiums for endowment policies are relatively high because the full face amount will normally be paid sooner than for whole life insurance. Endowment policies are useful in meeting known future expenses, such as college tuition or a retirement fund.

Family Income Policies

Family income policies combine whole life insurance for permanent protection with decreasing term insurance for additional temporary protection. Typical coverage for the head of a family might be a $100,000 base policy with a fifteen-year family income provision. If the policyholder dies within that time, his beneficiary would receive $100,000 in benefits plus 1 percent of the face value, or $1,000, a month for fifteen years. If the policyholder lives longer than fifteen years after the start of the policy, the decreasing term portion of the policy that provided the monthly income expires, but the whole life portion providing $100,000 in coverage remains.

Family Policies

Family policies offer coverage with different amounts and provisions under one contract to all the members of an immediate family—husband, wife, and children until they reach a certain age. With coverage normally sold in units, the primary breadwinner's protection is typically for the largest amount, the spouse's for the next largest, and the children's for the least. Under family insurance, which reduces the need for multiple policies within the family, the general pattern is for the husband to have whole life insurance and the wife and children to have term coverage. In addition, the children are guaranteed the right to convert their coverage to whole life without a physical examination when they are no longer eligible for the family plan.

Variable Life Insurance

Variable life insurance incorporates some features of whole life insurance—level premiums, low-rate loan privileges, and cash accumulations. But it also offers the possibility of investment and death benefit growth. This occurs because the investment portion of variable life premiums is invested by the insurance company in a separate portfolio of stocks or bonds. If the portfolio performs well, the death benefit will increase above the guaranteed level—and cash values will rise faster than under conventional policies.

However, the anticipated growth of the cash value is not assured, since there is no guaranteed floor. Furthermore, the amount of the death benefit may fluctuate from year to year. And when you borrow against a variable life policy, you may reduce the long-term return.

Universal Life Insurance

Universal life insurance, with policies that typically mature at a specified age, is a relatively new variation of long-term insurance that separates the insurance and savings elements. Universal policies are split in such a way that part of the premium pays for yearly renewable term insurance, while the rest is typically invested in a fund consisting of short-term, often high-yielding securities that help to build up cash value.

Universal life has the advantage of flexibility of both premiums and death benefits. You can raise or lower your coverage, subject to certain minimums, by increasing or reducing premiums. And as with whole life insurance, you can also pay premiums by borrowing against the cash value without losing the policy.

But the high advertised interest rates on the savings portion of a universal life policy, which are usually tied to prevailing money market rates, are not the complete story. These rates apply before the insurance companies deduct various charges to meet their expenses. There may be a load, or charge, of 5 to 10 percent of each annual premium, as well as one-time fees in the first year of the policy. There may be corresponding charges if the policy is surrendered. Most companies also pay just 4 percent interest on the first $1,000 in the savings fund. Many insurance specialists believe that because of these factors, the beneficial impact from the savings portion comes only over the long haul. Moreover, the law provides that flexible-premium universal life contracts have the same tax treatment as traditional level-premium whole life insurance only as long as the policies are substantially comparable and the universal contracts are not overly investment-oriented.

Annuities

An annuity, although sold by insurance companies, is the opposite of death-benefit life insurance. Rather than paying benefits after death, an annuity is a contract that provides periodic payments, normally on a monthly basis, for a specific period—either for a certain number of years or for the life of the insured, formally known as the annuitant. Annuity payments, based on life expectancy and the amount contributed by the insured, protect individuals if they outlive the period for which their financial resources might otherwise last. Annuities can supplement Social Security benefits and other retirement income.

Many varieties of annuities are on the market. For instance, a straight life annuity pays a specified regular income to the owner of the contract for life, with no further payments to anyone after he dies. A ten-year (fifteen-year, or twenty-year) certain and life annuity pays off to the insured, or to his beneficiary, during the first ten years (fifteen years, or twenty years) of the contract. It also continues payments as long as the annuitant lives. An installment refund annuity pays an income to the annuitant for life, but if he dies before getting as much money as he contributed, his beneficiary receives additional income until total payments equal the purchase price. And a deferred annuity, which can be bought with a single premium or, as is more likely, paid for over a period of time, calls for income payments beginning at a specific future date.

LIFE INSURANCE AND TAXES

Life insurance proceeds from the death of an insured are generally income tax–free. Thus no taxes are usually due on a lump-sum payment of the full face value of a policy, including endowment contracts, employers' group insurance plans, and workers' compensation insurance. What's more, interest paid on proceeds left with the insurance company is also nontaxable in most cases.

However, there is a different tax treatment for installment payments spread over the life of a beneficiary or received for a fixed number of years of an amount that could have been paid in a lump sum. The part of each installment attributed to interest may be taxed. To determine how much is tax-free, divide the face amount of the policy by the number of years that the installments are to be paid. A surviving spouse of an insured can also receive tax-free up to $1,000 of interest paid with the annual installment before subtracting the interest and dividend exclusion.

Dividends paid by an insurer as a reduction of premiums—whether taken in cash, left at interest with the company, or used to accelerate the maturity of the policy—are not taxable. And if you surrender your policy for cash, the money is taxed as ordinary income if the amount received exceeds the premiums paid minus dividends.

PROVISIONS OF LIFE INSURANCE POLICIES

Most life insurance policies contain key provisions that have an important effect on policyholders. Among them are:

Incontestability

An incontestability clause states that an insurer cannot, because of misrepresentations by the applicant, challenge the validity of a policy during the lifetime of the insured after it has been in force for a specific time—usually two years. Unless the policyholder committed outright fraud in taking out the policy, the insurer usually cannot refuse to pay the death benefit after the end of the contestability period. Because of this clause, beneficiaries will receive the proceeds due them regardless of any illegal acts of the insured, who is not alive to defend a possible challenge by the insurance company.

Suicide

A suicide clause states that after a specified period—normally a year or two—a suicide becomes a risk covered by the policy and the beneficiary gets the same benefits that would have been received owing to death from any other cause. During this one-

or two-year waiting period, though, the death benefit in the event of a suicide is no more than the total of the premiums paid.

Grace Period

A grace period in most policies normally gives a policyholder twenty-eight to thirty-one days after the premium is due to pay his bill without a penalty. Afterward, the policy may lapse. Although the insurance remains in force if the insured dies during the grace period, the overdue premium is deducted from the benefits that would otherwise be awarded.

Reinstatement Clause

A reinstatement clause gives a policyholder who lets his coverage lapse the right to have it reinstated within a fixed period, usually five years, as long as the cash value has not been withdrawn and the individual is still insurable. Although you would have to pay all of the missed premiums with interest, the annual cost of your reinstated policy will be the same as when you first bought it—and cash values will correspondingly be built up as rapidly.

Misstatement of Age Provision

In the event that an insurer discovers the insured has incorrectly stated his age on the insurance application, the company is allowed to pay only the amount of death benefit that such premiums would have bought at the correct age. Some companies even have a misstatement of sex provision in their policies because females, who have a longer life expectancy, are usually charged lower rates than males.

CLASSIFYING LIFE INSURANCE POLICIES

Participating Policies

With participating policies, also called par or dividend-paying policies, sold primarily by mutual insurance companies, the premium is fixed at a considerably higher rate than necessary. Usually two or three years after the origination of the policy, policyholders may get an annual dividend—actually a refund of a portion of the premium—on the basis of the company's loss experience during that period. This dividend is made, however, at the company's discretion. If you get one, it can be used to reduce the annual premium, purchase more insurance coverage, or accumulate at interest with the insurer. Insurance companies include future dividends in their sales illustrations, but these dividends are not guaranteed because changes in the economy and the investment climate can markedly change the dividend scales.

Nonparticipating Policies

In the case of nonparticipating policies, also called guaranteed cost or non-dividend policies, sold principally by stockholder-owned companies, dividends are not paid. Instead the premiums are set at a level that the insurer expects will adequately meet its expenses. These premiums are typically fixed at the time of issue, in which case the policyholder knows from the outset exactly what his insurance cost will be. Premiums for guaranteed cost policies are generally lower than those, before the payment of dividends, for participating policies. After the dividend payments, the costs are generally similar.

COMPARING COSTS

You cannot assess the cost of a life insurance policy by its premium alone. When comparing the cost of policies, you must consider the time value of money; the interest that the premiums would have earned if invested elsewhere; the cash value, if any; and, in the case of participating policies, the dividends a policy may pay during the period in question.

The most widely used method of comparing costs that encompasses all of these considerations is the interest-adjusted cost index. This index—also called the payment cost index—offers a means of taking into account the time value of money and converting it into a dollar figure that reliably estimates the average annual cost of insurance protection over ten or twenty years.

The interest-adjusted method utilizes the accumulated premiums, how much you might get back in dividends, and what cash value would be available at the end of a period of years. The lower the index number, the lower the cost of the policy.

This index number, which is usually given per $1,000 of life insurance, can be used only to compare similar plans of life insurance. Thus you cannot compare a term policy with a whole life policy through the cost index, but you can compare similar policies offered by different insurance companies.

Comparisons of Term Policies

For term policies, there is a single interest-adjusted index for any given period of time. Most companies prepare indexes for a ten- and a twenty-year time span. This index is derived by accumulating the annual premiums year by year at a specific interest rate, say 5 percent, subtracting the accumulated illustrated dividends, if any, and dividing by a constant determined by actuaries to arrive at an equivalent annual outlay.

Comparisons of Whole Life Policies

For whole life policies, there are two interest-adjusted indexes also typically prepared for both ten and twenty years. One, the net-cost or surrender index, determines your projected cost if you hold the policy for the specified period and then surrender it for the cash value. The second, the net-payment index, measures the projected cost of holding the policy until you die without cashing it in. The former accounts for cash value, while the latter ignores it. Therefore you should calculate both the net-cost index and the net-payment index as part of your cost comparison.

For example, the median net-cost index for a woman purchasing a $50,000 nonparticipating whole life policy might be 2.55 at age twenty-five, 4.05 at age thirty-five, and 7.53 at age forty-five. For a similar participating policy, the indexes might be 3.81 at age twenty-five, 5.71 at age thirty-five, and 10.43 at age forty-five.

Even though a dollar sign sometimes appears in front of the interest-adjusted cost index, it is an index and not necessarily the actual cost for your insurance. Most states now require insurers to provide cost-comparison indexes when selling policies, along with a simple explanation of how the cost-comparison method works. But remember to compare the relative strength of the insurers and the reputation of their agents, as well as the index, before selecting a policy. Small differences in index numbers could very well be offset by other policy or service features.

RIDERS TO INSURANCE CONTRACTS

Insurance contracts often have riders that offer options to the policyholder beyond the principal features of the policy, usually for an additional charge. Here are some of the most common:

Waiver of Premium

This rider normally waives the payment of any premiums prior to the age of sixty or sixty-five during the period that the insured is totally and permanently disabled. The waiver typically goes into effect, allowing policy benefits to continue without charge, when the insured's disability lasts for four to six months, although the premiums paid during that period are later refunded. Insurance companies have different definitions of disability, ranging from the inability to perform the duties of your regular occupation to the inability to perform any job at all.

Accidental Death Rider

Also called a double indemnity benefit, this rider pays an additional benefit equal to the face value of the policy if the insured dies from an accident. Accidental death, however, must generally occur within ninety days after the injury and before a certain age—also sixty or sixty-five. Although some insurance companies also provide a triple indemnity rider, for a total benefit of three times the face amount, this benefit is usually available only if the insured dies in certain types of accidents like airplane crashes.

Disability Income Option

When the insured is totally disabled, a disability income option pays a fixed monthly amount based on a percentage of the insurance coverage. Normally these payments begin after a waiting period of, say, six months and end on a specific date.

Guaranteed-Insurability Option

Available generally to people in their twenties and thirties, this option lets the policyholder purchase specified additional amounts of insurance at fixed intervals without proof of insurability. With it, a policyholder can increase the amount of insurance in force when his income rises, even if his health is not good enough to pass a medical examination. The guaranteed-insurability option states the different ages at which additional insurance can be purchased and the maximum amounts of available coverage.

SETTLEMENT OPTIONS

After the death of an insured, the proceeds pass to his beneficiary. Normally the person taking out the insurance has the right to choose how these proceeds shall be distributed and does so by selecting one of the settlement options available. But since no one can tell with certainty what your family's circumstances will be like after your death, the best alternative may be to give your survivors the opportunity to decide how the funds should be used.

The usual options include:

- Leaving the money with the insurance company, with interest paid to the beneficiary from time to time until the money is withdrawn. Many families like this option because it gives survivors an opportunity to make a final choice, without forcing them to keep the money with the insurer indefinitely. However, the interest rate will probably be lower than you could obtain through another type of investment.

- Taking the funds in a lump sum. This is the standard method of payment if no settlement option has been selected. And if you have created a trust into which your insurance proceeds will go, the full-payment option provides for the money to be automatically transferred to this trust.

- Accepting the proceeds in periodic fixed amounts. With this option, a specified amount of the benefits is distributed at certain designated periods until all of the funds are paid out. The insurance company also pays interest on the amount it holds for the entire time. Again, this rate is likely to be relatively low.

- Spreading receipt of the proceeds over a given period. In this event, the amount of each payment depends on the face value of the policy, the rate of interest, and the number of years income is to be paid.

- Buying an annuity, whereby the insurer will pay the beneficiary a fixed monthly amount for life. These monthly payments depend upon such factors as the policy's face value, the rate of interest, and the age and sex of the beneficiary.

It makes sense to talk over the various settlement options with your beneficiary at the time a new policy is purchased. The important point is that the survivor should have plenty of time after the death of the insured to make a decision as to the disposition of the proceeds.

GUIDELINES FOR BUYING LIFE INSURANCE

Using common sense is the best rule for selecting the most appropriate life insurance for any family, but every consumer should bear in mind a number of basic guidelines:

- Shop around before you buy an insurance policy. There are substantial variations in life insurance prices and shopping may help you find a low-cost policy with the same features as a high-priced one. For instance, in some states, savings bank life insurance is sold at lower rates than those charged by most other companies in the industry.

- Beware of switching policies from one company to another. If you already have a policy in force, it may not pay to drop it and choose another, even if the existing policy charges higher premiums for the same benefits. Front-end administrative and commission expenses for a new policy are high, dividends frequently get larger every year that you have a policy, cash values of whole life policies build up faster in succeeding years, and the incontestability and suicide provisions of a new policy generally require two-year waiting periods. At the very least, get a second opinion on the switch from the company or agent who sold you the first policy. And if you finally decide to replace a policy, don't drop the old one until you are certain that the new one is in force.

- See if you are eligible for group life insurance through your employer, union, professional, fraternal or alumni association, or another group with which you are associated. Some forms of group insurance—which often does not require a medical examination—almost always cost less than insurance purchased individually, although the maximum coverage available may be less than desired. With employer group insurance, your premium may be paid wholly or partially by the employer. Group policies are usually for term insurance, with many plans structured so that coverage decreases in later years and ends at a specified age. Since group policies can be canceled by the insurer and you can lose your insurance if you are no longer connected with the group, they are best used as a supplement to your other coverage. But particularly for younger people, they often meet a need at a bargain price.

- Buy as comprehensive a policy as fits your pocketbook. It makes no sense to purchase more coverage than you can afford and that you will have to drop after a few years.

- Pay your premiums on an annual basis, rather than monthly, quarterly, or semiannually. You will usually save money by doing so because, as a rule, the more frequently you pay, the greater the expense.

- In most cases, it is better to have as few policies as possible. Try to plan your life insurance program so that you will not have to purchase new policies on a regular basis. It will usually cost less to buy one $50,000 policy than five $10,000 policies.

- Before making a final decision, check *Best's Insurance Reports* in your local library for its ratings of the financial stability of various life insurance companies. If possible, pick a company given one of the two top ratings—excellent and very good. And in selecting an agent, look for the Chartered Life Underwriter, or C.L.U., designation. It indicates that the salesperson has passed a tough examination and shown a strong degree of professionalism, so he may be better qualified to advise you than one without that designation.

- Whatever life insurance program you have is subject to change. Review your policies every few years to determine if your coverage should increase, decrease, or remain the same. Similar reviews should also take place when your financial responsibilities or circumstances are modified. In other words, keep your insurance up-to-date.

Chapter Seven

Health Insurance

PERSONAL HEALTH INSURANCE GIVES YOU peace of mind: You know that some or all of your hospital or medical expenses will be paid for in the event of injury or illness. It is the life preserver that offers security and can save you from financial disaster when a serious medical problem strikes your family.

However, the soaring cost of health insurance is a major problem for Americans. Too often individuals learn the details of their health insurance program the hard way after a medical bill is rejected by the insurer because the service was not covered by the policy. Some individuals lose out in other ways, by failing to use a service that is included in the policy or by not filing or following through on a claim properly.

Most people have some coverage under group programs established through their employer, labor union, or professional, fraternal or other organization. Because of the advantages of mass marketing, this coverage generally costs less than individually purchased insurance. And millions more are covered by Medicare, the federally operated insurance program primarily available to people over sixty-five.

For those ineligible for a group plan or not covered by Medicare, or for those who wish to supplement group coverage or

Medicare, protection can be purchased with individual health insurance. Individual policies are sold in a wide range of prices and coverages, but all key buying decisions must be made by the purchaser, since there is no "group" involved to negotiate benefits and premium costs.

A large segment of the public still lacks the essential knowledge of what is included in their health insurance plans. To start to get a handle on the concept, remember that protection exists on three principal levels: basic, major medical, and disability. Each has its own characteristics and advantages that should be recognized by everyone interested in the cost of personal health care and ways to reduce it.

BASIC PROTECTION

Basic protection falls into two broad categories: basic hospitalization and basic medical-surgical. Both categories are designed to provide at least the initial health coverage in certain situations for most families.

Basic Hospitalization

This coverage pays benefits for a variety of services performed in and by a hospital. Among the charges usually covered are semiprivate room and board, regular nursing, operating room fees, X-rays, laboratory tests, drugs, and medication. Certain outpatient procedures, like kidney dialysis, emergency room care, and radiation therapy, may also be fully covered. But cosmetic surgery, in or out of the hospital, is rarely included in these plans.

With a basic hospitalization plan, you are normally covered for hospital services for a specific period, ranging from twenty-one days to a year or more, with the benefit period renewed after a lapse of, say, three months. The general pattern is that the longer the coverage, the more expensive the policy.

The most widely used, and normally the best buy among the basic hospitalization programs, are the plans operated by units of the nonprofit Blue Cross Association—a national federation of some seventy locally governed autonomous corporations in different parts of the country that are joined by a common name, symbol, and operating philosophy. Blue Cross started in Dallas, Texas, in 1929 to provide prepaid health-care services to subscribers. Today there is a wide range of Blue Cross programs from lower-cost coverage to a higher-cost, more comprehensive package of benefits.

Although the quality of Blue Cross plans varies from state to state, Blue Cross service benefits are always paid directly to the hospital. These benefits typically provide for all necessary hospital services, so you don't have to get involved with payments and claim forms.

Other kinds of basic hospitalization plans, based on a system of indemnity benefits, are also offered by private insurers. These policies typically provide a specified per diem amount under a fixed fee schedule toward hospital room and board, with the remainder paid by the individual.

Basic Medical-Surgical

Basic medical-surgical coverage, usually offered in combination with basic hospitalization, is primarily for doctor bills incurred as a result of surgery or hospitalization. It also sometimes includes certain services of a doctor at a private office, in your home, or at a nursing home. But there may be a number of exclusions listed in the policy, like preexisting conditions, length of coverage, and chronic health problems.

The biggest of the medical-surgical plans is the nonprofit Blue Shield, the sister organization of Blue Cross, a group of separate, autonomous corporations operating in specific geographic areas. While county medical prepayment bureaus came into existence late in the nineteenth century, Blue Shield—whose local groups are linked through the Blue Shield Association—traces its origins back to 1939 in California.

Some doctors agree to accept the full Blue Shield reimbursement allowance for their fees, but many do not. You should determine your doctor's policy in advance of any service by having a frank discussion about fees when you go to him for the first time.

MAJOR MEDICAL

Major medical policies, developed in the late 1940s, normally pick up where the basic hospitalization and basic medical-surgical insurance end. Major medical is essentially health insurance for catastrophes designed to cover the expenses of serious or lengthy injury or illness. Ideally you should have a basic plan with a supplemental major medical plan or, as an alternative, a comprehensive major medical policy that combines both plans.

Among the costs covered in a typical major medical plan are hospitalization, surgery, diagnostic techniques, doctors' fees, blood transfusions, private-duty nursing, drugs, medical devices, and rehabilitation services. Routine checkups are rarely included in major medical coverage, but patients sometimes get around that barrier if their doctor investigates a specific complaint during the examination. In addition, many of these policies have a waiting period before they become effective and others exclude coverage, at least for a specified period, for preexisting medical conditions.

Although some major medical policies pay for covered expenses from the first dollar, most have a deductible clause—generally from $100 to $1,000—that you must satisfy before the insurance is in force. Policies are structured so that the higher the deductible, the lower the cost of your insurance. Make sure that the deductible in your policy is an annual amount, rather than a separate sum for each illness.

Beyond this deductible, coinsurance usually goes into effect; the insurer will reimburse you for only a fixed percentage, perhaps 75 or 80 percent, of your covered expenses. Thus, if the medical-care bill for eligible costs amounts to $10,000, you would pay $2,000 or $2,500 over the deductible.

A number of policies, however, have a specified stop-loss limit of, say, $1,500 that you would have to pay annually. Beyond that sum, the insurance would cover all expenses up to the maximum for which you are insured. Many health insurance specialists believe that if you don't buy a policy with unlimited protection, a lifetime maximum for major medical should be between $100,000 and $250,000. Others say it should be as high as $1 million. With some of these policies, moreover, the maximum applies to each separate illness.

Because many people supplement their group health policies with individually purchased major medical plans, there may be duplicate coverage for certain medical or hospital expenses. But most major medical policies deduct the amount already paid by any other insurer, so that the combined payment will not exceed the total cost incurred.

DISABILITY INSURANCE

Disability or loss-of-income insurance provides a regular cash income in the event of disability through injury or illness that prevents you from working. The theory is that you will continue to collect a percentage of your normal earnings until you return to work. Most disability payments, moreover, are tax-exempt, as long as the individual policyholder pays the premium.

A look at the bewildering number of disability income protection programs reveals the complexity of the system. Yet without any disability protection, a family could suffer financially even with basic and major medical insurance, since they might have no income during the period of the disability.

Before investigating the various private plans on the market, check out the other sources of disability income that may be available to you at no cost or at a reduced rate. For example, there may be a group sick leave or wage continuation plan through your employer or union that provides partial or full salary for a set period. Disability resulting from an on-the-job accident may be covered by state workers' compensation programs, while some states also operate disability insurance funds for workers who become disabled due to nonoccupational injury or illness. There are also benefits to the long-term disabled and their dependents under Social Security for workers who qualify, as well as certain types of veterans' welfare and civil service disability benefits. If the total of all such benefits equals your after-tax income, then you probably don't need a private policy.

Private Insurance

When it comes to private insurance, you first should be aware of the many different definitions of disability. Some policies consider disability the inability to perform your regular line of work. Others, however, have a different definition, considering disability to be the inability to perform both regular or related duties for which you are reasonably suited. Still others will not provide disability payments unless you cannot handle any occupation at all.

With disability insurance, the general pattern is that you have to be totally disabled before benefits start. Depending on the policy, disability insurance pays these benefits beginning a day to a year after the onset of the disability and for a duration ranging from thirteen weeks to retirement age. The longer you wait before benefits start, the lower your premium for the policy. And the shorter the benefit period, also the lower your premium.

The most effective disability policies are noncancelable and have guaranteed renewable coverage, thereby protecting you—as long as you pay the premiums, of course—against being dropped by the insurer if a health problem develops. Furthermore, it is important to have coverage for both accidents and sickness, rather than just for accidents alone.

A good clause to look for in a disability policy is one that commits the insurance company to pay for the cost of a rehabilitation program. Another extra is a rider for partial disability, whereby benefits are paid when you cannot perform some of the important functions of your regular work. But in most cases, partial disability has to follow a period of total disability for the same cause.

The amount of disability insurance that you can purchase is usually limited to a percentage of your income, because insurers want to avoid creating a disincentive for returning to work. The maximum coverage tends to be around 60 percent of pre-disability income, including any Social Security disability benefits that you receive. High-income persons, though, are usually limited to a much lower percentage of pre-disability income, with the annual maximum in many policies set at about $5,000. Thus, the higher your income, the less likely that disability insurance proceeds will come close to covering your expenses.

HEALTH INSURANCE TIPS

Whatever health insurance policy you buy, here are some guidelines to keep in mind:

- When you pay your own premiums directly to the insurer, save money by paying annually, rather than monthly, quarterly, or semiannually.

- Take advantage of the "free look" option when you receive a policy. You have ten days to inspect it and ask for a refund, if for any reason you change your mind.

- Your policy should reach you within thirty days. If it does not, make inquiries to the insurance company in writing. If you do not get a response after two months, contact your state insurance department.

- Although switching policies could subject you to new exclusions and waiting periods, on some occasions a new policy offers better value or price. Just because you have an old policy with an insurance company does not mean that it gives you any special "credit" with that company.

- Overlapping coverage with two or more policies is not only costly but also sometimes futile. Many insurers have coordination-of-benefits clauses in their policies, limiting benefits to 100 percent of actual expenses.

- If you have a group policy and lose your connection with that group—if you leave a job or end an affiliation with a fraternal organization—see if you can convert your policy to an individual one. You will have to pay more and your benefits may be fewer, but at least you will have some health protection until you are able to join another group.

- Keep your insurance up-to-date by reviewing your policies annually. Make sure that your benefits have not been far outdistanced by inflation.

MEDICARE

Medicare is a health insurance program subsidized by the federal government through the Social Security Administration for people sixty-five and older—and for some severely disabled people under sixty-five. Even those who do not qualify for Medicare because they lack sufficient Social Security credits can purchase this protection for a monthly premium. Medicare's benefits depend on your health and are totally unrelated to your previous income level. They also have nothing to do with whether you are retired or whether you also have private health insurance.

Under Medicare, however, all of your health expenses are not picked up by the government. A percentage of the Social Security tax paid by employees and employers goes into the Medicare fund, and one part of Medicare is available only for a monthly charge. Then there are deductible and coinsurance amounts that you must pay before receiving any benefits. Nevertheless, Medicare is a good value for the out-of-pocket cost, and since the insurance does not go into effect automatically, it makes sense to file an application at a Social Security office a few months before you turn sixty-five so that you will be covered at the earliest possible moment.

Medicare consists of two parts: hospital insurance, or Part A; and medical insurance, Part B. Part A is geared toward rehabilitation and helps pay for a hospital stay in the United States and follow-up professional care in a skilled nursing facility or through a participating home health agency. The rule is that to receive Medicare payments, the care you get must be "reasonable and necessary" for the treatment of an injury or illness. It also must not be mainly custodial or primarily for the purpose of meeting personal needs, such as help in walking, bathing, or taking medicine.

Part B helps to pay for doctors' and outpatient hospital services and for specific medical services and supplies. But it does not cover such items as eyeglasses, hearing aids, the first three pints of blood, drugs, orthopedic shoes, private-duty nursing, and treatment in a foreign nation. Nor does it cover routine medical examinations, cosmetic surgery, acupuncture, and most chiropractic services.

Part A

With the hospital insurance, your hospital, skilled nursing facility, and home health-care bills are paid directly by Medicare. There is a deductible in each benefit period—a relatively small amount that has been rising steadily since the program was introduced—for which you are responsible. Then Medicare will pay the cost of the first sixty days in a hospital and all but a small proportion of the next thirty days. You are responsible for that proportion as a copayment. There must be a minimum of sixty days between each ninety-day benefit period of hospital stays for Medicare benefits to be applicable again. In addition, every Medicare participant gets an extra sixty hospital days, called reserve days, covering most costs, if he is forced to remain in a hospital for more than ninety days.

Part A also helps to pay for up to a hundred days in each benefit period for care in a nursing home and skilled home health care. But restrictive conditions exist before these services are made available under Medicare that limit their applicability to many people who might otherwise qualify.

Thus, to be covered under Medicare in a nursing home, five conditions must be met: (1) you have been in a hospital at least three days in a row before being transferred to the facility; (2) you are transferred to the facility because care is required for a condition that was treated in the hospital; (3) you are admitted to the facility within a short time after leaving the hospital; (4) a doctor certifies that you need, and you actually receive, skilled nursing care or skilled rehabilitation services on a daily basis; and (5) the facility's utilization review committee or a professional standards review organization does not disapprove your stay.

Similarly, for Medicare hospital insurance to pay for home health care, these six conditions must be met: (1) you were in a qualifying hospital at least three days in a row; (2) the care is for further treatment of a condition that was treated in a hospital or skilled nursing facility; (3) the care needed includes part-time skilled nursing care, physical therapy, or speech therapy; (4) you are confined to your home; (5) a doctor sets up a home health plan for you within fourteen days after your discharge; and (6) the home health agency providing the services is participating in the Medicare program.

Part B

As for medical insurance, the voluntary part of Medicare, a monthly premium is typically deducted from your Social Security check. There is also a small deductible each year, after which the government will pick up 80 percent of the "reasonable charges," leaving you to pay the remaining 20 percent with your coinsurance.

Many doctors, however, will not accept assignment of Medicare benefits as the total charge for their services. So unless you choose a doctor who agrees with the Medicare payment schedule, you will have to pay the entire amount of the difference, which could be significant.

When filing a Medicare claim, get a fully itemized bill from the doctor, including the diagnosis, a listing of each charge, the date of treatment, and the doctor's name and office address. Make sure that you fill out the Medicare form completely, or else your payments may be delayed.

If Medicare makes an adverse ruling against your claim or claims, there is a four-level appeals process. You can first ask for reconsideration by the Medicare system, then seek relief from an administrative law judge and later go on to the Appeals Council in Washington. If these steps are unsuccessful, you have the option of bringing a case in federal court. Appeals are time-consuming and can be costly when you hire a lawyer to plead your case, so they should be brought only when a substantial amount of money is involved and your chances of recovery are good. For smaller claims, a letter or telephone call to your United States Representative cannot hurt.

Although Medicare is a federal program, payments are handled by private insurance companies under government contracts. Companies that take care of claims under Part A are called intermediaries, while those handling claims under Part B are called carriers.

MEDIGAP

Because old-age coverage has many gaps, even with Medicare, it might be advisable for a person participating in the program to take out a private supplemental policy. This supplemental insurance, which is widely known as Medigap, comes in three basic forms: wraparound, hospital income, and dread disease. Many elderly health insurance buyers find that these gaps are difficult to understand because the policies are often so unintelligible.

Retirement associations sometimes offer Medigap coverages for a nominal membership fee. Typically, these plans permit enrollment regardless of previous health history and have fairly short waiting periods for preexisting health conditions. In addition, Medigap policies are offered on an individual basis through agents or directly from an insurance company, sometimes on a mail-order basis.

Two of the biggest difficulties with Medigap insurance are that you will be overinsured or that you will replace one policy with another. Medigap policies should complement, not duplicate or act as a substitute for, the coverage provided by Medicare.

Wraparound Policies

Wraparound policies are designed to supplement Medicare by paying for services that the government program does not cover. They typically pay for the deductible and copayment segments of Part A and the coinsurance portion of Part B. They may also pick up certain items not covered by Medicare, such as private-duty nursing and out-of-hospital prescription drugs. But they generally do not pay for custodial nursing home care.

Hospital Income Policies

Hospital income policies pay a fixed daily amount for a designated number of days, normally beginning after you have been hospitalized for a certain period of time. Such hospital confinement indemnity policies pay a flat fee rather than a percentage of the costs, so that you can use this income for any purpose. If you don't need the money for your bills, you can even put it in the bank.

Dread Disease Policies

Dread, or specified, disease insurance is usually the worst kind to buy because it is so narrow. These policies cover just one or a group of specified illnesses, like heart disease or cancer, and are typically limited to a fixed amount for each type of treatment. With dread disease insurance, you are usually gambling rather than insuring.

When you are in the market for Medigap insurance, try to buy a guaranteed renewable policy before you reach the age of sixty-five. Watch out for clauses excluding preexisting conditions—a mental or physical condition that began or originated before the policy was written—for a given length of time. And never make a check payable to a salesperson or pay him in cash; all payments should be made by a check to the insurance company.

HEALTH MAINTENANCE ORGANIZATIONS

Health Maintenance Organizations, also known as HMOs or medical supermarkets, are prepaid group practice plans. They are organized health-care delivery systems that promote early detection by having a single body responsible for institutional and doctor services to an enrolled group of people. With medical staffs on salary rather than working on a fee-for-service basis, Health Maintenance Organizations offer a range of treatments, are usually affiliated with hospitals, and emphasize preventive medicine. For example, periodic examinations and health education, which are rarely covered by private insurance plans, are encouraged at Health Maintenance Organizations.

Monthly premiums to Health Maintenance Organizations are typically higher than for most health insurance plans, although with some groups there is a small fee for doctor visits and pre-scription drugs. But a plethora of hospital and medical services are covered along with unlimited outpatient and emergency use of the medical center. Many Health Maintenance Organizations do have exclusions, however, with the most common being cosmetic surgery, chronic psychiatric conditions, and speech therapy.

A big plus often found in Health Maintenance Organizations is its one-stop shopping aspect because most of the medical specialists and laboratories are in the same building or complex. You can also accurately predict your annual medical costs, obtain twenty-four-hour-a-day, seven-day-a-week service from a doctor with ready access to your medical records, and get greater continuity of care at the same facility than you would otherwise.

Nevertheless, a disadvantage of a Health Maintenance Organization is having to use only those doctors affiliated with the group—although allowances are sometimes made if you need treatment far from home. You will probably not always see the same doctor within your group. And benefits also vary widely from group to group.

SHORT-TERM HEALTH POLICIES

Short-term health insurance is used to pay hospital, surgical, and medical bills for brief periods. Among those who might utilize such temporary insurance are a recent college graduate who has not yet found employment, an unemployed person who is searching for a job, an individual on strike against his employer, or someone in the probationary period established by his company for new employees.

By paying a one-time premium, you can get coverage for a specified period ranging from sixty days to a year. Some insurers' plans are even renewable. Your indemnity for hospital charges might be dependent on the daily room-and-board amount that you select, whereas other covered benefits might be paid on the basis of 80 percent of the actual costs.

Premiums for short-term insurance usually vary according to age and sex. Women in the same age group frequently pay more than men because many insurance companies believe that women at younger ages have a greater frequency of sickness.

MAIL-ORDER HEALTH INSURANCE

An enormous amount of mail-order health insurance is sold by many companies through extensive and aggressive direct mailings and broadcast and print advertising campaigns. But specialists advise extreme caution in dealing with these companies because their policies often contain inadequacies as basic protection plans.

As a rule, mail-order policies do not require a physical examination. They pay a fixed daily cash benefit while you are in the hospital and frequently make liberal use of preexisting condition exclusions. Most of them also deny a larger percentage of claims than other insurance companies. And some have a waiting period of up to eight days before cash payments for hospitalization begin, so that you could be out of the hospital before you even qualify for the benefits in the policy.

A mail-order policy with a maximum payment of $1,000 a month, for example, means that you will receive just $33.33 a day—much, much less than the daily cost of a hospital stay and far less coverage than you need. Some of these policies cover accidents but not illnesses; others lure you with unusually low introductory premiums that are quickly replaced by substantially higher prices. And buying a policy from a company that is not licensed in your state—which is easy to do with mail-order purchasing unless you check with the state authorities first—could leave you without state protection in the event of a claims collection problem with the insurer.

Mail-order policies therefore should not be a substitute for broader health policies. This insurance might have something to offer, however, if you need the additional benefits of a supplemental policy and make your choice carefully. For example, the daily benefits during a hospital stay provided by a mail-order policy—when added to those of your existing medical insurance—might be welcome at a time of high medical and hospital expenses.

Chapter Eight

Automobile Insurance

WHEN THE FIRST AUTOMOBILE INSURANCE policy was sold in 1887, one major concern was the damage that the newfangled cars might do to the horses on the road. Today the risks of driving an automobile are far different—and the potential damages that cars can inflict are infinitely more severe.

Some 30 million motor vehicle accidents occur each year, resulting in over 5 million injuries and about 50,000 deaths. The economic losses from such factors as damage to property, medical expenses, and lost wages stemming from these accidents amount to about $60 billion. Traffic accidents kill one person approximately every ten minutes. Automobile insurance is absolutely essential for any driver seeking protection from the threat of financial ruin in the form of a lawsuit.

Yet the cost of car insurance has increased significantly in recent years and has become a major consideration in the total cost of owning and operating an automobile. Buyers of automobile insurance should be aware that significant differences exist in premiums among the various insurance companies. Also to be considered are the other ways that insurers compete, including policy coverage variations, different types and quality of service, selectivity in accepting policyholders, and differences in non-renewal practices.

INSURANCE COVERAGE

Every automobile insurance company has policies that differ from other insurances to some extent. Your responsibility as an insurance buyer is to know which coverages to purchase and to find the best products available.

Liability Insurance

The most important auto insurance coverage is liability insurance, which pays for injury, death, or damage that you may cause to other people or property. This type of insurance covers accidents that occur whether the injured person is in your car, is in someone else's vehicle, or is a pedestrian. Without liability coverage, you could be financially wiped out in the event of a major accident.

When you have bodily injury liability coverage—and most states require owners or drivers to prove that they can pay with their own assets or with insurance a minimum amount in the event of negligence causing an accident—your insurance carrier will defend you in suits brought by others, even if these legal actions are fraudulent or groundless. This defense could include a trial on the merits of the case, although most suits are settled before they come to court.

In becoming a policyholder, you choose the limits, or the amount of insurance, that you want in each category. Some companies have a single liability limit, a flexible plan whereby you pick an amount, say $300,000, representing the maximum that the insurer would pay for all liability claims for both bodily injury and property damage. With a split liability limit you are covered for separate ceilings on each portion of the coverage. Thus coverage of 10/20/5 means that the insurer would pay up to $10,000 for all awards to one person for each accident, up to $20,000 for all personal injuries for each accident, and up to $5,000 for property damage liability.

Many individuals choose much higher limits, such as 100/300/ 25, because judgments in automobile accident cases are often six- and even seven-figure amounts. And if your coverage is not high enough, you are personally liable for the damages beyond the limits stated in the policy. The bigger your nest egg, the more you need.

Property damage liability applies when your vehicle causes damages to the property of another, whether it is a car, building, fence, or anything else. This protection, available in limits ranging from $5,000 to $50,000 or more, is in force even if another person is driving your car (as long as he has your permission) or if you or a family member are driving another car (also as long as permission has been granted).

Umbrella Insurance

As a supplement to both automobile liability insurance and the comprehensive liability insurance found in homeowner's and tenant's policies, insurers sell what has become known as umbrella insurance. This is a personal catastrophe liability policy that gives you excess coverage over underlying insurance amounting to $1 million, $2 million, or in some cases, up to $10 million worth of protection. A prerequisite for obtaining umbrella insurance, however, is usually a basic policy or policies for a specified amount of bodily injury, property damage, and personal liability insurance.

Medical Payments

Another important kind of auto insurance coverage is medical payments, which provide for the medical or funeral expenses of anyone injured or killed while inside or getting in or out of your car. Such payments also provide for members of your family who are injured while in someone else's car or when hit by someone else's car when walking.

Under medical payments coverage, it does not matter which party was at fault in the accident. Specified limits might be anywhere from $500 to $10,000 for every person covered by the policy, regardless of the number of people involved in a particular accident. Among the "reasonable and necessary" costs that are typically covered are surgical, X-ray, ambulance, hospital, dental, and orthopedic or prosthetic devices. Auto insurance carriers try to avoid paying a claim for expenses that have already been covered by your health insurance, but your medical payments coverage can be used to supplement health insurance or to pick up the deductible amount.

Collision Insurance

Collision insurance is purchased, on an optional basis, to cover damage to your own car, regardless of fault. Collision coverage is limited, though, in that the most the insurer will pay if the car is a total loss would be the cash, or depreciated retail, value just before the accident.

Collision insurance is sold only on a deductible basis—whereby the policyholder absorbs losses up to an agreed-upon amount—since its major function is to pay for larger, less frequent losses. Deductibles of $50 to $500 are generally available, through which you pay for losses up to that amount before the insurance comes into effect. The lower the deductible in your policy, the higher the premium. If your insurance company proves that the other driver was at fault and obtains from that driver or his insurer the amount paid out under your collision coverage plus the deductible, it will reimburse you for the deductible.

If you finance a new car with a loan from a bank or other lender, the institution will probably insist that you obtain collision coverage, at least until the loan is repaid, in order to protect its investment. But after the value of the car has declined significantly, usually four to six years after the purchase, it may be worthwhile to drop this coverage. The cash value of the automobile at this point is likely to be small, and in the event that major repairs are required you might not receive enough money from the insurance company to put the vehicle in running order.

132   INSURANCE

Comprehensive Insurance

Insurance for comprehensive physical damage covers most other losses to your car or its contents, including losses from theft, fire, glass breakage, malicious mischief, riot, vandalism, and falling objects. But although comprehensive coverage is quite broad, it usually does not provide for mechanical breakdowns and normal wear and tear. Nor is this coverage normally offered for tape recorders, CB radios, or other similar devices attached to the inside of your car.

Comprehensive is also sold only on a deductible basis, with deductibles typically ranging from $50 to $250. This part of the policy includes clauses for the reimbursement of renting a car—up to specific limits and for specific periods—if your car is stolen. There may be specified limited payments for clothing or luggage in your car at the time it is stolen.

Here again, the lower the deductible, the higher the premium. Take a typical six-month policy with collision and comprehensive coverage for a late-model midsize car, for which the premium with a $100 deductible would be $173; with a $200 deductible the premium would be $147, or 15 percent less; with a $250 deductible, it would be $134, or 23 percent less; and with a $500 deductible, it would be $101, or 42 percent less.

Uninsured Motorist Insurance

Uninsured motorist, or family protection, insurance provides payments to you in the event of injury by an uninsured driver or in a hit-and-run case. It may also apply to injuries caused by an insured motorist whose insurance company becomes insolvent. With this coverage, the insurer will assume responsibility for the medical expenses, pain and suffering, and, sometimes, property damage, up to the limit specified in the policy.

In certain states, uninsured motorist coverage with set limits of, say, 15/30/5 is mandatory, while in others, such protection is optional. And in some states, the payments may be reduced by the amount you get under your disability insurance, workers' compensation insurance, or other automobile medical coverage.

Other kinds of auto insurance coverage include underinsured motorist, wage loss—which makes up for at least a portion of the income you lose due to injury—and substitute services—which pays for services, like child care, that you cannot perform yourself while recuperating from an injury.

TAX EFFECTS OF USING DEDUCTIBLES

Until 1983, many taxpayers were able to write off part of their collision and comprehensive deductibles, and thereby let the government pay a portion of the cost. But since then, federal income tax itemized deductions of personal casualty and theft losses were restricted to the amount exceeding 10 percent of gross income. And this means that policyholders cannot rely on the tax law to subsidize an underinsured loss.

For example, take an unmarried individual with an adjusted gross income of $85,000 and a $500 deductible in the collision section of his automobile insurance policy. If that person were involved in an accident prior to 1983 that caused $1,000 worth of damage to his car, he would take a $400 deduction—the $500 uninsured part of the loss minus the $100 per occurrence base for reimbursed casualty losses. And since he was in the 50 percent tax bracket, the deduction has an after-tax value to him of $200. The result is a total out-of-pocket cost of $300—the remaining $200 plus the $100 base.

Since 1983, however, that individual would have to suffer a loss of at least $8,500, or 10 percent of his adjusted gross income, before claiming any deductions. So he would be able to deduct nothing following the $1,000 accident and would suffer a full out-of-pocket loss of $500.

NO-FAULT INSURANCE

The principle of no-fault automobile insurance, debated and proposed within the insurance industry for about fifty years, emerged in the mid-1960s with growing consumer discontent with the traditional ways of compensating injured victims of automobile accidents. Under the tort liability, or fault, system upon which insurance recoveries have been based since the nineteenth century, it was necessary to determine first who was guilty of negligence—generally defined as unreasonably risky conduct—and therefore legally at fault in any accident. And if the injured or deceased caused or contributed to the accident, he or his estate usually could not recover much beyond his medical expenses.

In order to determine who was at fault in an accident, a costly and time-consuming investigation by the two parties and their insurance companies was often required. When settlements were not negotiated by the parties, court trials prolonged the dispute and increased the expenses. And when some drivers had inadequate liability coverage, or no liability coverage at all, accident victims, particularly those who were seriously injured, faced a great deal of financial hardship.

Concept of No-Fault

No-fault automobile insurance therefore evolved as an attempt to reduce expensive insurance costs and to speed payment of claims by circumventing the adversary procedures of the courts. It recognizes that life insurance, health insurance, and property insurance are all based on the no-fault concept.

The major advantage of the no-fault system is not cost reduction, however, but a more equitable distribution of the automobile insurance dollar based on need rather than fault. With a true no-fault insurance system, all accident victims can be compensated for their injuries, not just those who can prove that somebody else was at fault.

The idea of a reparations system not based on determining who is responsible for the damage or injury has been a familiar feature of law and insurance practice since the start of workers' compensation legislation at the start of the twentieth century. But it did not become a factor in automobile insurance until a 1965 proposal highlighted the problem of the tort liability system and described a procedure whereby a person injured in an automobile accident would receive compensation for the economic loss from his own insurer, even when another person was at fault and therefore legally responsible for payment.

Although the state laws that have been enacted are frequently complicated, a true no-fault system has three essential elements: (1) benefits are provided to covered persons regardless of who is at fault; (2) no-fault insured persons are exempt from tort liability; and (3) individuals are compelled to buy no-fault coverage on registered automobiles. Thus in all of the no-fault states except Michigan—where this coverage also includes vehicle damage—the no-fault system covers only losses connected with bodily injury.

No-fault insurance is known as first-party insurance because the benefits are paid to the policyholder—the party of the first part in an insurance contract. In contrast, liability insurance benefits are paid to a third party, the individual injured through the policyholder's negligence. The second party, of course, is the insurance company.

In theory, the goals of the no-fault auto system are efficiency, speed, equity, and security. The object is to offer prompt, fair, and adequate compensation to anyone who suffers a major financial loss as a result of an injury or death in an automobile accident—regardless of fault. A secondary objective is to raise the percentage of the insurance dollar that goes to the victim and, by reducing the amount of litigation generated by automobile accidents, to lower the percentage that is used to pay legal and administrative costs. Among the categories usually covered are medical and rehabilitation expenses, funeral costs, and loss of earnings.

As envisioned by theoreticians, a pure no-fault law would provide financial protection for all of the costs resulting from an automobile accident and abolish the right to sue the driver who was at fault in an accident. It would be compulsory with no-cancellation clauses, eliminate all liability coverages from auto insurance policies, and prohibit duplicate payments for the same loss. It would also make no provision for the intangibles of pain and suffering, and allow for coverage only of actual economic losses due to injuries or fatalities.

In practice, however, most no-fault insurance has become principally a system for limiting the general damages that can be paid out under different circumstances when an automobile injury or death occurs. Those whose economic loss—and in some cases, whose noneconomic loss, also called pain and suffering— exceeds the state's compulsory no-fault benefit limits can still bring a suit alleging liability for the excess amount.

No-Fault in Use

A general consensus developed in the insurance industry during the early 1970s as to the key provisions that no-fault insurance should encompass. These include:

- The benefit package to the first party, or policyholder, should be in the range of $5,000 to $25,000.

- Automobile insurance should be primary, thereby paying benefits before all other insurance except state workers' compensation or disability coverage. Primary auto insurance results in greater savings than primary health insurance, since the former is compulsory and the latter is not.

- The traditional fault principles should still be used if, say, benefits paid to one person are larger than $1,500 or if a commercial vehicle is involved.

Massachusetts became the first state to adopt a compulsory no-fault law, the Massachusetts Bodily Injury Law, in 1971. Now more than two dozen states have such legislation. Each law is different, although all state no-fault laws require some coverage by drivers. The variations among states deal with such basics as the amount to be paid for medical or funeral expenses, the availability of deductibles, the amount of loss of income to be paid to an injured worker, the amount to be paid to someone hired to perform essential services for a non-income producer, and the conditions governing the right to sue.

The consequence has been that while no-fault was conceived as a no-sue situation, in most states where this legislation has been enacted, you still can bring an action if your injuries are larger than a set dollar threshold. In fewer instances, you can sue if you suffer certain injuries that exceed a disability threshold or what is known as a descriptive threshold. In some states, dollar thresholds are quite low, while in others they are substantial. Disability thresholds, on the other hand, are usually more difficult to abuse than dollar thresholds. A third category known as verbal thresholds allow suits only for situations explicitly mentioned in a law, such as death, permanent disability, or loss of bodily functions.

In most states, no-fault is an addition to, rather than a replacement for, liability insurance. A pitfall of this condition is a conflict among various laws in different states. But recently, pressure has been building for the creation of a national no-fault system in the 1980s.

There is no assurance, however, that a federal law—whether it sets national standards or minimum standards for the states—will be any stronger than most state laws are at present. Although a uniform national formula has yet to be created that would be likely to work in every state, a federal plan would be practically irreversible. Since lawyers predominate in both the federal and state legislatures, the prospects for a strong push in the next few years for no-fault—with its limitations on legal action—are slim.

ESTABLISHING RATES

Insurers take a large number of elements into consideration when setting automobile insurance rates. As a result, a person with an excellent driving record may sometimes be forced to pay high premiums because he fits into one of the statistical categories that an insurance company has determined constitute worse-than-average risks.

Age is typically one consideration, with under twenty-five- or under thirty-year-old drivers generally paying more for auto insurance than older drivers. Women often are charged less than men, while married men and women are charged less than single people of the same age and in the same general circumstances. Those engaged in certain kinds of work may be termed high-risk by some insurance companies, as may those who live in major cities or in parts of cities where an inordinate number of auto thefts occur. Other factors may include the kind of car being driven, total annual mileage, and whether the vehicle is used daily for commutation.

Insurers use these classifications because, while it is not possible to predict whether a specific individual will have one or more accidents in the coming year, the probabilities for certain groups of drivers can be predicted with a great deal of accuracy. Insurers have been compiling and analyzing such data for many years.

Among the ways to save on automobile premiums are to insure all of your cars with the same insurer and under the same policy to obtain a volume discount, insure a car primarily driven by a teenage child in your name, pay premiums annually if possible, and avoid the purchase of high-performance vehicles that are known for high speeds. Of course, look at the policies and rate quotations of at least a few automobile insurance companies, rather than one alone, before selecting an insurer.

FILING A CLAIM

Whenever your car is involved in an accident, it is usually best to notify your insurance company promptly. Even if the damage to both cars appears to be minor and no one seems to be injured, you may be unexpectedly sued for liability by the other party at a later date. If you are accused of being at fault, you will need all of the backup your insurer can provide.

The reason for quick notification is that insurance companies are required, under their liability coverages, to pay justifiable claims against you and defend you in court if necessary. Therefore the faster they receive the necessary information and prepare their case, the better this defense might be. Your interests are usually better served by cooperating with your insurance company than by putting roadblocks in the way. One important caveat: Don't deal with the other party's insurance company before discussing the matter with your own insurer or agent.

After you give the initial notification, usually by telephone or letter, the insurer may advise you about filing a formal claim. This claim is a demand for payment for loss from bodily injury or property damage, under the terms and conditions of the policy. You will be asked to list information about the date, time, place, and circumstances of the accident, the facts concerning the injury or damage, and the total expenses incurred. Some insurers even operate drive-in claim centers, where damages can be determined and settlements made immediately.

In no-fault states, your bodily injury insurance payments should come quickly after you submit doctor or hospital bills and proof of lost earnings. Other claims are usually slower to process and you may wind up with a long wait, regardless of the merits of your case. Some insurers might stall by failing to acknowledge claims, delaying correspondence, or making their adjusters unavailable. Often no settlement is made until a trial is about to begin, so the longer you can hold out, the better off you may be.

When it comes to determining the damage to your car after an accident, get an estimate from your mechanic or body shop—not your insurance company's—that will guarantee the work performed. Otherwise you could wind up with a poor repair job done by someone who had to cut corners to meet a fixed price. An insurer may insist on more than one estimate, but whatever procedure is followed, your goal ought to be having the car repaired to your satisfaction, rather than to someone else's.

Even when there is no bodily injury and damage only to your own vehicle, a claim should still be filed. If the damages exceed the deductible limit and if you have collision or comprehensive insurance, your insurer will pay the difference.

REPLACEMENT COST INSURANCE

In some states, insurance companies offer automobile replacement insurance. In many ways, such insurance resembles the replacement cost coverage for the contents of a home that is sold in connection with homeowner's policies.

With replacement insurance, the insurer promises to pay the

partial or full expense of repairing or replacing your damaged vehicle after an accident. In contrast, the standard collision and comprehensive coverage is designed to reimburse you for no more than the actual cash value of the car at the time of the damage.

The underlying concept of replacement cost coverage is that the current market price of a vehicle may not reflect its intrinsic worth to the owner, nor be the amount necessary to buy a new car. In fact, a person could owe more money on an automobile loan than he receives as a settlement for damages from his insurance company.

A damaged automobile is considered a total loss by the insurance industry not only when it is impossible to repair, but also when it costs more to repair than its current market value. With the rising expenses of parts and labor—coupled with the prevalence of complicated unibody construction and the larger percentage of smaller cars on the road—more and more cars are being designated as "totaled." Under standard policies, the insurer pays the owners the book value of these cars and then uses them for salvage.

Although policies vary, the typical procedure under replacement cost insurance is for the insurer to pay for repairs, if the car will still be safe and if the cost is less than buying a new model of similar size, class, and equipment. When the vehicle is damaged beyond repair—a determination normally made solely by the company—the insurer will pay to replace it with a new car of comparable quality.

Take the case of an automobile purchased four years ago for $8,000 that has depreciated to $4,000. Under standard policies, the owner would receive $4,000 in the event of a total loss of the vehicle, although it might cost $6,000 to repair and a comparable new model might cost $12,000. With replacement cost coverage, the owner would receive $6,000 if the automobile could be fixed and $12,000 if it could not.

Replacement cost insurance is typically about 10 percent more expensive than the standard combined collision and comprehensive premium, but you may find it worthwhile. Conditions usually must be met before the replacement insurance goes into effect. And the coverage normally does not apply to fire or theft, in order to avoid creating an incentive for misrepresentation by the owner.

THE SHARED MARKET

Individuals with a poor driving record could have problems buying insurance or find that an insurance company will not renew their policies. But laws in every state call for insurance to be sold to these drivers, although they may have to pay considerably higher premiums or accept only minimal coverage.

Millions of cars in the United States are covered by this automobile insurance shared market—the system devised by the industry to guarantee the availability of insurance to almost everyone. Also called the residual market, such a system offers a last resort to motorists who have difficulty obtaining auto insurance through normal channels.

There are four different shared market mechanisms in use among the various states. The concept calls for all companies writing business in a particular state to participate equitably, as ascertained by their competitive market share. Insurers participate either by the acceptance of individual risks or by becoming a member of a pool.

Approximately 7 percent of all insured vehicles in this country, around 7 million automobiles, are insured through the shared market. This amount is larger than the number of cars voluntarily insured by all but two companies and represents about 8 percent of all insurance premiums. Some 85 percent of the shared market coverage is for private passenger cars.

Assigned Risk Plan

The most common of the shared market mechanisms, operating in more than three quarters of the states, is the assigned risk plan, formally known as the automobile insurance plan. Under this plan, governed by a board representing the state's licensed insurers, applications for insurance by those turned down for regular coverage are distributed to all companies in proportion to the amount of business the company voluntarily writes in the state—although with credit and incentive programs the percentage may vary. Each insurer must then service these policyholders just as it services its other policyholders.

Joint Underwriting Association

Another type is the joint underwriting association, a pool in which all automobile insurance companies in the state share in the profits and losses, as well as the costs generated, by this business. Assessments are prorated on the basis of a company's premium volume in the state. The actual policies, however, are issued and serviced by just a few companies, known as servicing carriers, that are then reimbursed for bookkeeping and related expenses.

Reinsurance Facility

The third mechanism is called a reinsurance facility, whereby every automobile insurer is required to provide coverage and service to any applicant, no matter how bad his driving record. But carriers are also allowed to transfer a percentage of their worst risks to the facility. The facility's profits or losses are shared equitably among all auto insurers in the state, prorated on the basis of their overall volume.

State Insurance Fund

One state, Maryland, operates the Maryland Automobile Insurance Fund, which is in effect a state insurance company. High-risk drivers must be rejected by two insurance companies before becoming eligible for coverage from the fund. Private insurers do not participate directly in this fund, but they are required to subsidize any of its losses—with such expenses charged back in the form of subcharges against their policyholders.

FINANCIAL RESPONSIBILITY

A wide variety of state laws require drivers to furnish evidence, either before or after an automobile accident, of financial responsibility. And if you cannot prove that you have the resources to pay damages, your license and registration could be suspended or revoked.

Such evidence in most cases includes auto liability insurance with set minimum limits. Frequently the minimum in split-limit policies is $10,000 per person and $20,000 per accident for bodily injury coverage, and $5,000 for property damage coverage. The minimum for single-limit policies is often $25,000. However, in this era of large judgments after liability has been determined, it makes sense for most American families to have much higher limits as protection against financial disaster.

Financial responsibility can also be demonstrated by having specified financial assets or a specified net worth. In some states where neither adequate financial assets nor liability insurance are shown, your car may be impounded after an accident and held by the state until this financial responsibility is eventually proven.

AUTO INSURANCE TIPS

- Find out if you are eligible for any discounts from your insurance company. Some insurers, for example, offer compact car discounts, based on such factors as size, weight, and horsepower. There are also discounts based on such considerations as driver training, safe driving, age (over sixty-five), make and model experience, and a good scholastic record.

- Shop around for insurance, since rates can and do vary widely. A look at *Best's Insurance Reports* will reveal information about an insurer's financial soundness and a talk with representatives of three or more companies will indicate price differences. Remember that the lowest-cost company is not necessarily the best. Service, selectivity, and other standards should be weighed in choosing an insurer.

- Investigate whether you can participate in a lower-premium group auto insurance program. These plans are sometimes offered through employers, unions, and professional or social organizations and can often cut your premiums substantially.

Chapter Nine

Residential Insurance

A HOUSE IS PROBABLY THE most expensive purchase—and frequently one of the best investments—most families make. Homeowner's insurance therefore is essential to protect against the possibility of financial disaster caused by damage, theft, or liability.

Fire is the most feared disaster to a residence. But other common perils, such as windstorm, explosion, vandalism, and falling objects, can, and should, be insured against. In addition to these risks are the dangers of theft of personal articles in the home and personal liability suits brought by visitors and others alleging injury.

The so-called package homeowner's policies that are now so widely used, were first written by insurance companies in the late 1940s. Before then, insurers had been forbidden to sell both fire and liability, or casualty, insurance. With the elimination of those restrictions, package policies encompassing fire and liability insurance, along with theft insurance for the personal property in the home, were created by companies in the insurance industry.

145

The package policies provide these coverages for a lower cost than purchasing each one separately. Nevertheless, premiums for comparable coverage vary widely among different insurance companies. Among the factors considered by insurers are the construction, age, and condition of the home; the limits of coverage and deductibles; and the location of the property.

For example, a house twenty-five miles away from a fire station is considered a greater risk than a home much closer to a station. Frame houses tend to suffer more damage from fire than masonry homes. And theft coverage usually costs more in high-crime areas than in low-crime ones.

HOMEOWNER'S POLICIES

A homeowner's policy usually fits into one of four categories that insurance companies call HO-1, HO-2, HO-3, and HO-5. The categories differ in the kinds of coverage offered, with the simplest being Form HO-1—basic insurance against a limited list of perils—and the most comprehensive policy being Form HO-5—insurance against most risks on the dwelling and its contents.

Also generally included under the overall category of homeowner's insurance are special kinds of residential insurance policies for those who do not own houses. Among them is insurance for renters, for owners of condominium units and cooperative apartments, and for owner-occupants of mobile homes. These policies have special clauses related to the specific markets they serve, along with many standard provisions dealing with loss or damage to the contents.

As examples of different perils covered by the different policies, look at the differences in the perils covered by the basic Form HO-1 and the comprehensive Form HO-5. Form HO-1 insures the house and personal property against fire or lightning, windstorm or hail, explosion, riot or civil commotion, loss of property removed from the premises, smoke, vandalism or malicious mischief, theft, breakage of glass, and damage from vehicles and aircraft.

Form HO-5, on the other hand, not only insures the residence and personal property against those perils, but also covers such additional factors as falling objects, the weight of ice, snow or sleet, the collapse of the building, the freezing of plumbing, heating and air-conditioning systems, and accidental discharge, leakage, or overflow of water or steam.

Beginning in 1976, insurers began offering simplified versions of the various forms of their homeowner's policies with a form called HO-76. These policies are much easier to understand than the older, legalistic forms because of the substitution of straightforward language for the formal jargon that had been used for decades. The simplified policies, moreover, are much shorter than their predecessors, yet contain the equivalent information in as few as 5,000 words.

As for tenant's insurance, it serves as protection from severe financial losses in case of loss of, or damage to, furniture, appliances, clothing, and other valuable items. These household contents are not covered by the landlord's insurance policy, which covers the building but not tenants' personal belongings. The landlord's policy also does not cover tenants' liability to others.

The renter's or tenant's form, HO-4, is also a package policy encompassing both personal belongings and liability. Damage to the house is not covered under this policy, but the perils insured against include fire, theft, vandalism, breakage of glass, falling objects, and freezing of plumbing, heating, and air-conditioning systems.

Insurance on the Home

Potential damage to the home itself, of course, is the basis for the insurance coverage. The face amount of the policy is thus the basic amount that you would receive if your house were completely destroyed. In addition, you might receive money for the loss of personal property and household furnishings, additional living expenses, and the loss of other structures on your property. Conceivably, therefore, the amount paid by the insurer could be greater than the face value.

Most insurers use a coinsurance, or loss-settlement, clause that requires policyholders to carry insurance equal to 80 percent of

Perils Against Which Properties are Insured Under the Various Homeowner's Policies

Basic HO-1	Broad HO-2	Special HO-3	Renter's HO-4	Compre-hensive HO-5	Perils
					1. Fire or lightning
					2. Loss of property removed from premises endangered by fire or other perils*
					3. Windstorm or hail
					4. Explosion
					5. Riot or civil commotion
					6. Aircraft
					7. Vehicles
					8. Smoke
					9. Vandalism and malicious mischief
					10. Theft
					11. Breakage of glass constituting a part of the building
					12. Falling objects
					13. Weight of ice, snow, sleet
					14. Collapse of building(s) or any part thereof
					15. Sudden and accidental tearing asunder, cracking, burning, or bulging of a steam or hot water heating system or of appliances for heating water
					16. Accidental discharge, leakage, or overflow of water or steam from within a plumbing, heating, or air-conditioning system or domestic appliance
					17. Freezing of plumbing, heating, and air-conditioning systems and domestic appliances
					18. Sudden and accidental injury from artificially generated currents to electrical appliances, devices, fixtures, and wiring (TV and radio tubes not included)
					All perils except flood, earthquake, war, nuclear accident, and others specified in your policy. Check your policy for a complete listing of perils excluded.

–Dwelling and personal property
–Dwelling only
–Personal property only

* Included as a peril in traditional forms of the homeowner's policy; as an additional coverage in the simplified (HO-76) policies.
Source: Insurance Information Institute

the replacement value of the home in order to be paid in full for a partial loss up to the policy limits. If your insurance does not meet the 80 percent test, you will not receive full payment.

Thus a home purchased for $50,000 might have a replacement value of $100,000 and should be insured for at least $80,000. In the case of a fire causing $20,000 worth of damage to such a house with $80,000 in insurance, the claim would be paid in full. But if the house were insured for only $60,000, or 60 percent of the replacement cost, then the policyholder would be reimbursed for either 75 percent of the loss—60 percent divided by the 80 percent minimum required under the policy—or the actual cash value of the damaged structure, whichever is more. Your home may be underinsured if your insurance is not related to present-day costs.

Replacement Value

The effect of inflation on home costs has focused increasing attention on acquiring replacement cost insurance. In the decade of the 1970s alone, the cost of purchasing a home increased by 115 percent, the expenses of house maintenance and repair soared by 130 percent, and private residential construction costs zoomed by 156 percent. Indeed, the significance of obtaining insurance to full value has never been clearer.

Tens of thousands of homeowners are underinsured because they have not increased the amount of their homeowner's coverage from inordinately low levels. Homeowner's insurance should not be a "buy and goodbye" purchase. It requires continuous review in line with changing conditions.

Take the case of a house with an $80,000 replacement value insured under the broad form homeowner's policy—Form HO-2. If the home were insured to 80 percent of full value, as most insured homes are, the maximum coverage for the dwelling would be $64,000. But if it were insured for full replacement value, the dwelling would be covered up to the full $80,000.

A professional appraiser would probably most accurately determine the replacement value of your home. You could also calculate the square footage of the home and multiply it by a cost-per-square-foot factor. Do-it-yourself estimate worksheets that many insurance companies make available assign points to various features of the house, such as the number of rooms or the quality of the construction. The estimated replacement value is the total of these points multiplied by a cost factor depending on the square footage of the residence.

This value will probably change and your original policy limits are likely to be inadequate as the years pass, so it makes sense to update your coverage periodically. Many insurers sell an inflation-guard endorsement to their homeowner's policies that automatically increases the coverage every quarter, either by a specified percentage or in keeping with a predetermined index of costs. Don't forget that replacement value is not necessarily the same as market value; it can be more or less.

Homeowner's policies also offer coverage against damages to other structures on the same lot as the home, such as a detached garage or storage shed. But typically this coverage is limited to 10 percent of the amount of insurance on the home. Thus a home insured for $100,000 will carry $10,000 worth of insurance on the appurtenant structures.

Contents Insurance

Damage or loss to personal property inside the house is covered by these policies as well. Here, too, the coverage is a percentage of the face value of the policy, with contents insurance limited to 50 percent of the insurance on the house. Other coverages using a percentage of face value as the maximum include personal property off the premises at 10 percent and additional living expenses—the necessary increases incurred at hotels and restaurants while maintaining your standard of living when your house cannot be occupied—at 20 percent.

Most policies, though, have specified limits for certain categories of personal articles. Among these "special limits of liability" are $100 for money and gold and silver coins, $500 for theft of securities, jewelry and furs, and $1,000 for theft of guns and silverware.

Yet in many cases the contents of a home might include items that would push the real value higher than the personal property limits of a homeowner's policy. Among such hidden treasures in a home could be antiques, coin and stamp collections, musical instruments, camera equipment, oriental rugs, art, and other expensive or unusual merchandise.

These valuables can be insured separately by purchasing a personal articles floater policy, or rider to a homeowner's policy, that is widely available. Coverage applies wherever the articles are located at the time of loss, even if not in the home, and is therefore said to "float" with the property.

Appraisals of Household Goods

As for determining the value of household furnishings and personal belongings, an up-to-date written inventory can be helpful. A simple listing and description of the major items in every room, along with the serial numbers, purchase dates, and prices, and possibly photographs and original invoices, will go a long way toward establishing ownership and value if proof is required.

The undesirable alternative to keeping good records is for the homeowner to attempt to recall the contents from memory after a disaster. Most people cannot recall all items accumulated over a lifetime, and certainly not when they are under great stress. Therefore the more thorough the inventory, the greater its effectiveness and the better the chance that an insurance claim will be settled efficiently.

For a more sophisticated valuation of a particular item or items, professional appraisals can be obtained for a fee. In the event of a dispute with an insurer over the amount of a loss, this type of appraisal could expedite a quick settlement.

Both general and specialist appraisers are available. Their job is to study individual items, describe them, and place a retail value on them, as of the date of the appraisal. You can find an appraiser through recommendations, or select one from listings in the yellow pages. Another way to start might be to ask for information on the kind of appraiser for your needs from the two major professional appraisers' associations: The American Society of Appraisers, Dulles International Airport, P.O. Box 17265, Washington, D.C. 20041; or the Appraisers Association of America, 60 East 42nd Street, New York, NY 10017.

Professional appraisal charges vary, depending on location, and are established by the day, hour, item, or job. Some appraisers charge a percentage of the valuation, while others consider this kind of fee structure unethical and will have nothing to do with it.

Whether you undertake a simple homemade inventory or an appraisal by a professional, it is advisable to update or reappraise at least every two to three years to account for new or discarded possessions and changes in values. Above all, don't keep the original document in the home whose contents it is designed to help protect. Put the document in a safe and secure place elsewhere, such as in a bank safe deposit box, so that it will be available if necessary.

Liability Insurance

An accident may occur at any time in and around your home, and if it happens to someone outside the family, you may be sued. Liability insurance is designed to provide protection for you or members of your household against claims and lawsuits. This coverage is for accidents that happen not only at the home, but also—with few exceptions, such as automobile accidents—for accidents that occur off the premises.

There are two basic categories of liability insurance: protection against personal injury and protection against property damage. Coverage on the standard homeowner's liability insurance is usually limited to $25,000 per accident, but this amount can be increased at a modest additional cost.

Also available as an option is medical payments coverage for hospital and doctor expenses of those either accidentally injured on your property or injured by your family elsewhere. The basic coverage is $500 per person, although again, increased coverage can be purchased for an extra amount. Payments do not depend on legal liability and are made according to the no-fault concept.

A further supplement to the standard comprehensive liability coverage is separate umbrella insurance, which also supplements automobile liability coverage. Such a personal catastrophe liability policy—which has as a prerequisite a specified amount of basic liability insurance—provides excess coverage of $1 million or more for a relatively small premium.

In the standard homeowner's policies, as might be expected, the only injuries or damages covered are the unintentional ones. For example, the wording in a sample policy provided by the Insurance Information Institute is: "Medical payments to others do not apply to bodily injury or property damage which is expected or intended by the insured."

When a legal action is brought against you, your insurance company will pay claims up to the limits of the policy. The company also has the responsibility for providing a legal defense in court, negotiating an out-of-court settlement if possible, and paying the interest on contested judgments.

Remember that homeowner's liability coverage excludes business activities and the rental premises of the insured. If you buy additional property, it may be covered under the policy, but your premium will probably rise at renewal time. If a worker is injured while doing a job at your home, any claim arising from such an injury may also be covered in some states.

Liability Prevention

A number of steps can be taken by homeowners to minimize the possibility of fires or accidents at their homes. For instance, the observation of basic fire-prevention techniques can make your property much more secure. Among the most important are the installation of smoke detectors and fire extinguishers, as well as periodic checks of the electric wiring.

Other precautionary measures include the use of the proper size fuses, purchase of electrical appliances that have the Underwriters' Laboratories seal, and preparation of a plan for escaping from the house in case of fire. Keep escape ladders in upper-level bedrooms for emergency situations when no other exits are open.

As for the ways to diminish the chances of accidents occurring inside and outside the home, a safety-oriented attitude among members of the family is of the essence. Actions that you can take include clearing the sidewalk and driveway of snow, ice and wet leaves, keeping the stairs and halls clear of obstacles, and securing the rugs and carpets in order to prevent tripping and falling.

Additional Coverage

Insurance companies have added coverages to their policies for other expenses that affect homeowners whose houses are damaged or destroyed by a fire or other peril. The six additional coverages are:

- Reasonable temporary repairs that are necessary to protect the property against further damages.

- The reasonable cost of removing debris and other damaged property.

- The replacement cost of the loss of any trees, shrubs, plants, or lawns, up to $500, or a maximum of 5 percent of the insurance limit for the residence.

- The expense of removing rescued property from a home and protecting it for up to thirty days against any direct loss.

- Reimbursement for fire department service charges, in areas where homeowners must pay, up to $250.

- Reimbursement up to $500 for loss of credit cards, check forgeries, or the acceptance in good faith of counterfeit money.

HIGH-RISK PLANS

Special property insurance plans are intended for those who may not be able to get insurance elsewhere because of unusual hazards. They are operated in many states in order to assure the availability of insurance protection for high-risk properties in urban areas. These plans are also designed to cover properties in coastal areas where severe windstorm damage often occurs and where standard insurance could be hard to purchase.

In twenty-six states plus the District of Columbia and Puerto Rico, such plans are called FAIR plans, an acronym for Fair Access to Insurance Requirements. Also known as fire insurance pools, these plans provide coverage against losses from fire, riots, and vandalism. They were established after Congress passed the Housing and Urban Development Act of 1968.

FAIR plans, which are supported by the insurers that sell property insurance in the state, must offer insurance on inner-city properties at rates that are not higher than those on the voluntary market. The pools do so in order to qualify for federal riot insurance, but the result is that many of them have continual operating losses. FAIR plan applications cannot be rejected because of the location of the neighborhood or an environmental hazard beyond the control of the owner of the property.

All FAIR plans sell what is known as fire and extended coverage, which includes windstorm, vandalism, and specified other perils. And some of them also provide homeowner's insurance and miscellaneous coverages in addition to their primary protection.

HOMEOWNER'S INSURANCE TIPS

- Take advantage of homeowner's deductibles if they are available in your state, thereby assuming some of the risk yourself and saving on insurance costs. About one third of all damage losses on homes and contents is for under $100. By self-insuring for losses of, say, $100, $250, or $500, premiums can be significantly reduced.

- Don't leave your home empty for thirty consecutive days, because if a loss occurs while you are away, you may not be protected against such situations as vandalism or broken glass.

- If the plumbing, heating, or air-conditioning systems freeze, your damages may not be covered unless you can demonstrate that you properly drained the pipes or maintained the heat.

- Try to pay your homeowner's insurance premiums annually, instead of monthly, quarterly, or semiannually, and thereby save on premium costs.

- An important element in the fire insurance portion of homeowner's premiums is the rating of the local fire department. The installation of safety devices, such as sprinklers, smoke detectors, fire extinguishers, or alarm systems, can help to reduce rates further.

- Some companies offer discounts for security devices such as burglar alarms and dead bolt locks. Discounts may also be available from insurers if your house was built or renovated recently, or if it is insured for 90 or 100 percent of the replacement cost. Ask your company whether discounts are offered for any reason.

- Check out the possibility of purchasing less expensive homeowner's insurance through your employer, union, or professional organization. This coverage is quite rare, but it does exist in certain places. Some such groups have used their combined buying power to negotiate substantially lower premiums for eligible individuals.

- Compare the coverages and premiums offered by a number of companies, rather than accepting the first policy presented. Even if you already have a homeowner's policy, do some comparison shopping before renewal time to assure yourself of the wisest selection. Insist that the insurance company or agent answer whatever questions are on your mind. Of course, claims handling, quality of service, payment methods,

and the insurer's financial conditions are also important considerations.

- File a claim immediately after suffering a loss and en-
  close the necessary supporting documentation—such
  as a copy of the police report of a theft or photographs
  showing the damage from a fire.

Part Three

Investments

Chapter Ten

An Overview

INVESTING IS A WAY TO make your money grow. By buying stocks, bonds, mutual funds, options, futures, or other securities and commodities, you put your funds to work in an effort to obtain a return on your investment. As many people have discovered, such purchases can be a hedge against inflation and a basis for retirement.

If you are knowledgeable, skillful, and lucky, your investments will increase in value, perhaps rapidly, perhaps slowly. If not, you will have less than you started with. The odds are that the value of your portfolio will rise and fall at different times over the years. However, with proper preparation, frequent weighing of choices and opportunities, careful selection of an advisor or salesperson, and continual analyses of your holdings, you have a good chance of building an estate for the future.

But make no mistake about it. There is a risk in investing, whatever the form, since you can lose part or all of the amount involved. Yet if you put money in a bank, the interest rate may be lower than the inflation rate and the real value of your money will erode. And there is risk in holding on to cash, since the money can be stolen or its purchasing power can be worth far less in real terms when you want to use it than when you received it.

Therefore, how and when you invest depend to a great extent on your ability and willingness to take risks. If your financial resources are tight, there will probably be little in the form of discretionary funds for investing. If you are close to retirement, of conservative bent, or have irregular commission earnings, your investing pattern is likely to be different from that of the person who is beginning his career, enjoys taking a chance, or has a steady salary. You must make any investing decision based on your particular lifestyle, attitudes, and status.

Thus, fixed-income securities, such as corporate, municipal, and government bonds, are typically picked by individuals who seek stability of principal and a regular income. Money market funds and mutual funds that invest in blue chip stocks are among other categories of relatively safe securities. Stocks of growth companies with untested earning power are less secure investments, as are those of small corporations that have demonstrated problems in operations or management. And included in the speculative category of investments are options, financial futures, commodities, and tax shelters.

Whatever your choice, your basic needs should be well taken care of before any investing begins. Emergency funds in the bank, adequate life, health and property insurance, and a down payment on a home ought to come before even considering stocks, bonds, or other investments. The complexities of investing for the future must give way to the realities of everyday living.

Although investing certainly is a complex and demanding task, it should not be shunned for this reason. A time-tested approach for the novice might be to first learn the guidelines for investing, then look into the various alternatives available, and finally select the individual investments that you can afford and that meet your needs. Financial independence is a worthy objective and one that should be approached with intelligence, eagerness, and anticipation.

OBJECTIVES OF INVESTING

It pays to understand the differences among the various investment goals in order to determine which objectives best fit your requirements at each stage of your life.

Security of Principal

The possibility, and certainly the hope, of gain is, of course, the basic rationale for investing. But a corollary to this desire is the long-term retention of the capital undergoing risk, which otherwise could be partially or entirely lost when investments go sour.

Many investment advisors believe that the best way to preserve your funds is by following basic rules that offer the best chance of retaining the amount invested regardless of the short-term swings in the financial markets. Among them are diversification of portfolio, long-term investing, and a search for issues that have stood the test of time. With experience, you may determine additional rules of your own.

Growth of Capital

If your earnings cover your current expenses and you have provided for possible emergencies, your investment approach might well emphasize capital growth. Here, too, long-range results are most important, since annual average increases in an overall portfolio of, say, 10 percent for thirty or more years could leave you with a sizable nest egg for the future.

The bottom line could become even larger if all or part of the investment appreciation were carried out through one of the many tax-deferred plans available, such as an individual retirement account (I.R.A.) or a Keogh plan. Furthermore, if this growth of capital is sufficient, you might be able to maintain the same, or almost the same, standard of living after retirement as before.

Stability of Income

When a steady income is your most important consideration, bond interest or stock dividends should be emphasized. This might be the situation for retired people or individuals who need to supplement their earned income on a regular basis with income from their outside investments.

In seeking out such investments, you should study companies' past records and potential for higher earnings, as well as their current yields. Cyclical industries and newly established corporations should be avoided because the consistency of earning power will probably be absent in those cases.

SELECTING A STOCKBROKER

If you are picking a stockbroker for the first time, a good way to start is by asking for recommendations. Consult your lawyer, accountant, banker, or a trusted friend for the name of a brokerage firm, or an individual at a firm, that might handle your account. (The New York Stock Exchange, 11 Wall Street, New York, NY 10005, will send you on request a complete listing of the names and addresses of its member firms that do business with the public.) You might select two brokers at different firms and let each handle a portion of your business until you settle on the right one.

The broker who you eventually choose should have an investment philosophy regarding growth, income, and safety that is in line with your own. You should be aware of his pattern of working with other customers, along with some of his previous recommendations, and the results of this trading. And his ability to learn about your financial objectives and then attempt to help you achieve them should be determined within a one-year trial period.

If you think that the wrong broker is handling your account, it should be moved as quickly as possible to another broker at the same or a different investment firm. Among the signals that a relationship with a broker ought to be coming to an end are frequent claims of possessing inside information, investment results that are significantly below the appropriate market averages, failure to execute orders promptly, and excessive trading, or churning, in the account.

The best stockbrokers have many characteristics in common. They are aware of significant investment, corporate, and market trends and pass this information along to their customers. They analyze the risks, as well as the rewards, of the products they sell and make sure that their customers are not confused before placing an order. They are rational, careful, and consistent, with a good reputation among their customers and other brokers. And they do not lie, exaggerate, and mislead, nor hesitate to inform you about the difficulties that arise in your portfolio.

Such a paragon is naturally hard to find, particularly if you are not a large investor or frequent trader. But because of the importance of the relationship with your broker and its effect on your financial status, it usually pays to search out the best person available and follow him if and when he moves from one firm to another.

Full-Service Firms

Most brokerage business in the United States is done by what are known as full-service firms—both national "wire houses" and regional concerns whose offices are located in a single area. These full-service houses usually have extensive research departments that provide a constant flow of background material and ideas on companies and industries to their brokers and, through them, to their customers.

Brokers at these firms, also called registered representatives or account executives, essentially work on a commission basis, so that their income is based on the frequency and quantity of their customers' purchases and sales. Remember that fact when a broker calls with advice or information about a particular stock. And ask yourself whether you believe him to have your interests first and foremost.

Discount Brokerage Firms

Discount brokerage firms were created following the abolishment of the venerable fixed-rate commission schedule for buying
and selling stocks that pervaded Wall Street since the New York
Stock Exchange was founded in 1792. Once negotiated rates became possible, the large institutions were able to demand lower
commissions when they bought and sold, while the individual
investor found his commission costs higher than before. New
companies that promised no-frills service along with low commissions then entered the fray and have since become an important factor in the market.

Discount brokers usually provide no research or investment
advice, work out of simple offices, and pay their salespeople salaries rather than commissions. You make the investment choice
and the broker merely executes the order. There may be a minimum fee per order or minimum service fee and you may not
find it too convenient or comfortable in dealing with a discounter.
Nevertheless, your commission costs are substantially lower at a
discount brokerage firm than at a full-service house, especially
on larger orders, and this savings could make whatever difficulties arise from the no-frills service worthwhile.

PROFESSIONAL INVESTMENT MANAGEMENT

Many individuals and families reach a point where professional
investment management becomes a sensible alternative to do-it-
yourself investing. These investment managers charge a fee for
their advice, over and beyond the traditional brokerage commission costs for buying and selling securities or commodities.
But in return for that fee, they provide full-time management
of your securities.

It is difficult to find bank trust departments or investment
advisory firms that will accept an investment management account under $100,000 and some concerns have much larger
minimums. But certain investment companies will take smaller
accounts, and they can sometimes be located through recommendations or advertisements in newspapers and magazines.

Advisory firms typically charge on the basis of a percentage of the assets under management—generally between 1 to 2 percent—so that they have a financial incentive to perform well and increase your assets.

When using an investment counseling firm, the normal pattern is for you to establish a discretionary account at this company, signing papers that give it full responsibility for investments and carrying out transactions without consultation each time a trade is made. So determine in advance if the advisor's investment philosophy and objectives match yours and if his past performance is in keeping with your expectations. With most advisors, you will receive a monthly statement outlining all trades and listing the securities currently in your portfolio. Of course, you can close your account at any time if you are dissatisfied with the performance or the manner in which the investment manager operates his organization.

SECURITIES PROTECTION

When you purchase securities, you can, as many investors do, hold and store the certificates yourself. Other alternatives include having the securities registered in your name and held by someone else or kept by a broker in a custodian account. Or you can do what tens of thousands of investors do as a matter of course for trading convenience and leave the securities in your broker's possession and in his name as well.

Investors who want, or need, the feeling of safety that comes with physical possession of their securities should keep them in their own name and in their own safe deposit box. That will be inconvenient when the stocks and bonds must be stored and/or removed after a purchase or a sale. But there is no question of either ownership or possession when you can hold the securities in your own hands at any time.

Frequent or steady traders, however, usually keep their securities with their broker. If the securities were bought on margin, or on credit, they must be held in street name accounts— the term used when stocks and bonds are left with a broker and kept in that broker's name. When a broker holds your stock, it allows for ease of buying and selling: certificates do not have to be sent back and forth from customer to broker. The customer is also relieved of the bother and expense of safeguarding his securities certificates and continually checking maturity or interest-payment dates. And although there is no advantage for the customer, securities in street name are used by brokerage firms as collateral for their own loans.

At one time there was a much greater danger in leaving stocks and bonds with a broker, because if the brokerage firm went bankrupt, its customers' securities would often be lost as well. The Wall Street liquidity crisis in the late 1960s that led to the collapse of many securities concerns intensified these fears and led to the creation of the Securities Investor Protection Corporation to provide insurance against such catastrophes.

Securities Investor Protection Corporation

The Securities Investor Protection Corporation was established by Congress in 1970 to give at least partial protection to investors whose securities are held by their brokers. Operating in a manner similar to the Federal Deposit Insurance Corporation and the Federal Savings and Loan Insurance Corporation, the Securities Investor Protection Corporation, known on Wall Street as Sipic, insures such brokerage accounts for up to $500,000, including $100,000 in cash.

Unlike the other insurance agencies, however, Sipic is not a government agency. It is a federally chartered, securities industry–financed, nonprofit membership corporation. Moreover, it will not protect you against losses from price declines during the period between the brokerage firm failure and the release of your securities by the court-appointed trustee charged with liquidating the concern.

Depending upon the size of the firm and whether the securities are in your name or in a street name, that period during which your securities are tied up may be lengthy. If you have more than one account with the same firm, you would have $500,000 worth of protection for each when, say, one account was in your name, another held jointly with your wife, and a third held as a trustee for a child. Many brokerage firms also offer their customers additional insurance far beyond the limits of Sipic.

SECURITIES RECORD-KEEPING

Regardless of where your securities are physically located, accurate and complete records should be kept of all transactions. Every time you buy or sell stocks or bonds, you will get a confirmation slip listing all of the details—including dates of trade and settlement, price per share, commission, tax, and the total involved. It is important to retain these confirmation slips, not only because they are useful in matching your buy and sell orders, but also because they have the dates, prices, and other information you will need when filing your income tax return.

After you receive a confirmation slip, transfer this information to your own records. Some people maintain a chronological listing of purchases and sales. Others use separate loose-leaf sheets for each security, with spaces for inserting such additional information as dividend payment dates and amounts, buying cost, and market quotations. The name of the stock transfer agent or bank trustee, frequently obtained from the company's annual report, should also be listed in your records. If you have actual possession of your securities, the certificate numbers should be recorded, too.

Most brokerage firms mail monthly statements to their customers detailing the trading of that period. These statements should be checked for accuracy and held with your records as further evidence of the transactions, at least until you receive the next statement. The year-end statement compiled by many firms, listing all interest and dividends received by customers in their dealings with the brokerage house, is also helpful in meeting the requirements of the Internal Revenue Service.

If your securities certificates are lost or destroyed through theft or fire, precise record-keeping can be a benefit. In order to obtain a replacement, you will have to provide complete details about each certificate, including the certificate number, to the stock transfer agent or bond trustee. You will also be required to purchase a surety bond which typically costs about 4 percent of the value of the security to protect that company from losses if these certificates are later found and used. The process is likely to be long and arduous, since many corporations are extremely reluctant to issue new certificates and insist that specific conditions be met before proceeding to do so.

Re-registration of a stock or bond certificate also requires communication with the transfer agent or trustee. For instance, this would be necessary when changing ownership from a trusteeship to a child who has reached maturity or from the name of one person to the names of a husband and wife.

Chapter Eleven

Stocks

THERE ARE MORE INVESTMENT VEHICLES today than at any time in history. Some securities firms have over fifty different kinds of investments in their sales arsenal. In recent years, alternatives such as money market funds, financial futures, and options on futures have exploded upon the scene, with many other imaginative new investment products on the drawing boards.

Despite the range and variety of investments available, the general public is still most aware of stocks. To many individual investors, "the market" is only the stock market. Although daily bond trading far surpasses stock volume, and the other types of securities and commodities also have a significant effect on the economy, the ups and downs of the stock market have the greatest impact on public perception of the financial markets in general.

Stocks represent proprietorship of a corporation in its broadest sense. A share of stock is a segment of that company and gives the holder all of the rights and privileges that such proprietorship entails. Its price is determined by the value that the marketplace—one or more willing buyers and sellers—places on it at any given moment.

171

COMMON STOCK

Common stock is the basic ownership of a company. If you own common stock in a corporation, you participate directly in its success or failure in proportion to the number of shares you own. You can acquire common stock from the corporation itself when it sells a primary issue or makes a secondary offering to the public. But you are more likely to buy common shares from, or sell them to, another individual or institution that wants to make a trade.

The extent of your ownership of the company is based on the number of shares that you possess. Thus if a million shares are outstanding and you have 1,000 shares, you own one tenth of 1 percent of the corporation. Evidence of ownership exists in the form of a stock certificate, which is often registered in your name and always states the number of shares that you own. The certificate may also state the par, or face, value of the stock, but this amount is normally unrelated to the current market value as determined by buyers and sellers at a securities exchange or in the over-the-counter market.

Most common-stock holders, unless they own nonvoting shares, have the right to vote at the annual meeting in proportion to their ownership. Votes are normally held on such proceedings as the election of directors, the selection of a certified public accounting firm to audit the company's financial records, and proposals by individual stockholders. You can vote by proxy if you do not attend the annual meeting, since a proxy statement describing all business to come before the meeting and a voting card are distributed to stockholders in advance. As a practical matter, of course, small stockholders have little influence on the management of a corporation because the ownership generally is so diverse that management-nominated boards of directors rarely are challenged at the annual meeting or at any other time.

Common-stock holders are also entitled to receive whatever dividends are declared by the directors on a pro rata basis. Dividends, generally announced and distributed every quarter, are the portion of a corporation's earnings that is paid to its owners.

Some companies pay dividends in their own stock rather than in cash to conserve operating funds. Others have established dividend reinvestment plans whereby dividends are automatically reinvested in the corporation's common stock for any stockholders who so desire, with no commission charges added.

If directors of the company declare a stock split of, say, three-for-one, you will receive additional shares, but your relative interest in the corporation remains the same. Thus if you owned 100 shares before the split, you would own a total of 300 shares afterward. But the total value of your holdings would be unchanged, since the market price of each new share is likely to be one-third the value of the old ones at the time of the split. Sometimes, though, stock prices will rise after a split because the lower marketable trading range encourages demand.

When a corporation is liquidated or goes bankrupt, its common-stock holders are the last to receive whatever assets remain. Bondholders and other creditors who have lent money to the corporation are paid first, followed by owners of preferred stock, who are entitled to the par value of their shares. In those relatively rare cases where anything is left, it is distributed to the common-stock holders in proportion to their ownership.

Classifying Common Stocks

Investors, brokers, and investment advisors tend to classify common stocks that have similar characteristics into certain categories. While these categories are somewhat imprecise, they broadly describe the type of security under consideration.

Blue chip stocks are those that generally have maintained a dominant position in an established industry for many years and are held in high esteem by investors. However, stocks move on and off the roster of blue chips, in keeping with changes in the market. Blue chip stocks are typically issued by major corporations with unbroken records of earnings and cash dividend payments, solid prospects for growth, and a conservative financial base.

Cyclical stocks are issued by corporations that are directly and immediately affected by overall business conditions. When the business cycle moves downward, so do the fortunes of cyclical companies. The opposite normally occurs when general business improves. Consumer goods and capital equipment companies are examples of businesses strongly influenced by cyclical activity.

Income stocks are issued by mature companies in stable industries. They have minimal price fluctuations and pay a large percentage of their earnings to stockholders in the form of dividends. Since a relatively small part of net income is retained in the business every year, such stocks are usually of interest to those desiring current income, as opposed to long-term capital gains.

Growth stocks are issued by companies in rapidly expanding industries with favorable long-term potential. To achieve consistent sales and above-average earnings increases, these companies put particular emphasis on management, research, and new products. The result is often a high return on stockholders' equity. With much of the earnings of these companies usually reinvested in the business, growth stocks typically pay low dividends and have a below-average yield.

Special situations generally refer to corporations with stock profit potential based on a forthcoming development affecting the company. Investors who find special situations stocks do best when this development is not yet widely recognized by the general public since prices have not yet risen along with expectations. Special situations could be influenced by a commercially feasible new product, technological breakthrough, earnings turnaround, merger announcement, favorable court ruling, or other indication of fundamental change. There is a big risk in special situations investing, since your analysis of the pending development may be premature or erroneous and the anticipated upward stock movement may never occur.

PREFERRED STOCK

Preferred stock, just like common stock, represents part of the ownership of a corporation. Its name is derived from the fact that it has a preference over common stock in such matters as dividends and distribution of the company's assets in the event of liquidation.

Dividends on preferred stock, which in contrast to common stock are set at a fixed rate, must be paid before any dividends can be distributed to common-stock holders. Moreover, preferred stock usually takes precedence over common stock when a corporation is dissolved and remaining assets are parceled out to stockholders. Bondholders, however, are first in line for payment at liquidation.

Preferred-stock holders normally do not have the right to vote for directors or participate in other voting at the annual meeting. And since dividends on preferred stock, known on Wall Street as a senior security, usually do not fluctuate, higher earnings will not boost dividend payments. Nor will a preferred-stock market price advance or decline as rapidly as the price of the common stock.

Preferred stock is, in effect, a hybrid security with characteristics of both equities and debt. Like an equity, it has a claim on the company's earnings up to the fixed amount of the declared dividend. And since preferred shares are usually cumulative, skipped preferred-stock dividends must be made up later before any common-stock dividends are allowed to be paid.

But like a debt instrument, the overwhelming majority of preferred stock also has a fixed-rate payment. Although relatively few corporations have participating preferred stock that permits dividend increases, the general pattern is to pay fixed dividends annually, in the same manner that bonds pay fixed interest each year. Therefore preferreds are said to be interest rate–sensitive securities. And like bonds, preferred stock typically pays a generous current yield, but is a poor hedge against inflation.

Corporations, however, can exclude 85 percent of the dividend income of most preferred stocks from federal income taxes. As a result, corporations are the largest holders of preferred stock and are major competitors with individual investors when new issues come on the market. In recent years, corporations have become particularly interested in adjustable-rate preferred stock, which, although it has a ceiling and a floor, pays dividends indexed to Treasury securities and adjusted every quarter.

Convertible preferred stock is a preferred stock that can be exchanged for a specific number of common shares at a specified time and price. Convertibles thus have maximum opportunity for price appreciation if the common stock gains significantly. They also have limited downside risk because prices of convertible preferreds usually level off when yields are equivalent to that company's other preferred stock or bonds.

The conversion value of convertible preferred stock is the number of common shares into which the preferred stock is convertible, multiplied by the market price of the common stock. If the convertible is trading above its conversion value, then it has a conversion premium, which is described as a percentage of the preferred stock's market value. Normally, the lower the premium, the more attractive the convertible.

WARRANTS AND RIGHTS

Warrants and rights are among the more speculative investments and, as a general rule, should be traded only by sophisticated investors. They are securities whose value is derived from their relationship to an underlying common stock, with which they are generally issued initially.

Warrants are brought out by corporations in an effort to make their underlying stock more desirable to investors. Some warrants are detached from the common stock so that they can be bought and sold independently, while others remain attached to the stock with their value included in the price.

Warrants give their owners the privilege of buying additional shares of a company's stock—usually on a one-for-one basis—at a specified price at any time before a specified expiration date. This exercise price for conversion is typically higher than the market price of the common stock when the warrant is issued, but often changes during the life of the warrant. Nevertheless, warrant holders are protected from any dilution of value that may be caused by stock splits or stock dividends.

An important element in the value of a warrant is the period of time before expiration of the conversion privilege. Warrants are worthless on the expiration date, when their holders will lose their entire investment, if the exercise price is higher than the market price of the common stock. The result is that warrants with more time before expiration normally have a greater value than those with less time before expiration.

Rights are shorter-term instruments than warrants, typically permitting holders of a common stock or another kind of security to buy additional shares at a favorable price. These rights have a value, so that if you do not want the additional shares, you can sell your rights during the period of the offering. If rights expire unexercised, they become worthless.

Holders of warrants and rights do not have any privileges of ownership of a corporation. Although they are equity-related instruments, warrants and rights carry neither voting nor dividend privileges. You benefit only if the price is higher when you sell these issues than when you bought them.

BUYING ON MARGIN

Although the majority of investors buy stocks for cash, a substantial group of Americans, including professional traders on the trading floors of securities exchanges and in the over-the-counter market, take out loans for securities purchases. Such speculative use of credit is called buying on margin, and accounts at brokerage firms established for that purpose are called margin accounts.

When you buy on margin, the securities are held by the brokerage firm in its own, or street, name, although you are credited with all dividends and stock splits. The advantage of margin buying is that you obtain leverage—the ability to acquire stocks without putting up the full purchase price. If the price advances, your profit percentage will be higher than if you paid for the stocks entirely in cash.

For example, if you bought 200 shares of a stock selling for $10 a share, you would have spent $2,000. If that stock rose to

15 and the market value of your shares totaled $3,000, your gain would be $1,000, or 50 percent. But if you bought 400 shares at 10 for $2,000 in cash and $2,000 in credit, you would have $4,000 worth of the same stock. Then if an increase in the stock price to 15 gave you shares with a market value of $6,000, you would have $4,000 more than your original cash investment of $2,000, or a gain of 200 percent.

When the price of a stock bought on margin declines, however, the dollar loss is larger than it would have been otherwise. If this drop is large enough and the value of the stock approaches the minimum requirement, your stockbroker will send you a margin call by telephone or letter, asking that more cash or securities be added to your account as collateral in order to continue the loan. If you don't comply, the broker has the right to sell the stock to obtain the amount necessary to satisfy this loan.

Along with the risk of buying on margin is the interest cost of borrowing. For purposes like margin buying, brokers borrow funds from banks and other sources, and then lend the money at a higher interest rate to their customers. In addition to the interest charges, customers also pay the regular commission costs.

The maximum amount that can be borrowed for margin buying is set by the Federal Reserve Board and is changed by the board in keeping with national credit conditions. This margin requirement, which has ranged from 50 to 100 percent of the value of the shares purchased over the last few decades, has been 50 percent since 1974. Various brokerage firms also have their own margin requirements that may be stricter than those of the Federal Reserve, while the New York Stock Exchange has rules regarding the initial down payment and margin maintenance requirements for customers of its member firms. The exchange can also require extra margin or forbid margin trading altogether in a particular stock because of wide price swings or heavy volume.

SELLING SHORT

Short selling, a widely misunderstood technique, is the reverse of the usual stock market pattern. Most investors first buy stocks and then hope to sell them at a higher price, which is known in the securities business as going long. But with short selling, you first sell stock that you do not own at the current price, known as shorting the stock, by borrowing shares from your broker. Then you hope the price will decline so that you can buy an equal number of shares on the open market, use them to re-place—or cover—the borrowed stock, and pocket the difference.

For instance, if you sell short 100 shares at $25 a share and the price of that stock falls to $15, your profit is $10 a share, or $1,000. Conversely, if the price turns upward and reaches $35, your loss is also $10 a share, or $1,000.

The major danger in selling short is that theoretically the price of any stock can continue to rise indefinitely. When you purchase a stock, your maximum loss is limited to the purchase price. But when you sell short, your maximum loss is indeterminate. One way to limit possible losses is to place a stop order at the same time as the short sale, telling your broker to buy the stock as soon as it rises to a specified level.

In an attempt to prevent continual selling waves from en-gulfing short sellers, a rule was made by the New York Stock Exchange that no short sale is allowed except after a trade in which the price was at least one eighth of a point higher than the previous sale. This means that a stock can be sold short only in a rising market, even if that rise occurs for just a brief time.

Every month the New York Stock Exchange reports the total number of shares that were sold short in every stock traded. When the short interest rises, analysts view it as a bullish sign, since every short seller must return to the market at some point and purchase the shares in order to make delivery. Thus a cush-ion of forthcoming buy orders exists that helps to keep prices higher than they would otherwise be.

To make a short sale, you operate under procedures similar to those governing margin buying. There are initial margin and margin maintenance requirements established by the Federal Reserve Board, along with rules set by the New York Stock Ex-change and individual brokerage firms.

Short selling is even more risky than margin buying, and both the name and the technique still have a questionable connotation.

You will be going head-to-head against professionals in the securities business, primarily full-time specialists on the floor of the New York Stock Exchange, who study overall market conditions and the potential of various stocks. Although regulations governing short selling offer some protection, this tool is best used by sophisticated investors who have carefully considered the possible risks and rewards.

Chapter Twelve

Fixed-Income Securities

FOR ANYONE WHO WANTS THE security of a fixed-income return on an investment, a variety of instruments are on the market. Among them are corporate bonds, municipal bonds, and United States government securities.

Although there are many differences among the various fixed-income obligations, they all share certain characteristics. Such securities are contractual credit obligations through which the issuer agrees to pay a specified sum on a regular basis until maturity. In short, they are loans at a fixed rate of interest from the holder of the security to the issuer of the security.

When you buy a fixed-income obligation, the issuer also agrees to repay the loan in full on the maturity date. But if you need or want your money before then, you can sell the security in the open market to another investor. In that event, you may get more or less than the face value, or your purchase price, since fixed-income prices are directly related to current interest rates.

There are two key guidelines for investors in fixed-income securities to keep in mind. When interest rates rise, fixed-income securities prices fall; when interest rates fall, fixed-income securities prices rise. And short-term interest rates tend to fluctuate more than long-term rates.

CORPORATE BONDS

Corporations issue bonds, a tradable evidence of debt, for reasons that include building factories, financing equipment, or even acquiring other companies. In contrast to stock, which represents ownership of a corporation, a bond is an I.O.U. that can be readily bought and sold, by which the issuer pledges to repay the funds that were loaned. Corporate bonds are sold in minimum denominations of $5,000 or $10,000, but quoted as a percentage of par, or 100.

Most corporate bonds are debentures, backed completely by the general faith and credit of the issuer. Other kinds include first mortgage bonds, which are high-grade issues backed by liens on specified property of the company; and equipment trust or guaranteed loan certificates for the purchase of railroad cars or airplanes, where the backing is the value of the equipment used as collateral. There are also convertible bonds that, like convertible preferred stock, can be converted into common stock of the company under certain conditions. The term "junk bonds" applies to low-grade, high-yielding bonds.

Corporate bonds are outstanding in two forms, registered and bearer. Registered bonds are those registered in the name of the owner, who receives interest payments automatically and is protected against loss or theft. Bearer bonds do not identify any owner and may belong to whoever has them in his possession. With bearer bonds, owners can detach interest coupons periodically from the certificate and present them to a bank for payment. Bearer bonds are generally a disappearing breed in the United States and corporate bonds, in particular, have not been issued in this form since the mid-1960s.

From a company's point of view, bonds do not dilute the equity of the already existing stock. The expense and difficulties in issuing bonds are often much less than in selling stock. And economic conditions may indicate that it will be less costly to come out with a bond issue than a stock issue.

Investors in bonds have a different viewpoint. They see corporate bonds as a secure investment in which the principal is relatively safe and the periodic interest is fixed. And they know that if liquidation or bankruptcy occurs, they will be repaid when funds are available before one cent is distributed to preferred- or common-stock holders. Bond interest is payable even before federal, state, and local income taxes.

Bonds normally pay interest at a fixed rate, or coupon, established at the time of issue, stated on the certificate and unchanged thereafter. This interest is distributed on fixed dates—usually semiannually, but sometimes quarterly or annually—until maturity, unless repayment is made under certain conditions before this expiration date. Since bonds are normally issued in minimum denominations of $1,000, a 10 percent bond will pay interest of $100 annually per $1,000, with payments made, say, on February 1 and August 1 each year.

There are, however, a number of relatively rare variations to the fixed-income pattern of corporate bonds. For example, some bonds pay a floating interest rate adjusted periodically to the prevailing market rate as measured by short-term Treasury securities or other money market instruments.

With fixed-interest bonds, the current yield, or interest payment as a percentage of the current value, is determined by market conditions, the maturity of the issue, and the financial strength of the issuer. All of these factors may change during the life of a bond, affecting both its price and its current yield.

Take the case of the 10 percent bond that pays $100 annually. If interest rates on comparable bonds rise to 11 percent, the market value of the 10 percent bond might fall from $1,000 to about $900, since potential buyers of the bond will want to get that same 11 percent rate.

Correspondingly, if interest rates fall to 9 percent, the market value of the 10 percent bond might rise to $1,100. Bonds that are priced below par are said to sell at a discount, while those priced above par sell at a premium.

When investors buy bonds at a discount, or less than face value, the yield to maturity—a complex mathematical calculation—will be greater than the current yield, since the total return includes the difference between the purchase price and the face value, along with the annual interest rate and reinvestment of interest. Bonds bought at a premium have a lower yield to maturity than current yield because investors lose on the difference between the purchase price and the face value paid at the expiration date.

The quality of corporate bonds is assessed regularly by rating services that examine the issuing company's financial statements, debt structure, credit rating, and other factors. The two best-known services, Moody's Investors Service and Standard & Poor's Corporation, use letter and/or numerical ratings to evaluate the investor's risk of purchase, ranging from Aaa or AAA for the best quality to C or D for the lowest quality. Moody's lowest investment-grade rating is Baa3 and Standard & Poor's is BBB−.

Ratings change frequently, but the general rule is the higher the rating, the lower the yield, and vice versa. So when you see a yield that is significantly higher than the current market, check out its rating and determine if you want to take the risk of a speculative offering.

Most bonds are sold with call protection, whereby the company guarantees for a certain number of years that it will not call in the issue prior to maturity and redeem it with one paying a lower interest if rates decline. But protection against such redemption usually does not exceed five or ten years, which may be unsatisfactory to long-term investors. However, if you purchase deep discount bonds that trade for much less than their face value, they will probably not be called and will also provide a capital gain as well as current interest when held to maturity.

Bonds may have a sinking fund, requiring companies to redeem a certain number of issues every year before maturity according to a predetermined schedule. The good news for investors about sinking funds is that the principal of a bond may be repaid earlier than maturity. The bad news is that you may not want to be repaid early because you are unable to invest these funds at the same or a higher rate of interest. Bondholders are generally notified of sinking fund requirements by mail from the issuers or by advertisements in newspapers.

Most bonds, moreover, are not as liquid as stocks. Although there is a listed market for certain bonds on securities exchanges, more are traded in the unlisted over-the-counter market where there is a lower bid price and a higher asked price for every issue. Furthermore, some bonds are inactive and therefore very difficult to trade, while others have an unusually wide spread between the bid and asked prices. Normally the smaller the quantity traded, the wider the spread.

Corporate bonds are considered a more defensive investment than stocks, because of their fixed annual return. But in an inflationary period, interest from fixed-income investments generally will not buy as much as it did before. In addition, the market value of a portfolio of corporate bonds may be as affected by changes in Federal Reserve policy, bank loans, credit availability, and other overall economic conditions as by the credit standing of the issuer.

MUNICIPAL BONDS

Municipal bonds are the biggest part of the bond market, with more than a million different issues outstanding—more than every other category combined. Municipals are debt obligations issued not only by cities, as the name might indicate, but also by states, counties, and authorities for a broad range of purposes.

The big plus of municipal bonds, issued only in registered form, is that interest from these securities is exempt from federal income tax. Interest from bonds issued by a state or one of its municipalities is also usually exempt from state and local income taxes for residents of that state. The result is that municipal bonds, also called tax-exempt bonds, are usually attractive investments for those in middle to high tax brackets seeking income rather than capital appreciation, even though the issues pay lower interest than most corporate and federal government bonds.

Even under the 1986 Tax Reform Act, which reduced the maximum tax rate from its previous high of 50 percent, a taxable security would have to yield significantly more than a municipal bond to equal the take-home yield for many individuals. For example, a tax-free yield of 7 percent would be equivalent to a 9.7 percent to someone in the 28 percent tax bracket, 10.4 percent to someone in the 33 percent tax bracket and 11.4 percent to someone in the 38½ percent bracket. Other taxable yield equivalents of tax-exempts are:

Tax Exempt/Taxable-Yield Equivalents
(Individual income brackets—thousands of dollars)

Single Return	$0–$17.9	Over $17.9	See Note 1	1987 Only See Note 2
Joint Return	$0–$29.8	Over $29.8	See Note 1	1987 Only See Note 2
Tax Bracket	15%	28%	33%	38.5%

Tax-Exempt Yields %	Taxable Yield Equivalents %			
4.0	4.7	5.6	6.0	6.5
4.5	5.3	6.3	6.7	7.3
5.0	5.9	6.9	7.5	8.1
5.5	6.5	7.6	8.2	8.9
6.0	7.1	8.3	9.0	9.8
6.5	7.6	9.0	9.7	10.6
7.0	8.2	9.7	10.4	11.4
7.5	8.8	10.4	11.2	12.2
8.0	9.4	11.1	11.9	13.0
8.5	10.0	11.8	12.7	13.8
9.0	10.6	12.5	13.4	14.6
9.5	11.2	13.2	14.2	15.4
10.0	11.8	13.9	14.9	16.3
10.5	12.4	14.6	15.7	17.1
11.0	12.9	15.3	16.4	17.9
11.5	13.5	16.0	17.2	18.7
12.0	14.1	16.7	17.9	19.5

Note 1   The Tax Reform Act phases out the benefit of the 15% rate for taxpayers with high taxable income. This provision in effect imposes a third top rate of 33% for those taxpayers on a portion of their taxable income. This is done by use of an additional tax of 5% on taxable income falling within certain ranges. In general, the 5% additional tax applies to taxable income levels between $71,900 and $149,250 for joint returns and $43,150 and $89,560 for singles.

Note 2   Special Rates for 1987

Tax Rates	Joint Returns	Single Individuals
11.0%	$0–$3,000	$0–$1,800
15.0%	$3,000–$28,000	$1,800–$16,800
28.0%	$28,000–$45,000	$16,800–$27,000
35.0%	$45,000–$90,000	$27,000–$54,000
38.5%	Above $90,000	Above $54,000

Source: Weber, Lipshie & Co.

Tax-exempts, which have maturities of up to thirty years, also are considered a relatively safe investment for preservation of principal. Although different governmental units or agencies have varying degrees of safety, the viability of a taxpayer-supported body attests to the health of most municipal issuers. And with a diversified portfolio, the security of municipal bonds is greater still.

However, certain criteria should be weighed by potential investors in municipals to assure themselves of the issuing body's guarantee to make timely principal and interest payments. Among these criteria are the revenue stream, the relative weight of the tax load on property owners, the economic background of the community, the level of tax burdens, and the percentage of current tax collections.

If you desire to sell your municipal bonds before maturity, be prepared to receive less than what seems at first glance to be the market price. There may not be much demand for bonds of relatively low amounts, and you are often at the mercy of the broker or dealer making the trade.

Types of Municipal Securities

The largest group of municipals are general obligation bonds, or GOs. These issues are backed by the full faith and credit of the issuing body, which can increase real estate, sales, or income taxes, if necessary, to obtain the funds to meet bond payments. GOs have unlimited taxing power behind them and, in effect, place a lien on unencumbered municipal revenues. Facilities built with long-term general obligation bonds include streets, state and municipal buildings, and schools.

Revenue bonds raise funds for a specific project that will throw off the income necessary to both pay the interest and repay the principal to bondholders. For instance, revenue bonds might produce funding for hospitals, water systems, or public housing projects. Borrowings are repaid not from taxes on the general public, but are secured by revenues or user fees generated by these facilities.

Hybrid, or double-barreled, bonds have characteristics of both general obligation bonds and revenue bonds. Thus a revenue bond to finance a state highway might be secured first by the income from tolls and then by the proceeds of a gasoline tax.

Industrial revenue bonds are issued by a governmental body but backed by the lease payments of the corporation that uses the facilities. An example might be a pollution-control bond secured for the benefit of a company for which the system was built.

Municipal notes are short-term financings ranging from one month to three years for such purposes as construction or temporary cash flow shortages. Some of these issues are rolled over a number of times before finally being redeemed. Among the categories of municipal notes are bond anticipation notes, tax anticipation notes, revenue anticipation notes, and project notes for urban development and redevelopment projects that are secured by the full faith and credit of the federal government.

The two kinds of municipal bond repayment schedules are serial issues and term issues. With serial issues, usually used in connection with general obligation bonds, part of the outstanding obligation is paid off semiannually or annually. But with term issues, associated with revenue bonds, a sinking fund is created into which funds are placed for ultimate repayment of the full issue at a single stated maturity.

If interest and principal payments on municipal bonds are delayed or in arrears, they are said to be in default. Such an action could be taken by the issuer if tax collections are lower than anticipated or the facilities do not generate the projected revenues. Moody's and Standard & Poor's also rate municipal bonds, and the Municipal Bond Insurance Association and the Ambac Indemnity Corporation are among the organizations that insure the timely debt service on certain issues. If a bond has such third-party backing, Standard & Poor's will give it an AAA rating, higher than it might otherwise earn. But the bond's yield will probably be reduced slightly to pay for the insurance.

When borrowing money to invest in municipal bonds, the interest on the loan is not tax-deductible. Even if you borrow for other purposes but own municipal bonds, your interest deduction may possibly be disallowed by the Internal Revenue Service. Caution and the assistance of a tax advisor could help to avoid this problem.

Unit Investment Trusts

Unit investment trusts have become a popular way for small investors to buy municipal, as well as corporate, bonds, because of their convenience, simplicity, and relative safety. The trusts are prepackaged, diversified portfolios of anywhere from a few to dozens of issues that remain constant, except for redemptions, during the life of the trust, which could be from three to thirty years. Usually no bonds are added or changed at a trust, but sometimes bonds may be sold if the sponsors are concerned about their safety. As a general rule, risky bonds are rarely bought for a trust portfolio.

You can purchase units, or pro rata shares, in tax-exempt unit trusts, with each unit costing from $1 to $1,000 and a minimum purchase requirement of between $750 and $5,000. The interest rate is normally fixed when the trust is sold and is not altered. You also have liquidity, because you can redeem your units before maturity through the secondary market maintained by most sponsoring brokerage firms. In those situations you will probably be paid the lower bid price, rather than the higher asked price, for your shares.

Unit trusts are not designed for in-and-out traders. Although they have no management fees, there is typically an initial sales charge and an annual fee for the trustee and evaluator factored into the quoted yield. If you want to sell your shares in the secondary market when interest rates are higher than at the time of purchase, the value of your units will be depressed, perhaps sharply if rates have risen substantially during this period. Of course, if market rates have dropped, the value of your shares will be higher.

There are also floating-rate unit trusts in which the rate, though guaranteed at a certain minimum, is pegged to the prime interest rate. In such a trust, with the fluctuation in the rate, the market value of each unit remains at about the same level during the trust's lifetime.

With unit trusts, you will probably receive interest income checks monthly, instead of semiannually as in the case of most bonds. A number of sponsors also have reinvestment plans whereby this interest can be automatically reinvested in mutual funds or new unit trusts. Remember that with some trusts, the checks you receive or are credited with each month can represent a return of principal, as well as interest.

Many trusts, moreover, consist entirely of the bonds of a single state. If you live in such a state and it also has an income tax, you may get the benefit of triple-tax exemption, since most states exempt their own residents from state and local income taxes on their bonds.

UNITED STATES GOVERNMENT SECURITIES

Securities of the federal government—bills, notes, and bonds— are debt obligations backed by the full faith and credit of the United States, and are therefore considered the safest investments around. Securities issued by federal agencies have a slightly higher risk, since they generally carry a moral obligation or an implicit, rather than explicit, government guarantee. But here, too, safety is a key consideration in pricing and selling the securities.

This safety is based on the simple, unarguable situation that Uncle Sam has both taxing power and the control of the presses that could print more money. Investors who lend to the federal government at a specified rate of interest do not have to worry about bankruptcy or default that could occur if they were to purchase corporate or municipal bonds. Nor are they concerned about premature redemption, since most government securities are not subject to a call provision.

There is a trade-off, however, in that government securities, or I.O.U.s, frequently pay lower interest rates than corporate bonds and have lower take-home yields after taxes than municipal bonds. But no state and local taxes are imposed on government securities and most agency securities, which could be important to high-income individuals in such heavily taxed states as California or New York.

All of these securities are borrowings by the Treasury Department to pay the bills run up by Washington. The government, through the Federal Reserve Board, is continually buying as well as selling securities, as it attempts to manage the nation's monetary and credit supply.

If you retain a government security to maturity, you know that you will always be repaid on schedule. But if you sell such securities before maturity, their prices may be higher or lower than your cost. That's because Treasuries, like other fixed-income securities, rise and fall in an inverse relationship to interest rates. Price quotations on recent issues can be obtained from any local office of the Federal Reserve.

Treasury Bills

Treasury bills are short-term obligations, issued with initial maturities of three, six, and twelve months, and sold in minimum amounts of $10,000 and additional increments of $5,000. A new batch of three- and six-month T-bills is auctioned publicly every Monday, while new issues of one-year bills are sold every month.

The government issues bills only in book-entry form, so that ownership is signified in an account at the Treasury, rather than through the more familiar engraved certificate. Prices of new bills are not set by the Treasury, but by the competitive bidding of investors soon after the announcement of an offering.

The easiest way to buy a Treasury bill is by asking your broker or bank to handle the details of the transaction, for which there will be a small commission fee. You can also buy a bill in person or by mail at no charge from one of the thirty-seven Federal Reserve banks or branches around the country. When you do so, you are assured of getting the entire amount desired because you are making a noncompetitive tender in which you agree to pay the average price of all the competitive tenders accepted.

Treasury bills are sold and quoted at a discount, whereby at the time of purchase you pay less than the full face value you will receive at maturity. Thus the coupon equivalent rate of a Treasury bill—the rate you would receive if the funds were invested in a bond or other security sold on a coupon interest basis—is higher than the quoted rate. For example, a three-month Treasury bill sold at a 13 percent discount is equal to a 13.62 percent bond equivalent yield.

Treasury Notes and Bonds

Treasury notes and bonds are similar federal instruments but with longer maturities. Notes mature from one to ten years from the date of issue, while bonds normally mature in more than ten years. Although the minimum denomination for notes and bonds is $1,000, the Treasury sometimes sets higher minimums for particular issues.

There are also periodic auctions for Treasury notes and bonds, although not as often as for Treasury bills. Notes and bonds have been sold only in registered form since 1982.

Tigers, Lions, and Cats

Tigers, lions, and cats are variations of the zero-coupon bond concept applied to government securities. A zero-coupon bond is issued at a large discount, sometimes at a price that is one third to one quarter of the face value, and redeemed at full face value when it matures many years later. You get no regular cash interest payments during this period, since all of the income is paid at maturity.

One major attraction of a zero in a time of fluctuating interest rates is that you do not have the problem of reinvesting cash interest payments, since that reinvestment is computed into the price of the security and the interest compounds semiannually. Yet although you don't receive the interest in cash, you are still liable for the income tax on the amount accrued annually. By locking in a fixed return, you benefit if interest rates fall, but you will be faced with declining values if interest rates rise. Zero-coupon bonds have been designed primarily for retirement plans, such as individual retirement accounts and Keogh plans, where interest compounds on a tax-deferred basis.

The government securities with the feline names of tigers, lions, and cats are Treasury bonds that have been stripped of their coupons by the brokerage firms selling them, thereby separating the interest payments from the principal payments. You can then buy what are technically receipts representing claims on the future interest payments at a sharp discount. The original securities are held in trust by a custodian bank, which will pay you the total interest in one lump sum at maturity.

Agency Securities

Along with the direct obligations of the Treasury, a number of federal agencies or instrumentalities created by Congress and operating under federal charter also issue securities. Among them are the Federal Home Loan Bank, the Federal Home Loan Mortgage Corporation, the Export-Import Bank, the Federal Intermediate Credit Banks, the Banks for Cooperatives, the Tennessee Valley Authority, the Student Loan Marketing Association, the Federal Land Banks, and the Government National Mortgage Association.

Since the guarantee of these securities by the federal government is not explicit—in many cases they carry only a moral obligation—their yields are often fractionally higher than those of comparable Treasury securities. In addition, the secondary market for agency securities is not as large as the market for Treasuries, so liquidity is less. Agency securities have varying maturities from one week to thirty years and minimum denominations ranging from $1,000 to $25,000.

Savings Bonds

In contrast to all of these marketable Treasury securities, there is a special kind of registered, nontransferable government obligation called United States savings bonds. Long familiar to millions of Americans because they have been sold through payroll deductions, they have undergone many changes over the years and now pay money market interest rates in line with other Treasury instruments.

Savings bonds combine the advantages of safety, low denominations, and simplicity of purchase and redemption. The Series EE savings bonds, the most popular category, are issued in minimum face value denominations of $50 and sold in minimum denominations of $25, with the full faith and credit guarantee of the federal government behind them. They can be purchased not only through payroll deduction, but also at thousands of locations, including most banks, where redemption tables outlining rates and values are available. In addition, they can be redeemed on the spot at the same location.

These variable-rate EE bonds yield 85 percent of the average return on five-year marketable Treasury securities if held for at least five years, with interest compounded semiannually. However, you are guaranteed a minimum return of 7½ percent if you hold these ten-year bonds for this five-year period, even if market rates fall lower. Interest is exempt from both state and local income taxes, and federal income tax is deferred until redemption. If you don't redeem the bonds at maturity, they go into an automatic extension period until the final maturity date forty years from the date of issue.

A tip for buyers of Series EE bonds is this: Since interest is received on the first day of every month for the first eighteen months, don't cash in such bonds in the middle of the month or you will lose about two weeks' interest. Buy bonds at the end of the month, because no matter when the purchase is made, interest is credited from the first day of that month.

Another category is Series HH, which provides a regular cash interest payment of 7½ percent twice a year until a ten-year maturity, when the principal is returned to the investor. But HH bonds are available only in exchange for EE bonds or similar Treasury securities and cannot be purchased for cash. By acquiring them, you can postpone reporting the accumulated interest from the EE bonds and thereby delay paying the tax on them for as long as ten years.

Chapter Thirteen

Mutual Funds

MUTUAL FUNDS, A TERM THAT many people use to include all of the various kinds of investment companies, have one major function: to acquire a broad range of assets and manage them. If the management of a fund can increase the value of these assets, its stockholders will benefit. If not, then the stockholders in the fund will suffer a decline in their holdings.

This concept of managing the funds of many investors with the same, or similar, investment objective dates back to the Scottish and British investment trusts of the nineteenth century. The first American mutual fund, Massachusetts Investors Trust, was established in 1924, and nineteen were in operation when the Depression struck in 1929. The Investment Company Act of 1940 established regulations for the industry and restrained some of the abuses that existed in mutual funds, such as excessively trading the securities portfolio. Growth was rapid after World War II, and hundreds of funds are now operating in the United States.

Formally, mutual funds are open-end investment companies whose capitalization is not fixed, so they issue and redeem new shares in keeping with customer demand. One category, money market funds, has become so popular that its total assets far exceed those of all other kinds combined. Although they are not mutual funds, because their capitalization usually remains fixed and their shares are bought and sold on the open market, closed-end investment companies are often grouped in this category.

MUTUAL FUNDS

The basic feature of mutual funds is that they are constantly creating and selling new shares whenever an investor wishes to buy. At the same time, the funds stand ready to redeem or repurchase the shares of any stockholder, whenever he wants to sell. Thus the number of shares outstanding in a mutual fund on a given day will very likely differ from those the day before.

Each share, sold on a net asset value basis, represents a proportionate interest in many different companies. The dividends and interest that the fund gets from its holdings are distributed to its stockholders, typically once every three months. The fund's capital gains are also distributed the same way.

As provided for in the 1940 law, mutual funds that qualify for investment company status cannot acquire control of the corporations in which they invest. But if they distribute at least 90 percent of their income annually to stockholders, the funds do not have to pay corporate income taxes. These stockholders, in turn, pay income tax, based on their personal tax bracket, on the income received from the funds.

Advantages

Diversification is perhaps the number-one advantage of mutual funds, because the danger of poor performance inherent in any single company or industry is minimized. By purchasing shares in corporations in a variety of industries—electronics, utilities, transportation, food, apparel, and many more—funds spread the risk of declining stock prices or corporate bankruptcy among many issues. Most individuals could not otherwise participate in such a broad range of securities.

Professional management is another major reason to invest in mutual funds. To keep a continuous watch over their portfolios, these funds engage full-time investment managers who study both general economic conditions and particular opportunities in the financial markets. The money managers make all of the necessary buying, selling, and holding decisions, and most have tallied long-term results that surpass the most widely followed market averages.

Another point in favor of mutual funds is that they offer liquidity, which means you can redeem any portion of your shares during any business day. The amount you get will be your pro rata share of the fund's net assets that day. Since securities prices move up and down regularly, the net asset value per share—the value of the fund's investments minus expenses, divided by the number of shares outstanding—could be higher or lower than your cost.

Dollar-cost averaging allows investors to put the same amount of money into a mutual fund at regular intervals. The result is that you buy more shares when prices are lower and fewer shares when prices are higher. You can also have your income dividends and capital gains distributions automatically converted to additional shares and invested in the fund.

Exchange privileges are offered by many funds that are members of a family or funds operated by one sponsoring organization. For little or no cost, a stockholder can move all or part of his assets from one fund in a group to another. Such privileges may be helpful when a stockholder's investment objectives change or a new type of fund is offered by the organization.

Freedom from excessive paperwork is a virtue of mutual funds, since you have no stock certificates to safeguard, sign, or forward to a broker. Most funds send their stockholders monthly statements of the transactions that took place in their account, and this is the only piece of paper that you need to retain for accounting and tax purposes.

Efficiency of scale is still another advantage, and one of the most important, since mutual funds have lower transaction costs than individual investors. Because they buy and sell large amounts of shares in a single transaction, funds pay less brokerage commissions and pass those lower rates on to their stockholders.

Load Versus No-Load Funds

The two basic kinds of mutual funds are load funds and no-load funds. "Load" refers to the sales commission on some funds, usually about 8½ percent of the total purchase price. No-load funds charge no commissions, and are sold principally via direct mail and through advertisements in newspapers and magazines.

The percentage of the mutual fund investment dollar put into no-load funds has been rising in recent years. The bottom line, of course, is the investment performance of the fund after all expenses, including the sales charge, have been deducted. In some instances, the performance of some load funds has surpassed that of some no-loads.

Nevertheless, the mutual fund sales charge that covers the commission to the salesperson and cost of distributing the shares does prevent you from putting all of your investment dollars to work immediately. For example, when you make a $1,000 purchase of shares in a fund with an 8.5 percent load, $85 would normally be used for selling expenses and just $915 would be invested. Computing the $85 commission as a percentage of the $915 investment, the load is even larger at 9.3 percent.

Whether you invest in a load or a no-load fund, certain fixed costs affect all shareholders. Funds charge management fees related to the size of the net assets, in many cases around one half of 1 percent annually. There are often other charges against the fund for such items as administrative services and legal fees that are added to the mangement fee to constitute the fund's expense ratio. This ratio should fall as the assets of the fund rise, because some charges are fixed and therefore unrelated to the size of the portfolio.

Goals of Funds

Choose a mutual fund that meets your investment goals. As required by the Securities and Exchange Commission, each fund's prospectus summarizes the primary objective at the outset and elaborates upon it within the document. The major classifications are:

Growth funds, the largest category of mutual funds, are primarily aimed at long-term growth of capital, rather than income. Dividends are often low since the primary emphasis is on selecting companies expected to have a rapid earnings increase and a corresponding rapid advance in the stock price.

The best-known subcategory of growth funds is long-term growth funds, designed principally for young investors willing to assume risk with the goal of creating future equity. Others include performance funds, which take more risk with the hope of achieving more capital gains; aggressive growth funds, which specialize in smaller companies and therefore entail an even greater risk; and hedge funds, which sell stocks short as well as buy them and thereby attempt to profit regardless of which direction the market moves.

The primary objective of income funds is current income as opposed to capital gains. They invest in securities that produce high dividends and interest. Diversified income funds place their funds in stocks and bonds, whereas others concentrate solely on bond holdings.

Growth-income funds strive for a combination of income and long-term growth. They generally do not fluctuate in value as much as the more speculative funds, since they tend to invest in major corporations that participate in overall market growth and pay a reasonable return.

Balanced funds vary their portfolios by purchasing common stock, preferred stock, and bonds. Through this conservative buying policy, they reduce risk and provide income and capital appreciation.

Bond funds fluctuate inversely with interest rates and their prices normally rise as these rates fall. If rates increase though, share prices of bond funds may decline enough to offset any possible gains from the higher interest.

Municipal bond funds invest in a group of tax-exempt bonds and pass along the interest to their stockholders on a tax-exempt basis. In contrast to unit trusts, which have fixed, self-liquidating, and unmanaged portfolios, municipal bond funds are fully managed, with purchases and sales made periodically. In line with this management, for which an annual fee is paid, bond funds are more liquid than unit trusts, allow for the reinvestment of dividends, and make it easy for stockholders to buy and sell shares.

There are also specialized funds of many kinds. These include industry funds that concentrate on stocks in a certain field, such as chemicals, utilities, or insurance; venture capital funds that invest in new high-risk businesses; option funds that buy and sell options; and social funds that look for investments that further specific social programs.

MONEY MARKET FUNDS

Money market mutual funds were not invented until the early 1970s, but they quickly became one of the best-received investment products ever created. Before long, total assets invested in money market funds surpassed the assets of all other categories of mutual funds combined. And even the subsequent establishment of money market deposit accounts at banks and savings and loan associations with federal deposit insurance did not make the money funds obsolete.

Hundreds of money market funds, making short-term, higher-interest debt securities indirectly available to individual investors who desire immediate income and safety of principal, have made their mark on the American financial scene. Initially gaining ground at a time when the stock market was soft and interest rates were high, money market funds continued to advance in later years when market conditions changed, as new versions were developed and existing ones were refined.

Money funds invest in a variety of money market securities—loans made by the federal government, leading banks, and blue chip corporations for relatively brief periods. Such conservative instruments include Treasury bills, government agency notes, repurchase agreements, commercial paper, letters of credit, and commercial bank certificates of deposit.

In addition to the general money market funds, certain types specialize in particular short-term securities. Some that invest only in high-quality federal government and agency securities provide an extra degree of safety and therefore usually offer investors about one or two percentage points less in yield. Others buy only municipal securities and offer tax-free income primarily to investors in the upper-income brackets who would benefit from it.

Like other mutual funds, money market funds are managed by professional portfolio managers who attempt to limit risk by diversifying their investments. Risk is also limited by the fact that securities in a money market portfolio are generally short-term interest-bearing instruments, most of which mature in sixty days or less. Short average maturities add safety to the money funds.

Money market funds usually require a minimum initial investment of about $1,000 and value their shares at a constant price of $1. The income received on your pro rata share of the assets is considered the return or yield on your investment. The income fluctuates daily based on the general level of interest rates as they affect the assets of the fund. There are virtually no capital gains and losses, so shares are usually redeemed for the same $1-a-share purchase price.

One major feature of money market funds is the check-writing privilege, which lets stockholders redeem shares by writing a money fund draft, similar to a bank check. Money funds typically require a minimum amount of $500 for checkwriting, though some have a lower minimum and others have none at all. Even after you write such a draft, your money continues to earn dividends until the draft clears, allowing you, rather than a financial institution, to take advantage of the float. Other features often include immediate telephone or wire redemption and exchange privileges with other funds operated by the same sponsoring organization.

Most money funds, moreover, are no-load investments, so they have no sales charges for opening and adding to a fund. But management and other fees are common to all mutual funds.

Risks of Money Funds

Investors in money market funds should be aware of three different kinds of risks:

The first is the risk of maintaining yield. Since this yield fluctuates daily, there can be substantial changes in the rate paid to investors, both on a short- and a long-term basis. In contrast to money market accounts and savings certificates at banks and savings and loan associations that announce their rates in advance, money funds report the results to their stockholders after the interest has been earned.

Second is the risk of default. Some investments in a fund could go sour and fund participants would then take a loss. For example, a fund may own a kind of unsecured promissory note called commercial paper or it may own foreign certificates of deposit, and certain portions of either classification may not be able to pay off at maturity. In those situations, fund shareholders have no recourse to Uncle Sam because no government deposit insurance is involved.

Finally there is the risk of market fluctuation. Those funds that do not have a constant share value present their stockholders with the possibility of upward and downward changes in the price of the shares. Sometimes downward market fluctuations are counterbalanced by current income credits, making it difficult for shareowners to keep track of the monthly adjustments in their share accounts.

CLOSED-END FUNDS

Closed-end investment funds, like open-end mutual funds, use professional managers to invest in a variety of securities funds according to a stated purpose, thereby minimizing the risk and maximizing the potential return. But unlike mutual funds, they are not open-ended. As their name indicates, the funds themselves are closed off to future contributions after a specified amount of money has been raised through an initial offering. There are no further investments in a closed-end fund and no redemptions by the fund. All buying and selling then takes place among investors on a securities exchange or in the over-the-counter market, with as much ease as trading in any other publicly owned security.

When you buy shares of closed-end funds, also called investment companies or investment trusts, you are buying part of a diversified portfolio of stocks or bonds with a fixed number of shares outstanding. These portfolios can be quite specialized since many funds are concentrated largely in a specific industry or a foreign country.

The idea of closed-end funds originated in Belgium in the early nineteenth century and spread later to England and Scotland. The first American fund was established in 1893, but the 1929 market crash brought their growth to a virtual halt. Since then, open-end mutual funds have eclipsed them in popularity.

There is a major difference in the way closed-end funds and open-end funds are priced. Open-end funds are traded at prices based on their net asset value per share, with a sales charge added to buy orders in the case of load funds. But prices of closed-end funds are governed by supply and demand, so that trades generally take place either at a discount or at a premium from the actual net asset value.

In the majority of instances, closed-end shares are bought and sold at a discount from the underlying value of the securities in the fund's portfolio. For example, if the net asset value of a closed-end fund were $10 a share and the stock traded at $9 a share, there would be a 10 percent discount from this net asset value. Sometimes the discount is substantially greater.

One of the most important reasons for closed-end funds to typically trade at a discount is the lack of sponsorship by a brokerage firm. In a very competitive marketplace, such firms are inclined to sell mutual funds or unit investment trusts paying much larger commissions than closed-end funds. Other reasons include the high management expenses of closed-end funds, an overhang of competitive issues, and the expectation that prices always tend to fall when they approach their net asset value.

Although some closed-end funds show volatile price movements, most share prices move in a narrow range over the long term. Nevertheless, there are a number of ways in which investors are able to benefit from this discount valuation. By buying closed-end fund shares at a discount, you may be buying assets for, say, 80 cents on the dollar, thereby increasing your effective yield. If the discount from net asset value then narrows from 20 to 10 percent—a phenomenon that tends to occur during bull markets, as buyers are attracted to closed-end fund values and prices advance—you get added leverage on relatively small price moves. And when purchasing a fund with a steep discount from net asset value, you have some downside protection because the securities are acquired for less than their actual value.

Types of Funds

Like open-end funds, there are a variety of closed-end funds to meet specific investment requirements. Among the most widely purchased categories are:

Stock funds, the first to come on the scene, are the best known of the closed-end funds. Most of these stock funds, which primarily seek capital appreciation, invest in a diversified portfolio of stocks. However, some specialized closed-ends limit their holdings to specific areas of investor interest.

Bond funds are designed primarily to produce current income and high yields. Convertible-bond funds try to combine income and capital appreciation.

Dual-purpose funds have both common and preferred stock. The common-stock holders share in the fund's capital gains, while the preferred shares pay a guaranteed minimum dividend. At a specific date, perhaps fifteen years after the fund is established, the preferred shares are redeemed at a specific price. The remaining assets are then owned by the common-stock holders, who vote to either "open-end," thereby continuing the company as a mutual fund, or to liquidate.

Chapter Fourteen

Options

STOCK OPTIONS, WHOSE ORIGINS DATE back more than a hundred years, were once a mysterious trading vehicle, largely restricted to the most sophisticated investors who dealt with specialized brokerage firms. But since listed option trading created a continuous public auction market in the mid-1970s, much of the mystery has disappeared. Regulated by the Securities and Exchange Commission, options have now become widely used by all kinds of investors, particularly as a hedge against disastrous moves in stock prices.

Nevertheless, options are still not usually recommended for those whose paramount concern is a minimal exposure to loss. About 25 percent of all options purchased are allowed to expire with a complete loss of the investment. Buying and selling options requires a basic knowledge of the technique, a concentration on market developments, and a willingness to speculate on often-volatile short-term movements in the price of particular stocks.

Yet the increasingly broad range of options strategies allows investors to use a number of different trading devices, depending on whether they are bullish or bearish. Often the attraction of options is their relatively limited exposure to risk—all you can possibly lose in a trade that goes wrong is the cost of the option plus the commission charged by your broker.

In addition to stock options, the concept has been broadened to non-stock categories. There are now debt options, commodity options, foreign currency options, and others on the scene. Even options on stock indexes are being traded. However, stock options, the first and largest category of option trading, have been the big lure for investors thus far. The enormous growth of stock options indicates how much it has permeated the financial markets and how greatly it has affected investors in virtually every walk of life.

STOCK OPTIONS

Options are the right, but not the obligation, to buy or sell a hundred shares at a set price within a specified time. This finite lifetime is important, because when that time passes, the option becomes totally worthless.

The two basic types of options are puts and calls. A put is an option to sell, or deliver, a hundred shares of the underlying stock and a call is an option to buy, or demand, a hundred shares. Investors generally prefer to buy calls rather than puts, just as they generally prefer to buy stock rather than sell short.

With a call, you are betting that the price of a stock will rise with a particular velocity; with a put, you are betting that it will fall with a particular velocity. If your prediction is correct, the value of your option will increase because you are using leverage whereby you don't have to make a big investment to earn a big percentage gain. At the same time, you are putting at risk whatever investment you do make in the options market because you are competing against the expanding number of full-time professionals in the field.

A stock option is essentially an unbalanced contract, in which only one party is obligated to fulfill the terms. The person with the choice pays for this right by acquiring an option that expires on a preset date. The time and price at which the stock can be bought or sold do not change during the period that the option is outstanding, but market conditions may change considerably.

Therefore the price that you would pay for a particular option to buy or sell a stock could fluctuate during the trading day. Options can be purchased or sold at any time during their lifetime.

The cost of an option, called the premium, is based principally on three factors. The first is the difference between the current market price of the underlying stock and the specified option price, also called the striking or exercise price. Second is the exercise period, because options are bought and sold in three-, six-, and nine-month maturities, with the premium generally increasing along with the expiration date. Third is the anticipated volatility of the underlying stock, since those with rapid price movements are typically more expensive than those with a more stable price performance.

When you acquire an option, you stand the possibility of benefiting in one of two ways. If the market moves in your favor, you can either sell the option at a profit—closing it out as most individuals in the option market do when they are ahead—or exercise the option and buy or sell the underlying stock at an advantageous price. In contrast, if the market turns against you, you can sell the option before expiration and limit your loss. You must, of course, add the sometimes substantial brokerage charges to your overall cost of trading options.

When the striking price of a call option is lower than the current market price of the stock, the call is said to be trading in the money. If the reverse is true, the call is out of the money. And if the market price and the striking price are the same, the call is at the money.

In a mirror image, when the striking price of a put option is greater than the current market price, the put is in the money. An out of the money put is when the striking price is below the market price. The put is at the money when both prices are identical.

Calls

Calls are bought if you think that the price of a stock will rise significantly during a certain period. For example, if you acquire a three-month call option to buy a hundred shares of a stock now selling at $45 a share and with a striking price of $45, the premium, or option purchase price, might be $3. If the market price of the stock increases to $50 after thirty days, the value of the option would also rise and the premium might then be selling for $5. At this point, you could sell the option at $5 for a profit of $2 a share, or a total of $200.

If you had guessed wrong and the market price of the stock fell to $40 by the expiration date, it would be pointless to exercise your option, which would then become worthless. Your only expense would have been the $3-a-share cost of the premium, or $300, plus brokerage commissions. On the other hand, if you had purchased the stock at $45 a share and sold it at $40, you would have lost $5 a share, or $500.

Puts

The arithmetic is similar when it comes to puts, which are bought when you think a stock price will decline sharply. In the case of a stock selling at $50 a share, where you acquire a three-month put with the same striking price, a typical premium might be $3 a share, or $300 for a hundred shares. If the stock price dropped to $45 a share in a month, the premium might advance to $5 and the option could be sold for $500—for a $200 profit. Alternatively, you could buy a hundred shares in the open market at $45 a share and exercise your option to sell them at $50. By subtracting the $300 cost of the option from your gross profit of $500, you would again be ahead by $2 a share, or $200.

If you are the holder of a put option, and the market goes the wrong way, you simply do not execute the option and its value becomes zero at the expiration date. The result in this example would be an out-of-pocket loss of $300, the price of the premium.

As a put buyer, you have a major psychological edge over a short seller, who is also gambling that the price of the stock will fall. The short seller has theoretically unlimited exposure as the price of the stock rises, since he must replace the shares he has borrowed at the market price, whatever it may be.

Option Strategies

After you develop an initial awareness of the uses of options, the next step often is an understanding of the intricacies of option strategies. These strategies range from simple procedures for buying and selling to complex arrangements that are best undertaken with advice from an experienced options broker or professional investment counselor.

For instance, if you own shares of a stock for which options are available, you can sell, or "write," options on them. In return, you will receive the premium paid by the buyer of the option and thereby may increase your rate of return on the investment by 10 percent or more.

Such a step would be possible if you wanted to keep certain stocks for the long term, but also wanted to earn some extra income from them. By writing an option, you immediately get a premium—a price that usually starts off at about 5 to 10 percent of the stock's market price—that will raise your return on the investment if the buyer does not exercise his right to buy. If he does, you can then replace the stock at the higher price by using the premium to offset the higher cost. Option sellers retain the ownership of the stock and receive all dividends paid until the option is actually exercised.

When you sell an option on shares that you own, the strategy is called covered options. Here's how it works: Say that you own stock in a company selling for $50 a share and paying an annual dividend of $3, representing a 6 percent yield. You write an option at a strike price of $55 that expires in six months and receive a premium of $2 a share, equal to an 8 percent annualized yield. If the price of the stock does not exceed $55 by the expiration date, the option will not be exercised and you will retain the shares. If the price rises beyond $55, it will be called by the option buyer at the $55 price. But in either case, the option sale will have increased your current yield to 14 percent.

A more dangerous maneuver is writing a naked option where you have no underlying stock to back it up. If you sell a naked call option and the stock price declines or remains steady, you simply keep the premium. But the risk is that if the price increases, you will be called upon to deliver the stock and will have to go into the open market to do so. In a bull market, this could be quite an expensive undertaking.

A naked option—an option bought or sold without having physical possession of the stock—is regarded as the most speculative of all options strategies. Writers of naked options should keep enough cash or securities in their account as collateral to meet possible demands for the stock in case it is called away or put to the writer.

Another often-used device by option traders who anticipate wide fluctuations in the price of a stock is a hedging tool known as a straddle. Straddles are double stock contracts involving the purchase of a put and a call on the same underlying stock with identical striking prices and expiration dates. If the stock either rises or falls to a degree large enough to cover the brokerage commissions on the trades, you will come out ahead, as one option theoretically becomes worthless at expiration and the other creates the gain. But if the stock moves sideways, you lose money on both the put and the call. In that event, it is the straddle seller, expecting only a narrow movement in the stock before the expiration date, who is the winner in this battle of wits.

Then there are spreads, which take advantage of the broadening or narrowing of the price differential of two options on one stock and can involve either calls or puts. With a price spread, you could buy a call and at the same time sell a call on that stock with a different striking price. The same procedure could be followed by buying and selling puts. If the two options in a spread have the same expiration date, it is a vertical, or perpendicular, spread; if there are different expiration dates, it is a horizontal, or calendar, spread.

Still another combination strategy is variable hedging, or ratio writing. With this technique, you write calls on more shares than you actually own. But if the market price advances beyond the striking price, you will have to buy the additional shares on the open market.

The sophisticated use of stock options involves many maneuvers that not only offer the possibility of rewards but also entail a substantial amount of risk. If you don't learn how to get in and out quickly to limit your losses, and don't make the effort to master the details of this subject, you could be badly damaged financially. Nevertheless, the idea of using limited cash for extensive purchases and of knowing the full loss potential in advance of every trade has encouraged, and will undoubtedly encourage more, recruits to the world of options.

NON-STOCK OPTIONS

The proliferation of stock options trading has led to further usage of this type of contract for non-stock categories. As a result, a much wider spectrum has opened for speculators who are willing to take certain risks in exchange for new profit opportunities.

Debt Options

Options on United States Treasury securities were the first non-stock option to appear. These debt, or interest-rate, options on fixed-income obligations were first publicly traded when some of the nation's options exchanges or divisions of securities exchanges listed them in 1982.

Put and call options on Treasury bills, notes, and bonds are traded for many of the same reasons that individuals buy and sell stock options. Debt options can also be tools to manage, reduce, or transfer risk, as individuals seek to protect the market value of their debt portfolios. The high and volatile interest rates of recent years have caused many owners of these portfolios to attempt to hedge against price changes, and these options have provided a means of doing so.

In addition to the Treasury securities, options are also being traded on jumbo certificates of deposit, representing a deposit of $100,000 or more with maturities of ten years or less. Thus options on CDs with a face value of, say, $1 million issued by the nation's largest banks can be bought and sold for a tiny fraction of that amount by those who anticipate upward or downward changes in interest rates.

Debt options are similar to stock options, but they have many differences with financial futures contracts. The basic variation is that the premium paid by the buyer to the seller is the maximum liability incurred by anyone who acquires an option. In contrast, a purchaser of a futures contract may be required to meet margin calls if the market turns against him and he has insufficient collateral in his account. Another difference is that interest-rate options can be exercised at any time during the life of the contract. But in the futures market, exercise is permitted only near the end of the trading cycle.

If you anticipate a significant decline in the period ahead and a corresponding increase in prices of debt obligations, you might consider purchasing call options on these underlying securities. But if you believe that interest rates will rise substantially and that debt securities prices will fall, you might decide to buy put options on these issues.

Commodity Futures Options

Commodity options were outlawed by the federal government in 1933 because of a rash of dishonest dealings that corrupted the market. But fifty years later, after becoming convinced that conditions had changed and that surveillance would ferret out any wrongdoing, the Commodity Futures Trading Commission, the government agency charged with regulating the commodities industry, authorized the trading of these options again on a pilot basis.

Options on physical commodities (such as sugar, silver, and gold), financial futures, and stock index futures thus joined debt securities in the panoply of non-stock options available to the public. Such options are also instruments that confer on the holder the right to buy or sell the underlying futures contract at a stated price during a stated time.

These options, traded on regulated commodity and securities exchanges, are designed to offer traders the opportunity to seek the large gains often found in commodity markets while avoiding the large losses that are also a possibility. As in the other options dealings, commodity futures option buyers cannot lose any more on a transaction than the cost of the option. Yet the option also gives the buyer the price protection that he desires.

Because trading in commodity futures options is not as generally understood as many other brokerage transactions, some particular requirements must be met before opening an account. Brokers must inform their clients of the difficulties they may face in these transactions, and clients must then sign a specially prepared statement detailing the risks of futures options. The object is to avoid a repetition of the earlier abuses perpetrated by swindlers in the over-the-counter market and boiler-room operators.

Most individuals who take the plunge into commodity futures options are likely to simply buy calls with the expectation that prices will advance. But those who become more sophisticated in the complex use of these options can combine positions in a futures contract, an option on that contract, and even the commodity itself—and thereby reduce their risks in such trading.

Foreign Currency Options

Options on foreign currencies have been created for individuals with a speculative bent who seek another opportunity to profit on changes in foreign currency movements. These options are now traded on exchanges in the United States and elsewhere on currencies like the British pound, the Japanese yen, the Swiss franc, the West German mark, and the Canadian dollar.

The advantage of foreign currency options is that they offer a relatively low-cost hedge against currency fluctuations in relation to the United States dollar. The chances of such fluctuation have risen sharply over the years because of the increased volatility of relative currency values and the volume of world trade.

There is a key difference between options and the more widely known and riskier forward and futures markets in foreign exchange. As is the case with all options, a currency option does not have to be exercised when the exchange rate moves against the holder. Unlike futures trading, there are no margin calls in currency options trading to cover a possible loss on a contract.

A buyer can hold a foreign currency option for a specified period, regardless of how steeply the currency moves in the wrong direction from the contracted price. And like other kinds of options, the potential loss is limited to the cost of the premium.

Options on Index Futures and "Homemade" Indexes

Options on index futures and other indexes give buyers a way to speculate or hedge on widescale changes in the stock market without the nightmare of margin calls for more money. A willingness to take some risks, though, is still a prerequisite for traders of these options.

Index options are a means of speculating on whether the stock market as a whole is going to rise or fall, rather than betting on the fortunes of any particular stock. These options are the right but not the obligation to buy or sell a theoretical basket of stocks, as represented by the index, during a fixed period at a fixed price. If you are wrong, your loss is predictable and limited to the premium, or amount paid for this basket of shares, and the brokerage commission.

Options available on index futures, which serve as the "underlying goods" for the contracts, include those based on the New York Stock Exchange composite stock index of about 1,500 stocks traded on the New York Futures Exchange, a subsidiary of the New York Stock Exchange, and on the Standard & Poor's 500-stock index, traded on the Chicago Mercantile Exchange. Among the cash settlement options on indexes are the Standard & Poor's 100-stock and 500-stock indexes, traded on the Chicago Board Options Exchange; the Major Market Index of 20 stocks and the Market Value Index of all stocks traded on the American Stock Exchange; and the New York Stock Exchange composite index.

Such trading might involve the purchase of an option nominally valued at, say, $100 multiplied by a specific value of the index. If the index rose above this value, the holder could exercise the option and make a profit of a hundred times that increase. But if the index did not advance to at least that value, the option would be worthless and would not be exercised.

Some of the index and subindex options, like the ones traded on the Chicago Board Options Exchange and the American Stock Exchange, are "homemade" and based on blue chip or specific industry shares chosen by the exchanges, rather than on a stock market average. Now, for example, many narrow-based index options are traded, each typically containing about twenty-five stocks. These options must be settled in cash upon expiration, because they are not anchored to any futures contracts. If the option shows a profit, your broker pays you; if it shows a loss, you pay your broker.

Chapter Fifteen

Futures

THE FUTURES MARKET IS SO arcane and intricate that for generations most Americans have not known or cared anything about it. Nevertheless, an investment in futures is not only one of the most uncertain of ventures, but also one of the most profitable financial activities in which the general public can participate. The excitement of rapid and dramatic price fluctuations is ingrained in this field because commodities respond to factors such as weather, inflation, politics, and technology. Yet sizable rewards may flow to those willing to assume the risks inherent in such investment.

Much of the public's reluctance to become involved in the volatile world of futures is because this kind of investment usually requires substantial financial reserves. In addition, steady nerves, extremely quick trading judgment, the ability to take losses in stride, and enormous self-discipline are needed to avoid the stresses of the marketplace.

Playing the futures market is basically speculation by individuals who seek to benefit by anticipating price swings accurately. Whether you buy and sell commodities, financial instruments, or even stock indexes, the periodic movement of prices gives this trading its opportunities, thrills, and dangers.

HISTORY

The futures market is a refinement of first the cash or spot market and then the forward market of trading products that allows traders either to take delivery or to otherwise make a profit at a specific date in the future. Its origins can be traced to the empires of the Phoenicians, Greeks, and Romans, which developed ways of contracting for future delivery of products from their colonized territories.

Later, the agricultural marketplaces of the Middle Ages and the European medieval trade fairs stimulated mercantile activity that led to the codification of trading practices known as the Law Merchant. Because of the distances required in traveling to and from the fairs, and the vulnerability to robbery of merchants carrying gold received from cash transactions, exhibitors started to display only samples of the merchandise, promising delivery later. Dealers at these fairs signed a *lettre de fair* stating that the item offered for sale really existed in a distant warehouse. This procedure eventually led to the codification of futures trading systems to regulate transactions and to minimize disputes.

Among the arrangements of a standardized futures contract that were developed during this period and that have remained an important part of futures trading were quantity, minimum and maximum price fluctuations, grading, inspection, and delivery. Organized futures trading also came into existence in Japan during the seventeenth century, where warehouse receipts for rice became an accepted form of currency in business transactions by the early 1700s.

The modern futures contract is said to date from the establishment of the Chicago Board of Trade, the first United States commodities futures exchange, in 1848. Within two decades, the Board of Trade, now the largest commodity exchange in the country, issued rules dealing with such key factors as margin requirements, daily price limits, delivery, and payment terms.

About ten more exchanges were later formed to give members a central place to trade for themselves and for others, and to provide a supervised auction market for futures contracts. The major ones include the Chicago Mercantile Exchange, the Commodity Exchange in New York, and the New York Mercantile Exchange.

In addition, clearinghouses to guarantee all contracts were created by these exchanges. Standard, simplified commodity contracts were also developed as the legal agreement governing the transaction between the buyer or seller and the clearinghouse. Such matters as quantity, grade, trading and position limits, and delivery date and location also became standardized. And as an indication of the modern-day pervasiveness of futures trading, a 1974 law led to the creation of an independent federal agency, the Commodity Futures Trading Commission, to regulate the industry. Futures trading has indeed become an important segment of American economic life.

COMMODITIES FUTURES

A futures contract, the fundamental unit of trading, is an obligation to buy or sell a specific quantity and quality of a commodity—which can be any product that is bought and sold—on a specific date at an agreed-upon price. Therefore you are contracting to buy or sell something that may or may not exist at the time that the contract is made. The trading of these contracts for delivery in the future, with low initial margin controlling a large amount of money, is the essence of the modern-day commodities futures field.

Futures contracts have long been traded in dozens of commodities, each of which exhibits a great deal of price independence. Among them are agricultural commodities (corn, soybeans, wheat), live cattle and hogs, frozen pork bellies, precious metals (gold, silver, platinum), nonferrous metals (copper), tropical products (coffee, sugar, cocoa), and energy products (heating oil, gasoline, propane).

These contracts can be bought and sold only on regulated commodity exchanges, where all orders are executed by open outcry and hand signal. An exchange is a third party to every transaction, thereby facilitating entry into the market and improving the market's liquidity. The exchanges also tabulate the number of outstanding futures contracts and combine them into what is called "open interest"—a closely watched indicator of overall market activity.

With typically low sales commissions paid just once when a futures contract position is terminated and with market information readily available to the public, commodities are steadily drawing the attention of more and more individuals. In recent years, the mystique of commodities has become less and less forbidding to those who have never before been a part of this trading process.

Futures traders are often classified as either speculators or hedgers. Individuals who trade commodities in an attempt to make a profit are essentially speculators. Hedgers are primarily companies that make or use the commodities traded and utilize the futures markets in an effort to reduce the damages that could arise from price fluctuations. This hedging is a form of insurance against adverse prices.

Speculators take a position based on an expectation of price changes, either up or down. If you expect the price of a commodity to rise, you would take a "long" position by purchasing a contract to buy that commodity at a fixed price lower than the anticipated market price at the agreed-upon future date. If you expect the price of a commodity to fall, you would take a "short" position by selling a contract to deliver the product at a fixed price on a future date, anticipating a profit by buying it back at a lower price and thus closing out your position.

Regardless of horror stories about thousands of bushels of wheat or thousands of cattle being trucked to the home of a speculator who held a futures contract too long, delivery is usually by warehouse receipt. In fact, most speculative positions are held for just a matter of weeks. The normal pattern is that the position is cashed in or, more likely, that an equal and opposite position is taken in the same delivery month. Such offsetting, which nullifies the original trade, can be made at any time before the contract terminates.

In dozens of actively traded commodities markets there is a great deal of liquidity, providing for generally efficient and orderly trading. As a result, participants in these markets can shift their positions rapidly and at prices near the most recent quotation.

Many types of orders placed by individuals in the commodities markets are similar to those used when buying and selling securities. For example, an order placed at the market is executed at the best price immediately available, while a limit order is restricted to a specified price or better—and may not be executed for some time, if at all. A good-till-canceled, or GTC, order remains open indefinitely, as opposed to the routine orders that are automatically canceled at the end of a trading day.

Stop-loss orders, perhaps the most important special-order category, are placed as a safeguard above or below the current market price to limit a loss or protect a profit in an open position. With a stop-loss order, you decide in advance when to liquidate a position and are forced to abide by that decision unless you change the order before it is executed.

Margin Buying

One of the most difficult concepts for novice traders in commodities to grasp is margins, which are considerably different than in the more familiar securities trading. In the securities business, margin represents a down payment to purchase securities, with the remainder an extension of credit by a broker who charges interest on borrowed funds. But in the commodities business, margin is a good-faith, or security, deposit—a relatively small amount required to ensure fulfillment of the contract, with no interest charged on the remainder. The customer is liable, though, for any deficits that may occur.

A buyer and a seller of a futures contract must each post an initial margin, a performance bond in a specified dollar amount to guarantee that the contract will be fulfilled. The initial margin—whose level is established by the exchange where the commodity is traded and which generally ranges between 5 and 20 percent of the contract value of the commodity—is a good-faith payment that must be given to the broker before the trade is executed. In addition to cash, this margin can be in the form of Treasury bills, enabling you to earn interest on your deposit.

Afterwards brokerage firms may require customers to add funds to reach a minimum maintenance margin, since all gains or losses attributed to the contract are added to or subtracted from the margin daily. And if that margin call is not met, the broker may close out the position and bill the customer for any shortfall in the account.

Because of this margin system, a commodities trader enjoys a considerable amount of leverage, with a small price change having a large effect on the equity balance in an account. If the margin for a particular commodity is 10 percent, a 10 percent increase in the price of that commodity offers a speculator a gain of 100 percent in his trading equity. Leverage works both ways, though, and a 10 percent decline in a commodity price would give a margined trader a 100 percent loss of his equity.

Whenever you buy or sell a futures contract, you have what the professionals in the field call an open position until you offset that trade or settle it by delivering the commodity. After each trade, your broker will send, along with a confirmation slip, a list of all of your open, or uncompleted, positions, your gains and losses on each position, and the total equity balance in your account. Your net account balance—the best indication of the value of your commodity holdings—is the amount you would have left after closing out, or selling, all open positions at the settlement prices on any given day and paying all commissions due.

Daily Limits

The futures price of each commodity is usually permitted to rise or fall only by a specified maximum amount each day, known as the daily trading limit. These limits, set with respect to the previous day's closing price, are established to prevent extreme one-day changes resulting from any unusual circumstances.

Maximum fluctuation limits mean more orderly markets. Commodities exchanges can keep margin levels low because market participants are unable to overreact to new information. Although there is a suggestion that prices might change more whenever a market closes at a limit, traders prevented from further buying and selling have another day to assess the available information and to seek further data. Buyers and sellers can also get caught in a losing position by the daily limits and may be unable to trade their way out of it. It does not necessarily mean that trading is stopped, however, when the price of a commodity reaches the daily permissible limits. The significance of reaching the limit is that no additional orders will be filled beyond that price. Trading may be extended at the limit, although such activity is rare.

If a commodity hits either of its limits for two consecutive days, the following day's limits are increased by a specified amount. This amount will continue to rise if the commodity continues to reach the daily limits, but will return to the original limits immediately after the first non-limit day. Commodity exchanges also set minimum price fluctuations for the products traded in their pits.

Many commodities traders utilize a mechanical trading plan to guide them in their buying and selling, rather than making decisions on impulse. Some position traders use a fundamental analysis of basic economic principles to determine what the gross national product, supply and demand forces, economic outlook, and other factors will be, and whether the market forces have judged them accurately. Market fundamentalists believe that long-term trends are dependent on national or international considerations, while short-term movements are influenced by local conditions and minor price changes.

Others, called chartists, use technical analysis to identify and interpret the past behavior of the marketplace—through such devices as moving statistical averages and chart formations—as a guide to current and future price trends. This forecasting technique measures buying and selling pressures so that chartists can go along with the trends until a new one appears to be in the offing.

Whichever system you use, there are three fundamentals of commodity trading to remember. All commodity positions are marked to the market daily, whereby accounts of every customer are tallied every day by their brokers, and price changes are immediately reflected. A futures contract does not represent the actual transfer of proprietary rights, since ownership changes only when delivery is made or received. And you cannot hold a contract longer than the time remaining until the delivery month.

For those who don't wish to make their own decisions in this complex marketplace, a couple of alternative ways to participate involving professional management exist, although commodity managers often require that accounts be of a certain minimum size. One is a managed account with a brokerage firm, granting it the power to trade the account based on its own analysis. Although you are solely responsible for the losses generated from such an account, the account manager may share in the profits over and above the commissions generated by the trades.

Another method is shares in a commodity mutual fund, which holds positions in a portfolio of futures and is similar in some respects to the open-end investment companies that invest in stocks or bonds. These funds offer great diversity, since a large number of contracts are being handled under professional guidance. But in contrast to the securities mutual funds, commodity funds are self-liquidating and wind down when net assets fall below a specified level. The participants, who generally acquire units in a form known as limited partnership, cannot lose any more than their initial investment.

Even with such trading systems or professional guidance, the hazards of commodities speculating are enormous. More non-professionals lose money in trading commodities than make money because their price forecasting skills and their discipline in the marketplace are inadequate. The watchword when buying and selling commodities—perhaps more so than with any other investment—is caution.

FINANCIAL FUTURES

Financial futures, introduced in the 1970s, brought a new and different element to the traditional futures contract: speculation on price movements in a number of different securities. With traders buying and selling the new contracts as they buy and sell other commodity contracts, financial futures have captured a significant percentage of those seeking above-average profitability in return for above-average risk.

Widely known as interest-rate futures, financial futures refer to contracts based on financial instruments whose prices fluctuate with changes in interest rates. Included in this category are Treasury bills, notes and bonds, bank certificates of deposit, commercial paper, and certificates guaranteed by the Government National Mortgage Association. A separate category of financial futures is that based on foreign currencies.

The idea behind financial futures is that interest rates, which represent the cost of credit, can be examined as an opportunity for profit in the same manner as the prices of other commodities. Because of popular acceptance, broad-scale trading in these contracts is now going on at such exchanges as the Chicago Board of Trade and the Chicago Mercantile Exchange.

As with other futures contracts, an advantage of financial futures is that contracts are standardized. This means that the terms of coupon rate, maturity, issuer, and quantity are among those explicitly stated. The only variable is price.

Also as in other futures trading, the overwhelming majority of all market participants do not intend to make or take delivery of the underlying financial instrument. Most contracts are closed out at a profit or loss before the delivery date.

With interest-rate futures, as with the underlying fixed-income securities, prices rise when rates fall and prices fall when rates rise. Therefore speculators in these futures watch the same market indicators as fixed-income investors, including the money supply, changes in the government's economic policy, unemployment statistics, and the producer price index.

Competing against the individual speculator in the financial futures market are the money managers and financial institutions that use these contracts to protect themselves against interest-rate increases and decreases. Those professional hedgers who assume a conservative posture attempt to insulate themselves from interest-rate moves by taking an equal and opposite position in the financial futures market to the one established, or about to be established, in the cash market. The difference between them—cash price minus futures price—is known as the basis, which can be either positive or negative.

Because interest rates have been so volatile in recent years, financial futures are even riskier than the traditional commodities futures. With the possibility of controlling, say, $1 million worth of securities with a margin requirement of about $1,000, you had better have a strong grasp of yield curves and other rate theories. Yield curves plot the relative yield of money market instruments over a period of time, with the normal curve showing that yields rise as maturities lengthen. The reason: Time creates uncertainty, particularly with regard to future inflation.

STOCK INDEX FUTURES

Stock index futures, another kind of financial futures, were created in 1982. These contracts let risk-takers bet on overall market swings by speculating on stock movements or insulating their portfolios against market slumps. Moreover, individuals can bet on this abstraction at a fraction of the cost of buying a diversified equity portfolio.

The big advantage of index futures is that they allow for direct participation in the movement of the overall stock market. Participants undertake an obligation to buy or sell a mythical standardized portfolio of stocks that matches the composition of a published index. Then without selecting among the various stocks, they try to predict the direction of the market and the timing of its moves while enjoying the same high leverage of other commodities futures trading. Traders can thereby insure their stock holdings against a market decline or protect themselves against an advance if they are holding short positions.

Here, too, knowledge of the field and the ability to move rapidly are essential for even a chance at success. For every trader who wins, another must lose in this zero-sum game.

Stock index futures contracts mature four times a year. Such trading is taking place at such exchanges as the New York Futures Exchange, where contracts are based on the New York Stock Exchange composite index; the Chicago Mercantile Exchange, where they are based on the Standard & Poor's 500-stock and 100-stock indexes; and the Kansas City Board of Trade, where they are based on the Value Line average. The Standard & Poor's and New York Stock Exchange indexes are market-value weighted and take into account the number of shares outstanding, while the more volatile Value Line index, containing fewer large capitalization companies, is unweighted.

The contract price on stock index futures is figured at a multiple of 500 times the index number itself. Each one-point move represents $500 a contract. Unlike the case in all other commodities markets except Eurodollar futures, however, there is no possibility whatsoever of physical delivery if you reach the expiration date without closing out your position. Settlement on these contracts is only for cash, since no shares are ever delivered or accepted.

With the development of index futures to wager on the whole stock market in one stroke, a number of sophisticated trading techniques could be used by those with enough knowledge and financial resources to engage in such speculation. For instance, you could hedge one stock index against another based on how you believe the stocks that constitute the two indexes will perform. If you were bullish on bonds and bearish on stocks, you could go long on a financial futures contract in, say, Treasury bonds, while going short on one of the stock index contracts.

In addition to the contracts on stock indexes, futures contracts on subindexes, or more specialized groups of stocks, are also being offered. The subindex contracts let futures traders match more precisely the composition of their equity portfolios and act on their belief about the trend of a particular industry, such as financial services, in the near future.

FUTURES BUYING TIPS

- Don't speculate unless you can afford to lose. The futures market is a place for high-risk capital, since the necessary objectivity for trading decisions comes only when you are using surplus funds. A minimum account size for futures trading should be between $5,000 and $10,000, even though some brokerage firms have lower minimums, because smaller accounts will probably not be sufficiently flexible to tolerate the perils involved.

- Risk only a small proportion of your capital on a single trade. Furthermore, restrict your open positions to the number that you can adequately follow.

- A motto in the commodities business is, "Cut your losses and let your profits run." That's because retaining winning positions may be as difficult as eliminating losers. If you are on the right side of just 30 percent of your trades, you can be successful by using this technique, since you will make more money when you are right than you will lose when you are wrong.

- Stay on the sidelines and wait for attractive situations. You cannot participate in every market move, so don't try to be active all the time. Pick your spots carefully—and have patience.

- No one can choose only the tops and bottoms of the various market moves. Nor does it generally pay to fight trends, which are easier to recognize than define. Price movements usually possess a lot of momentum, which you should try to have working for you, rather than against you.

- Learn the basics of how the markets work and why prices move as they do. Study newspaper and magazine articles on commodities, read the commodity letters of brokerage houses, and perhaps attend a commodities seminar before making your first trade. When you begin trading, start on a small scale and expect to make many mistakes.

- Don't trade in thin markets or inactive delivery months. If the price moves against you and you are forced to liquidate when there are relatively few buy and sell orders, the differential between the bid and the asked prices could be five or ten times the minimum price change.

- Be careful about overtrading—either trading in quantities that are too large or trading too frequently. If you overcommit your trading capital, you cannot afford to be wrong and all traders are wrong sometimes. Moving in and out of the market continually is an expensive luxury, since the commissions on short-term trading can add up to such a large percentage of your capital that your profits will disappear.

Chapter Sixteen

Collectibles

COLLECTIBLES HAVE BECOME AN OUTLET for fun and potential profit for increasing numbers of Americans. But the potential for profit also brings the potential for loss—and this is certainly true in the case of collectibles.

The word "collectible" generally refers to an item in finite supply that was not inherently valuable when first produced. Only in recent decades have collectibles come into broad public consciousness. With the growing affluence of the middle class, many individuals turned to collectibles as a way to express an interest in a subject, as well as a means of investment. For some, collectibles became not only a personal and absorbing activity, but also a status symbol by which they could be judged by others.

Whether you are interested in collecting art, antiques, gold coins, stamps, precious stones, comic books, or any of the dozens of other collectibles, it makes sense to be careful. You will be buying and selling in competition with professionals whose knowledge of the field is likely to be far superior to yours. Fakes and frauds also abound in many kinds of collectibles.

In addition, collectibles are not liquid investments and therefore may tie up an investor's funds for lengthy periods. Collectibles also do not pay interest or dividends. Nevertheless, many individuals believe that these items are an attractive investment alternative to preserve capital from inflation and pass on something of increasing value to their descendants.

Today there are collectibles in virtually all price categories, from the inexpensive to the stratospheric. There are bargains in all of these categories, although nobody really knows what a bargain is until he tries to sell the item.

GUIDELINES FOR COLLECTORS

Certain guidelines can increase the pleasure and potential for gain of both novice and experienced collectors. These guidelines are no guarantee of profit, of course, but they can be helpful to anyone who hopes to make money from collectibles.

- Learn as much about the field as possible before plunking down your cash. Successful collecting usually takes time and effort. Read a book or two about the specialty and subscribe to the leading magazines and auction catalogues that cover this subject. Find out if there is a collectors club nearby where you can meet and talk to other enthusiasts. Visit dealer showrooms and auctions where the collectibles can be inspected and evaluated.

- Buy only those items that you like and enjoy having around you. Because collectibles are illiquid investments, they usually have to be retained for many years before there is an opportunity to realize a meaningful profit. Since you will probably be living with the collectible for a long time, if not forever, make sure that it is not a product you detest. If you don't like a piece, don't collect it—regardless of how much of a bargain it appears to be.

- Pick the best quality items that you can afford. Aesthetically and financially, you are better off with a smaller collection containing finer units than one that is larger but mediocre. Superior quality collectibles tend to increase in value faster in up markets and to hold their value or buck the trend in down markets. Masterpieces are always underpriced.

- The value of a collectible depends largely on its rarity, condition, and its desirability to others. A one-of-a-kind item or a limited edition usually is priced higher than comparable ones that are not as scarce. But regardless of the rarity, collectibles must be desired by others—preferably many others—if there is to be any real opportunity for capital appreciation.

- Don't be influenced by a short-term fad. Trends often have short lives and an item in demand one year may fall out of fashion the next. Since you probably cannot keep completely on top of the market, regardless of how long you collect, stick with quality collectibles for the long term.

- Be patient and businesslike. If you rush into buying, you are likely to get burned. Start with small purchases to discover the market, and after you have purchased some collectibles, don't sell them too quickly. You probably will have to buy at the retail price and sell at the wholesale price—and you may have to wait for a surge in demand before selling. Keep careful records of your collectible transactions, including invoices, checks, and supporting material, just as you would for any other transaction.

LIQUIDATING COLLECTIBLES

Selling your collectibles is usually much harder than buying them. Generating the cash that you want, or need, may require contacting many dealers or auction houses—and even then, the return could be less than expected. If overall economic conditions are poor and a recession is under way, there could be a scarcity of buyers at any price. There may be a stiff commission involved, too.

Before actually disposing of all or part of your collectibles, shop the market to determine selling prices for comparable items.

You may also do well to consult a professional appraiser, especially if there are some expensive items in the collection.

Once you have established a realistic asking price, find out if the dealers from whom you originally bought the items would be interested in repurchasing them. Check with any auction houses that may have sold you collectibles about offering them for sale there. Then inquire whether any other selling outlets may possibly be interested in your sale. Be prepared to compromise on the price.

By selling to a dealer, you may be able to obtain a fixed price for the items that change hands. Many dealers are willing to make a quick sale that is concluded for cash as soon as an agreement is reached. The dealer is probably buying with the intention of reselling the collectibles to someone else, so he will pay no more than a self-imposed price limit, beyond which his profit margin would not be adequate. Some dealers, moreover, will accept your collectibles only on a consignment basis, with a fee ranging from 10 to 30 percent of the sales price.

A sale through an auction house will take more time than a straight sale, because your items must be scheduled for an auction at some future date. Auctioneers generally charge a commission to the seller of 20 to 25 percent of the sales price, although some major auction houses that sell fine works of art and more expensive collectibles charge 10 to 15 percent to the seller and 10 percent to the buyer. Sales commissions are often negotiable, however, especially when an auction house wishes to sell your collectibles.

If you decide to take the auction route, be sure to get a written contract that spells out the details. The contract should state the sales commission, the reserve or minimum bid that will be accepted, the additional charges (if any) for insurance, photography, pickup, moving and storage, and the date of the sale. Other details to be negotiated that may not be included in the contract are when payment will be made to the seller and whether the auctioneer will assume the expenses of advertising the sale.

If you cannot sell your collectibles through a reputable dealer or auction house and all else fails, you can still obtain some value for the collection by donating it to a charitable or educational organization. You must be able to document the value of the donated items for the Internal Revenue Service if requested. But with such a donation, you will be able to deduct this value on your federal income tax return.

TAX CONSEQUENCES

One of the tax aspects of collectibles is the federal income tax deduction available if you make a profit from buying and selling. Normally there is no deduction for money spent on a hobby, because this is a personal expense. However, there may be times when you sell a piece of the collection, or even the entire collection, and your income is greater than your outgo.

In any year that your collection is profitable—and you can prove that you are collecting for investment and ultimate sale—you can deduct expenses related to the collection that would otherwise be considered personal. For instance, you can claim deductions for insurance premiums for the collectibles, appraisal fees, and specialized publications. These expenses are deductible, though, only up to the amount of your gross profit, so complete records of your dealings will come in handy in the event of an audit.

In addition, the profit from the sale of a collector's item that has been held for more than six months is considered a long-term capital gain. But with both long-term and short-term capital gains now taxed at the same rate, there is no longer any tax advantage to holding the item beyond six months.

Another tax matter for collectors to weigh is that most collectibles cannot be added to your individual retirement account or Keogh plan. Neither of these widely used tax-deferred retirement plans—the first for salaried employees or the self-employed and the second only for the self-employed—are permitted to be used for collectibles because the federal government believes that such investments do not increase the nation's productivity.

ART

In the art market, many individuals hesitate to make any purchases until they consider themselves qualified. Yet these individuals will probably never become qualified in the field until they have made a substantial number of purchases.

A good way to start acquiring this qualification is by purchasing relatively low-priced art—prints, posters, and similar works. For a couple of hundred dollars or so, you may be able to buy a decent item that can launch you into the world of art collecting. Try to find a reputable dealer and tell him what you want to buy and how much you want to spend. With inexpensive art, any mistakes that you make will be inexpensive ones.

Because the art market is so enormous, successful collectors generally specialize in a single field, such as Old Master drawings or classical artifacts. You can switch specializations, but you should stay with one area long enough to closely follow price trends, learn the nuances of this part of the market, and maintain a unified collection. In contrast to the stock market, where diversification of holdings is widely recommended, concentration usually affords the best opportunities for success in the art world.

When selecting an area of specialization, consider among other things your interest in that field, its prospects for capital appreciation, the availability of good local dealers, and the number of quality works on the market. The goal of the specialist collector is to develop the self-confidence to know values and to back up this knowledge with purchases when appropriate.

Serious art collectors often frequent auctions, if only to get a better handle on current price trends in their field. A key point to understand about auctions is that not every item is actually sold to the public. Many collectibles may be "bought in" by the auctioneer for the owner's reserve.

A reserve, which owners of items being auctioned often establish, especially for expensive items, is the amount below which the item will not be sold at auction. The amount of this reserve is determined by and kept secret between the owner and the auction house, so that participants in an auction will not know if a collectible has actually been purchased until the post-sale price list appears. Items that are bought in by the owner do not appear on this list. When many buy-ins take place for a particular category of art, it can mean that the market has weakened for that category and bargains are available for collectors.

Prints

Collectors who focus on prints usually find it a reasonably inexpensive way to participate in the art market. Print-making is the most democratic of the fine arts in terms of availability and accessibility. You can buy prints by recognized artists for as little as $100, although better-quality works cost more and Old Master prints sell in the six-figure range.

These prints, known as original, or rare, prints, are not reproductions made by printers who produce an unlimited number of copies of a work. In contrast, original prints are actual works of art, since the artist often makes an original design on a plate, stone, block, or other medium and has only a limited number of copies or impressions printed by a craftsman under his supervision. Prints have been made of works by some of the world's major artists, while others are the effort of men and women whose names are not household words. The value of prints is determined largely by the reputation and popularity of the artist, the condition of the print, the subject, and the number of copies printed.

Prints are typically produced in limited editions of a specific number of copies, with a code on each copy spelling out the total printed and the number of that particular copy. For example, 39/100 means that the work is the thirty-ninth copy of an edition of a hundred prints. Prints from smaller editions generally cost more than those from larger editions of comparable quality works. Editions in the thousands are not considered scarce.

The two best-known types of prints are lithographs and etchings. For lithographs, an artist draws on a slab of porous stone, moistens the surface with water, and applies ink with a roller to the moist stone. The inked stone is used to produce the prints, which typically look like crayon drawings.

For etchings an artist coats a copper or zinc plate with a thin waxlike resin and draws through this resin with a special etching needle. The plate is then immersed in acid, which etches the drawn lines into the plate. To the viewer, etchings look similar to pen-and-ink drawings.

Remember that fakes and misrepresentations are widespread

in the field of prints. Advertised "limited editions" could have 5,000 or more reproductions, while "hand-numbered" prints are sometimes numbered by someone else's hand, rather than the artist's.

In addition, many print tax shelters that promise big write-offs to investors have been attacked by the Internal Revenue Service as abusive. Although some art tax shelters are legitimate ventures, in which the objective is to produce both good art and an eventual profit for investors, others are established primarily to obtain the benefits of an investment tax credit and accelerated depreciation—and are being challenged by the I.R.S.

ANTIQUES

Regardless of what you pay for new furniture, its market value drops as soon as you buy it; antique furniture is often a much better buy. Many antiques are priced competitively with new furniture and also have a chance to appreciate in the years ahead. And furniture built centuries ago in the Chippendale and Goddard-Townsend workshops sells at prices that have reached beyond the budgets of most families.

Although in the long run, prices for antiques have gone up, selling prices fluctuate from year to year. Less expensive items can frequently be found at antique shows, country auctions, and dealer showrooms. At the other end of the scale, serious buyers generally continue to pay top dollar for top-quality antiques, thereby keeping volume steadily at a high level in this category.

Since an antique can be defined as a piece of furniture or decorative object made in an earlier period, a factor in its value is the limited supply of the item. In recent years, demand for antiques has also increased, thereby adding another positive element to the antique market.

No matter where your interests in antiques lie, be wary of getting involved too early with a style whose interest has recently resurfaced. It takes time for experts in a field to sift the quality works from the mediocre antiques of the period. You can therefore expect the secondary examples to decline in price from inflated levels, while the best works retain or increase their value.

Among the types of antiques that are good prospects for profitable long-term investments are basic pieces which have a specific use, like a bed or a lamp; an item in an identifiable series, like carnival glass or Royal Doulton figurines; pieces of unusual artistic or historical merit; and classic examples of a design period, like Art Deco or Art Nouveau. Collections that reflect a hobby or are rooted in one region of the country have better-than-average salability. The idea is to try to stay one step ahead of the crowd by locating an item so rare that its market value is most likely to advance.

Before buying an antique, either from a dealer or at an auction, study the piece carefully. Examine the furniture's construction, as well as the state of inlay and veneer, for signs of dry rot or infestation. After buying, don't refinish, replate, or restore any more than necessary, since restoration should be done in line with the original workmanship and excessive restoration may destroy value. And be wary of "instant antiques" created by unscrupulous operators who are out to turn a fast buck with shoddy merchandise.

GOLD COINS

Gold has been mined for some 6,000 years and has probably been a medium of exchange for just about as long. The metal is both rare and in continual demand, so it tends to retain its value better than paper currency, particularly during inflationary times. The most widely used technique in the United States of investing in gold is through the purchase of coins.

There are two basic kinds of gold coins for collectors: numismatic and bullion. Numismatic coins derive their value from their rarity, condition, and artistic value. Among the popular numismatic coins are the American Double Eagle, the French Napoleon, and the British Sovereign.

Since a major factor in valuing numismatic coins is their rarity, their prices can be astronomically higher than their actual gold content. Other considerations include historical importance and provenance. Rare coin prices can, and do, sometimes take a tumble, as many collectors have discovered to their regret. The better the quality, therefore, the more likely a coin will keep its value.

Bullion coins are official government restrikes designed for those who want to own gold in small convenient units. Prices of these coins, which have no numismatic value, are pegged directly to the daily wholesale gold price in London, with a commission of about 5 to 8 percent tacked on for coinage and distribution. The most heavily traded of these coins had been the South African Krugerrand—containing exactly one ounce of gold—but now others have become more popular, such as the Canadian Maple Leaf.

When buying bullion coins, shop around for the best price from banks, major auction houses, securities firms, coin dealers, or jewelry stores. And when selling, don't forget that some purveyors of coins will not purchase them unless they originally sold them to you. To keep you up-to-date on current gold market conditions, the daily gold price is quoted in many newspapers and on radio and television news programs.

STAMPS

Stamps have long been a popular collectible for many reasons. They have been a hedge against inflation, national and international catastrophes, and they are usually readily convertible into cash. Because they are small, they are also easy to hide. Recently the philatelic field has shown a growth in interest surpassing any previous surge.

You can get seriously started in stamp collecting with an investment of as little as $500. Once you have at least $10,000 or so invested in stamps, you can look forward to the possibility of major capital gains.

In collecting stamps, pick a specialty, such as a country or a particular period of time. Don't bother with mail-order packets of stamps, because there is little likelihood of any stamps in the packet having significant value. If you inherit or otherwise become the owner of a stamp collection, check with a few reputable dealers to determine its worth.

As with other collectibles, quality buying and holding for the long term are key factors in successful stamp collecting. Profits usually do not generally flow to the uninformed.

PRECIOUS STONES

For centuries, Europeans and Japanese have bought and held precious stones because of their combination of high value and portability. More recently, many Americans have followed the same approach, collecting precious stones as an investment for the future.

There are just fifteen categories of gemstones on the market. The most popular are diamonds and the colored stones, such as rubies, sapphires, and emeralds. Each stone's value is different, based on individual microscopic details that can be seen only by a trained gemologist.

When buying a gem, make sure that it is accompanied by a written certificate from an independent grading and testing laboratory. The four criteria for gem quality are the "4Cs": color, clarity, cut, and carats.

Color grades of diamonds are measured by a system running from D, or colorless, the most valuable, to the end of the alphabet, although investment grade stones go only to H, which is white to all but the trained eye. Clarity indicates a relative portion on a scale and also is graded, ranging from Flawless (F) to Imperfect (I-1 and I-2). Investment grade diamonds don't go beyond Very Slight Inclusions (VS-2).

Cut, or make, is least easily quantified because it describes the angles and proportions that give a stone its aesthetic values, sometimes described as brilliance and fire. The word "carat," or weight, is derived from the ancient carob seed. One carat weighs 200 milligrams and can be divided into 100 points.

Grading of colored stones is more primitive than diamond grading, although standards have been set by the testing labs. Any secondary colors in a stone, though, clearly reduce its value.

When trying to resell a precious stone, the most likely purchaser is the company from which you bought it. Some concerns do not hold inventories and thus will take the stone only on consignment for a commission. As a rule, selling takes longer than buying.

Therefore, if you don't want to be forced into a sale at a rock-bottom price, take the precautions of studying the market, shopping around, and selecting a dealer that backs its merchandise. Stay away from unknown companies that sell diamonds over the telephone, and be prepared to hold your investment for the long term—which in the precious stones market means at least three to five years.

COMIC BOOKS

It's a far cry from precious stones to comic books, but there are nevertheless tens of thousands of comic book collectors in the United States. These collectors are buying and selling comics for anywhere from 15 cents to around $15,000 for a mint condition Action Comics Number 1—the first superhero comic book, issued in 1938, that introduced Superman to the public.

In determining the worth of a comic book, an important consideration is whether it was a first issue. There is always a great price spread between the first and second issues of a series. Condition is significant, since you can expect to pay four or five times more for a comic book in mint condition (meaning virtually untouched) than for a well-read book. Scarcity also helps to determine value, with comics from the 1930s and the early 1940s, when fewer were issued and wartime paper drives decimated collections, the rarest on the market.

Comics from the Golden Age, from 1938 to 1956, appeal to a generation of older collectors. So do Classic Comics, but there is a danger in buying these books for investment. Since Classic Comics were used in schools, they were reprinted every six months from the original printing plates without changing the dates. That's why many individuals who believed they held valuable originals are now stuck with worthless reprints.

If you collect comic books, never store them flat, since there will be a great deal of handling and the spines of the bottom books will be crushed. Store them upright and keep your most valuable books in plastic cases for better protection.

Part Four

Real Estate

Chapter Seventeen

Mortgages

A HOME IS PROBABLY THE most expensive purchase that the average individual will make in his lifetime. Although most families consider a home as an investment rather than an expense, relatively few take the time and trouble to do the research that should be standard procedure before any major investment. However, the purchase of a home is more than a major expenditure; it is also the acquisition of the proverbial roof over your head. And there is no underestimating the care that ought to be taken in raising that roof.

Buying, as well as selling, a home is too often undertaken casually, without a "game plan" detailing the best steps to take in each circumstance. Professional advisors, like lawyers and real estate agents, are generally used for particular aspects of the transaction, but there is often no overall coordination among them to meet the long-range goals of their clients.

Furthermore, buying and selling a home cannot be purely an economic determination. Social and emotional considerations, such as your desire for privacy, your attitude about possessing property, your willingness to commute, your enjoyment of a garden, and your ability to handle minor and major repairs, should be carefully considered before reaching a decision.

MORTGAGE BASICS

For most people, buying a home means taking out a mortgage. A mortgage is a legal agreement between the purchaser of a property and an institution or individual who lends him the money, with the home itself as security or collateral. Most twentieth-century American mortgages have fixed monthly payments, a fixed interest rate, and full amortization, or transfer of equity, over twenty to thirty years.

The concept of realty mortgages as a loan security device goes back to ancient times; there is evidence of them as far back as 2000 B.C. in Babylonia. During the Roman Empire, many real estate conveyances were recorded, while the modern mortgage structure and usage began to evolve in the twelfth century. And by the 1600s, the mortgage had developed into a form that is quite recognizable by anyone familiar with those issued currently in the United States.

In today's standard home mortgages, payments of principal and interest are made periodically in equal installments, usually monthly. Although the amount of each installment does not vary, the proportion of interest and principal does. Under the process called amortization, the debt is repaid gradually through these combined interest and principal payments. During the early years, most payments are for interest and little is applied to principal. With the passage of time, more and more of the monthly amount is used for principal. Your equity accumulates gradually until the end of the mortgage period when the principal is fully repaid and no further interest is charged. Such loans are known as self-liquidating mortgages.

For decades, most lenders issued only traditional fixed-rate mortgages. But when interest rates became volatile and skyrocketed in the late 1970s, a miscellany of variable-rate mortgages came upon the scene. Federal regulators authorized these mortages to give banks, savings and loan associations, and other lenders wider latitude in writing loans more accurately reflecting the rates paid to depositors or investors. The term "creative financing" was used to apply to more than a hundred nontraditional mortgages that sprang up using variable interest rates and other new home financing techniques.

Most home loans issued by financial institutions are in the form of conventional mortgages. They are the fastest and easiest to obtain, but often require sizable down payments of 20 to 30 percent of the purchase price. Mortgages insured by the Federal Housing Administration or guaranteed by the Veterans Administration for eligible veterans generally have lower interest rates and lower down payments than conventional mortgages but are frequently enmeshed in red tape that stretches out the period it takes to obtain the loan.

Many lenders, though, require home buyers to pay an additional fee for a mortgage known as "points." This fee is essentially interest paid in advance at the time the mortgage is issued, with each point representing 1 percent of the mortgage amount. Points are an up-front charge imposed by banks to increase their stated interest rate, with borrowers usually having no choice but to pay the fee if they want the loan. But points are tax-deductible in the year they are paid, as long as it is for an original mortgage on your principal residence and the number of points does not exceed the amount usually charged in your area.

Also normally charged to the home buyer are the costs of the closing or settlement services, which must be paid in cash when the mortgage is issued. Among these costs, which vary depending on location and might easily run to more than $2,000, are such items as a loan origination fee, title search and insurance, appraisal fee, escrow account, bank lawyer's fee, and the mortgage interest and real estate taxes due between the date of the closing and the first regular monthly payment. You may also have to pay your lawyer's fee—generally about 1 percent of the sales price—when the closing takes place.

Of course, whatever kind of mortgage is obtained or whatever additional charges are added, the lender is primarily concerned with the buyer's ability to repay the loan. Different rules of thumb for determining this level have been applied over the years. Other families attempt to borrow on the basis of their personal priorities instead of any fixed rules.

When many lenders gauge the ability to repay these days, the standard formula is that the average family can afford monthly payments for housing, including mortgage amortization, insurance, taxes and utilities, of one third of their monthly take-home salary—up from the one quarter of take-home pay benchmark used not too long ago. For instance, with take-home pay of $1,500 a month, housing expenses should be no more than $500 monthly under this formula.

Another standard rule is that a family can afford a home if the purchase price is no greater than two-and-a-half times their annual gross salary. With such a formula, your limit for buying a home would be $50,000 if your income is $20,000.

From the buyer's point of view, the key factors to use in comparing sources of mortgage financing are the amount being financed, the length or maturity of the loan, the interest rate, the size of the monthly payment, whether or not payments or rates can change, how often and to what extent such changes can be made, and whether the loan can be refinanced at maturity if necessary.

TYPES OF MORTGAGES

A wide variety of mortgage loans are on the market. Among those that you are most likely to come upon are:

Fixed-Rate Mortgages

With fixed-rate mortgages, both interest rates and monthly payments are constant for the duration of the loan. Published amortization tables show precisely how each of these monthly payments is divided into principal and interest. Thus you know from the outset of a fixed-rate loan both how much interest will be paid if the mortgage is retained until maturity and the total amount paid during this period for both principal and interest.

The two key considerations in determining a home buyer's monthly payments for principal and interest are the interest rate, expressed as an annual percentage rate, and the repayment period. The higher the interest rate, the larger both the monthly payment and the total interest charge. The longer the period of repayment, the lower the monthly payment, but the larger the total interest charge.

Consider a thirty-year, $60,000 mortgage. Here are the different monthly payments and total interest charges over that period for mortgages with interest rates ranging from 11 to 13½ percent:

Monthly Payments* and Total Interest Charges for a 30-Year $60,000 Mortgage Loan at Different Interest Rates

Interest Rates (Expressed as an Annual Percentage Rate)	Monthly Payment	Total Interest Charges (over 30 Years)
11%	$571.39	$145,700.40
11½%	594.17	153,901.20
12%	617.17	162,181.20
12½%	640.35	170,526.00
13%	663.72	178,939.20
13½%	687.25	187,410.00

* Monthly payment figures shown include only principal and the interest charge—actual payments may also include taxes and insurance.
Source: "Managing Your Credit," Money Management Institute of Household International

As for the repayment period, here are the various monthly payments and total interest charges for a $60,000 mortgage at 11, 12, and 13 percent interest for fifteen, twenty, twenty-five, and thirty years:

Monthly Payments* and Total Interest Charges for a $60,000 Mortgage Loan Borrowed at 11%, 12%, and 13% with Different Repayment Periods

Repayment Period	11% Interest, Expressed as an Annual Percentage Rate		12% Interest, Expressed as an Annual Percentage Rate		13% Interest, Expressed as an Annual Percentage Rate	
	Monthly Payment	Total Interest Charge	Monthly Payment	Total Interest Charge	Monthly Payment	Total Interest Charge
15 years	$681.96	$ 62,752.80	$720.10	$ 69,618.00	$759.15	$ 76,647.00
20 years	619.31	88,634.40	660.65	98,556.00	702.95	108,708.00
25 years	588.07	116,421.00	631.93	129,579.00	676.70	143,010.00
30 years	571.39	145,700.40	617.17	162,181.20	663.72	178,939.20

* Monthly payment figures shown include only principal and the interest charge—actual payments may also include taxes and insurance.

Source: "Managing Your Credit," Money Management Institute of Household International

The interest rate on a fixed-rate mortgage is established by the bank, and an individual borrower can do little, if anything, to change it. Sometimes borrowers feel fortunate to obtain a mortgage at all, particularly a fixed-rate mortgage, since banks in a particular region often limit their lending to those in specific geographic areas who meet certain firm criteria. Once you have decided to buy a home and are seeking a mortgage, your recourse when faced with an unappealing fixed-interest rate from one bank is either to accept it or shop around at others in the hope of finding a better rate elsewhere.

Adjustable-Rate Mortgages

Adjustable-rate, also known as flexible- or variable-rate, mortgages have interest rates that rise or fall over the duration of the loan based on market conditions. Each bank's adjustable-rate mortgage is different, so the provisions of the appropriate documents should be carefully studied by you and your lawyer.

In general, the initial interest on adjustable-rate mortgages will be lower than the rate offered on a comparable fixed-rate mortgage. The reason is that your long-range risk is greater since your rate can increase along with changes in overall money market rates. As a result, lenders may offer an especially low rate at the outset as an inducement for you to choose the adjustable category.

Lenders use different indexes to determine when and how the interest rate will increase or decrease on their adjustable-rate mortgages. Such fluctuations in the index can change either your monthly payments, the length of your mortgage, or the balance of your principal. Because monthly payment changes in adjustable-rate mortgages do not always correspond to interest-rate changes, adjustable-rate mortgages may involve either negative amortization—adding unpaid interest to the principal of the loan—or accelerated amortization—higher payments than that necessary to repay the loan at the date of maturity.

With negative amortization, you are losing, rather than gaining, ground on equity, since the monthly payments are too low to cover all interest due. As the lender postpones collection of the money owed now, the borrower winds up making larger payments or more payments later. Moreover, the borrower will have to pay additional interest on the deferred interest.

In contrast, the monthly payments may be greater than those required to pay off the loan within the original term. In that case, accelerated amortization occurs, meaning a faster reduction of the principal of the mortgage.

Some banks include rate or payment caps in their adjustable-rate mortgages to limit the change in the interest rate or the monthly payment. There are both periodic caps, limiting the increase or decrease at any one time, and aggregate caps, limiting the increase or decrease over the life of the loan. Many lenders will not offer capped rates, however, and it may be necessary to make inquiries at a number of banks in order to find them.

Another variation of the adjustable-rate concept is renegotiable rate, or rollover, mortgages. Here the interest rate is fixed, typically for three to five years, and is then renegotiated based on current market conditions.

Although dozens of different indexing formulas exist, only a handful are widely used. These indexes are the interest rate on three- or six-month Treasury bills, or one- to five-year Treasury notes, both indicating how much the federal government has to pay for its borrowings; the national average mortgage rate for the purchase of existing homes reported by the Federal Home Loan Bank Board, indicating how much families are paying for new mortgages; and the average cost of funds to savings and loan associations insured by the Federal Savings and Loan Insurance Corporation, indicating how much lending institutions are paying for their borrowings.

Some banks utilize indexes that reflect the national marketplace, while others base their indexes on local trends or on the bank's own cost of funds. Whichever is used, it is important to understand exactly what formula is being applied to your mortgage. Make sure that you have studied the past performance of the index and that you can easily verify its current status. Look for the initial interest rate, the initial monthly payments, and the mortgage term. Check the bank's policy on the frequency and degree of rate changes and payment adjustments, along with the number of times that the rate and payments are allowed to move. In addition, determine how much advance warning you will get before a new rate or new payments are put into effect.

For instance, take a $67,000, thirty-year adjustable-rate mortgage indexed to three-year Treasury securities, with adjustments occurring every two-and-a-half years. If the initial interest rate were 16 percent, the monthly mortgage payment for the first two-and-a-half years would be $900.99. But for all subsequent two-and-a-half-year periods, payments will depend on the effective rate to the borrower. If the rate is 16 percent, payments remain at the same level. If it declines to 14 percent, monthly payments would be $795.71. And if it advances to 18 percent, monthly payments would be $1,008.21.

Balloon Mortgages

A balloon mortgage does not pay itself off as other mortgages do. At the end of the term, part of the principal remains and comes due in a single payment, often requiring you to take another mortgage. With such a mortgage, there is a series of equal monthly payments and a large final payment, known as the balloon. Generally these are fixed-rate mortgages, but the periodic payments are usually applied only to interest. The unpaid balance may become due after a short period, such as three to five years.

Thus if you take out a $30,000, five-year balloon mortgage at an interest rate of 15 percent, your monthly payments may be just $375. But in this example, the payments cover only the interest, so that the entire principal is due at maturity. And if you cannot make that final payment of $30,375 or obtain refinancing, you may be forced to sell the home for its then-current value.

Sometimes balloon mortgages are structured so that monthly installment payments are based on amortization tables for a longer mortgage than the one that actually exists. For instance, you may be paying off a mortgage over fifteen years, but with payments using twenty-five-year amortization as the basis. When the mortgage comes due and you want to remain in your home, the alternatives are attempting to obtain a ten-year extension of the loan or getting a new loan from the same lender or another.

Of course, when shopping for mortgage money again, the interest rate may be different from the original rate, depending on current market conditions, and there may be new front-end charges, like points and closing costs.

Graduated Payment Mortgages

Graduated payment mortgages are designed to help more individuals qualify for home loans, particularly young, first-time buyers who realistically expect to be able to make larger monthly payments in later years. In the initial years when a family's income is probably less and monthly payments pose more of a burden, mortgage payments are relatively low. Typically, this amount rises steadily for about five to ten years before leveling off for the duration of the loan. But the overall expense of these mortgages is higher than that of conventional mortgages in the long run because negative amortization is involved.

The usual pattern with graduated payment mortgages is that even though payments change, the interest rate is fixed. This means that in the early years payments are lower than dictated by the interest rate, with the difference made up by higher payments later. By maturity, the entire principal is repaid.

An example of a fixed-rate graduated payment arrangement is a $67,000, thirty-year mortgage at an interest rate of 16 percent, with payments increasing 7½ percent annually for the first five years. Monthly payments, which are $709.65 in the first year, rise steadily to $1,018.80 in the sixth year and remain at that level for the term of the mortgage.

There are, however, some graduated payment mortgages with adjustable interest rates. If rates rise quickly, more negative amortization occurs during the time that payments are low. If rates continue to advance after the initial period, payments will rise as well. But in the event that rates fall during the life of the mortgage, monthly payments may also decline.

Growing Equity Mortgages

Growing equity, or rapid payoff, mortgages represent a tradeoff of larger payments for a greater equity in a home. The key is that your income must keep pace with the increased payments. Although interest rates are fixed, monthly payments rise annually for a specified number of years or for the duration of the mortgage. And these increases can be either pegged to an index or established according to a fixed schedule, such as 4 percent annually.

Interest rates on growing equity mortgages are usually a few percentage points below current market rates because lenders anticipate being repaid faster. And after about six years of the mortgage term, borrowers are paying much less interest as part of their monthly payments than with a standard fixed-rate mortgage.

The reason is that with growing equity mortgages, the entire increase in payments is utilized for the reduction of the principal. So while the term of the mortgage may be thirty years, it may actually be shortened to around fifteen years, thereby reducing the amount of interest paid in the long run. The result is that equity in the home is accumulated at a faster rate.

To illustrate, a $67,000, thirty-year mortgage with an interest rate of 16 percent and an increase in payments of 4 percent annually would be paid off at the end of sixteen years. Monthly payments would range from $787 in the first year to $1,417 in the sixteenth year.

Shared-Appreciation Mortgages

Shared-appreciation, or shared-equity, mortgages describe a joint ownership between an owner-occupant and a nonresident lender or investor. For instance, when a buyer cannot afford to purchase a home on his own, an investor may pay all or part of the down payment and also contribute to the monthly mortgage payments in return for a proportionate share in the equity of the property.

When a lender is involved, a borrower gets a lower interest rate in return for providing a share in the later appreciation of the home. With such loans, the borrower agrees to give the lender a fixed percentage—usually about 30 to 50 percent—of the gain in the value of a home when it is sold or after a specified number of years.

Because of the shared appreciation feature, monthly payments are less than they are with many other kinds of creative financing. But you may be eventually required to pay the agreed-upon share to the lender or investor even if you don't want to sell the property at that time.

Another possible difficulty with these mortgages is that any improvements made by an owner that enhance the value of the property will ultimately be split with the lender or investor. Another party thereby shares in the benefits of the improvements that you have made without sharing in their cost.

Buydowns

A buydown is a subsidy of the mortgage rate that helps buyers meet the monthly payments and is generally made available during the initial years of a loan. Such subsidies can run for any length of time from one year to the full term of the mortgage, but they are most commonly offered for three years.

Buydowns are a tool used by developers and other sellers to help buyers qualify for a mortgage. They may be in the form of a lump sum paid to the lender in exchange for a lower interest rate or as funds deposited in an escrow account sufficient to reduce the interest rate and thereby supplement the buyer's monthly payments.

For instance, a $67,000, thirty-year fixed-rate mortgage with an interest rate of 16 percent might have buydown terms of 3 percent in the first year, 2 percent in the second year, and 1 percent in the third year. The borrower's monthly payments would, therefore, be $741.15 in the first year, $793.86 in the second year, and $847.18 in the third year, before leveling off at $900.99 for the remainder of the loan.

Whatever the amount, buyers should consider the pitfalls of buydowns, starting with an awareness that sometimes substantially higher monthly payments must be paid after the initial period. If the mortgage has an adjustable rate, moreover, and the index on which it is based has increased, the new monthly payments will be higher still.

When a buydown is offered by a developer of a new property, a buyer should try to determine whether or not this subsidy is contained in the contract with the lender. If not, then the lender may be able to hold you liable for the full interest rate if the builder changes his mind or goes bankrupt.

There is also the question of whether the selling price placed on the home was raised to cover this subsidizing of interest. The answer can be learned only by checking the price levels of comparable properties.

Zero-Interest Mortgages

With a zero-interest mortgage, the buyer makes a large down payment, typically about one third of the purchase price, and pays off the remainder over a short term. The equal monthly installments for zero-interest mortgages rarely run beyond five to seven years.

The high down payment puts such a mortgage out of reach for many home buyers, even though it is interest-free. But monthly payments are often commensurate with, or even lower than, a standard loan at current interest rates amortized over thirty years. And sometimes a portion of the down payment can be financed by a second mortgage.

Thus a $90,000 home might be sold with a seven-year zero-rate mortgage and a $30,000 down payment. You would then repay the principal—no interest is required—in eighty-four monthly installments of $714.29.

You should satisfy yourself in this situation, too, that the selling price of the home was not increased to reflect the elimination of interest. A careful study of other home prices in the area can help you decide if a zero-interest mortgage is really a bargain.

Reverse Annuity Mortgages

A reverse annuity mortgage, or home equity conversion, is not a mortgage in the strict sense. It is designed primarily for those who own their homes, particularly the elderly, and who want to continue living there but are having difficulty making ends meet. Individuals best suited for reverse annuity mortgages fit into the classification of "house-rich and cash-poor."

With this arrangement, you obtain a loan in the form of monthly payments over a long period, using your home as collateral. The most popular version is the lifetime reverse mortgage, whereby the borrower remains in the house as long as he lives, drawing funds regularly from the lender. When the owner dies and the home is sold, the lender gets a return of principal plus interest and all or part of any appreciation value. The monthly amount received by the borrower often depends on the owner's age and sex, interest rates at the time of the loan, and the value of the house when the reverse annuity mortgage is written.

Some lenders have worked out plans whereby these mortgages are issued at below-market interest rates. Others allow the borrowers to repay their loans if they suddenly receive a windfall. Still other banks refuse to participate in such programs because they don't want to be in the position of evicting an elderly person who outlives the number of monthly payments due under his mortgage contract.

SECOND MORTGAGES

A second mortgage is a loan on a home that is junior to a first mortgage in the event of default. It is riskier than a first mortgage because the first-mortgage holder has the opportunity to get all of his money repaid before the second-mortgage holder can make any claim on the property. Since the risk is higher, the interest rate on second mortgages is also usually higher than on first mortgages by two or three percentage points.

The history of second mortgages is replete with instances of unscrupulous operators, but regulations and legislation over the years have eliminated much of the negative stigma. Some states, however, still have laws that deter the issuance of second mortgages.

Many individuals take a second mortgage after they have paid off a portion of their first mortgage or their home has sharply appreciated in value. The equity that has built up in a home is the principal source of savings for millions of Americans and is thus converted into cash for purposes such as home remodeling, debt consolidation, or paying for a college education.

Second mortgages typically have shorter maturities than first mortgages and frequently have a balloon payment at the end. Banks and other institutions that grant second mortgages generally limit the amount that they will lend to about 70 to 80 percent of the value of the home, minus the existing first mortgage.

An example of a second-mortgage arrangement might be a $10,000 loan at 15 percent interest, with a balloon payment in three years but with monthly payments calculated as if the loan were going to be repaid in fifteen years. The monthly payments would thereby be $139.96, but at the end of three years there would be a balance of $9,325.07.

A newer variation of this borrowing method is the home equity loan offered by some brokerage firms, small loan companies, and banks. In contrast to second mortgages where borrowers usually get a lump sum, a fixed interest rate, and monthly amortization, equity loans are typically revolving lines of credit. The borrower gets a maximum sum against which he can draw down portions until the entire amount of the approved loan is used.

While the term of the equity loan is fixed, borrowers can make use of as much or as little of the available credit at any time during this period. Interest is paid only on the amount of the credit actually utilized. As the principal is paid back, it can be borrowed again during the lifetime of the loan. But at maturity, the entire amount must be repaid.

If you take out a second mortgage or home equity loan, your home is the collateral, and this property will be lost if you miss payments and the lender accelerates the loan or forecloses. Some homeowners are not aware of the potential danger of such borrowing, particularly on equity loans, because special checks or credit or debit cards are used to obtain needed funds. Be sure that you understand the conditions of such a loan if you use your home for its security.

SELLER FINANCING

When banks, savings and loan associations, and other lending associations are unable, or unwilling, to make a home loan, the potential seller is essentially left with two choices: either financing the mortgage himself or losing the sale. Thus the seller also may become the lender, with all of the privileges and problems such a role entails.

These situations occurred with increasing frequency in recent years as tight money, soaring inflation, high unemployment, and a decline in home building permeated the economy. Many families that had, or wanted, to sell their homes were forced to arrange the financing for the buyers, and those arrangements often meant that the sellers had to participate in one way or another. An understanding of the techniques of seller financing therefore has become important for both sellers and buyers of homes.

Among the various categories of seller financing alternatives are:

Buyer Assumes Seller's Mortgage

If a buyer can assume the seller's mortgage, the house may be sold much more quickly at a time when interest rates are high or rising. Otherwise the buyer will have to locate, and be approved for, a new mortgage that will probably be at a higher rate than the existing mortgage held by the seller.

Banks, however, are reluctant to allow such transactions and typically require in their mortgage contracts that the seller repay the lower-interest loan at the time the house is sold. The mechanism for such a requirement is the "due on sale" clause, which gives the lender the right to demand immediate repayment of the balance owed on a mortgage if the home changes hands. A typical clause would state: "If all or part of the property or an interest therein is sold or transferred by borrower without lender's prior written consent . . . lender may, at lender's option, declare all the sums secured by this mortgage to be immediately due and payable."

Such due-on-sale clauses have won a number of legal battles attesting to their legitimacy, as lenders increasingly insist on their right to raise the interest rate on homes they finance to the prevailing market level. Some states, though, have laws that prohibit lenders from calling in a loan when the home is sold. And all loans insured by the Federal Housing Administration or guaranteed by the Veterans Administration are assumable.

Seller Takes Back a Mortgage

Thousands of sellers are providing their own home loans—both first mortgages and, if necessary, second mortgages—when buyers cannot get them elsewhere. In the event of a default, a second mortgage, also known as a second trust, is satisfied after a first mortgage.

Seller take-back mortgages are generally for relatively short periods and may call for monthly payments for interest only. The principal of these mortgages would then be repaid at maturity as a balloon payment.

An example of an arrangement combining the two most common types of seller financing might be found in the sale of a $150,000 home where no bank financing is available. The buyer could make a $30,000 down payment and assume the seller's 10 percent mortgage with $70,000 still to be paid. For the remaining $50,000 the seller might give the buyer a second mortgage for five years at the below-market rate of 14 percent. Monthly payments on this second mortgage would be for interest only, so that a $50,000 balloon payment would be due at the end of the five-year period from the buyer, who would probably try to obtain a new loan at that time.

Some sellers who take back a mortgage and don't want to carry it for the full term before obtaining their equity, dispose of it as quickly as possible by selling the loan to another individual or corporation. Private companies around the country buy such seller take-backs, but usually at sizable discounts from the face value of the contract.

In situations where an approved institutional lender handles the paperwork and collection for a seller, and specific rules concerning credit checks, appraisals, and standardized forms are followed, the Federal National Mortgage Association will purchase seller take-backs. The advantage of such arrangements for the seller is that he obtains his full equity without the time and trouble of collecting monthly payments.

Furthermore, a number of mortgage insurance companies are insuring seller take-backs against defaults. These insurers generally work through banks, savings and loan associations, mortgage companies, and other institutional lenders that check the creditworthiness of the buyer, make sure that the transaction is drawn on an acceptable mortgage form, and service the loan. One drawback to this insurance is that if the buyer cannot make the required balloon payment or refinance the mortgage at maturity, the seller must agree to roll it over at the current market rate, thereby continuing the loan for a longer time than he may have expected. If the buyer refuses this refinancing offer or cannot afford the new payments, the mortgage goes into default and the seller is paid off through the insurance.

Wraparound Mortgages

Still another variation of the take-back is the wraparound mortgage. With such loans, a new second mortgage wraps around the existing first mortgage. The buyer makes all payments to the seller, who also holds the second mortgage and forwards the appropriate amount owed to the holder of the first mortgage.

As an example, take the situation of a buyer who can make a $25,000 down payment on a $75,000 home but cannot afford the monthly payments at the current interest rate of 18 percent on the remaining $50,000. The seller has a 10 percent mortgage with $30,000 still to be paid. So the seller might offer the buyer a $50,000 wraparound mortgage at 14 percent interest. The seller continues to make his scheduled payments to the lending institution to pay down his $30,000 loan, while the buyer pays off his $50,000 loan from the seller at a lower rate than would otherwise have been charged.

Wraparound mortgages can sometimes cause difficulties if the original lender is not informed about the new arrangement. Some of these lenders do not permit such wraparounds, which allow a buyer to pay a lower interest rate than if a new mortgage were issued, and demand that the old mortgage be repaid immediately.

Chapter Eighteen

Buying and Maintaining Property

EVEN AFTER YOU HAVE A basic knowledge of mortgages, there are still many other elements of real estate for an individual to understand. The financial considerations will vary, depending on each family's personal circumstances, but certain situations affect millions of Americans.

Prospective homeowners should weigh the advantages and disadvantages of buying versus renting. A home purchase could involve a condominium or cooperative and buyers should know the difference between the two forms of ownership. There are second home possibilities for vacations and for additional income. Some home improvements could add to the value of a home. And investment property may throw off income to the owner and show capital appreciation as well.

It is important to remember, though, that any involvement in real estate, whether on a minor or a major scale, involves both risks and rewards. Mark Twain once said, "Buy land, they aren't making it anymore." But not all purchases of land or buildings work out well. When becoming involved in the arcane world of

261

real estate, it pays to become familiar with as many possible alternatives as you can. Then when you invest, or even investigate, you will be doing so from a position of strength.

BUYING VERSUS RENTING

There has been a strong trend in favor of ownership by middle-class Americans since the end of World War II. Even in the metropolitan centers of New York City and Chicago, where apartment houses proliferate in the residential areas, condominiums and cooperatives have grown at a faster pace than rentals in recent years.

A number of reasons have been behind the home-buying phenomenon. For most of this period, lenders made mortgages easily available and interest rates were relatively low. Land for the building of new homes was being developed at a rapid pace and tract housing made for economies of scale. Families also discovered that homes were often valuable investments whose prices often climbed much faster than the rate of inflation.

Although the trend in home prices has been an upward one over the last three or four decades, there is no guarantee that the value of any home will continue to rise. Indeed, in parts of the country, home costs have been stable for some time and in other neighborhoods, property values have declined, because of such factors as changing demographics and the nearby construction of highways, factories, or commercial development.

Nevertheless, overall, owners have made rather than lost money when their house was sold. Even during the period of ownership, there is often a gain in value, at least on paper. Thus the investment aspect, with its potential for capital gains, remains a primary benefit—if not the primary financial benefit—of home ownership.

Leverage in Ownership

Another major plus of buying is leverage, since only a small portion of the owner's money is usually used at the time that the home is acquired. A small increase in the value of the property therefore equals a larger increase on the owner's capital. After making a down payment of 20 to 30 percent of the purchase price, the homeowner takes out a mortgage loan for the remainder. The balance, a fixed amount, is repaid over many years with dollars that, because of inflation, may be worth less than when they were borrowed.

In contrast, those who lease a house or apartment normally pay only a set monthly rental charge to the landlord. They do not have to come up with a down payment, a substantial sum in most residential real estate transactions. But while a renter's monthly rental costs will probably rise at the end of the lease period—usually one, two, or three years—the owner's total monthly payment for interest and amortization of the principal remains constant for the duration of the loan in most mortgages now outstanding. Any rise in the value of the home is kept solely by the owner, rather than the lender, in the overwhelming majority of mortgages.

Tax Benefits of Ownership

There are a number of tax benefits connected with ownership as well, starting with capital gains tax treatment at the time of sale. If you live in a home for more than six months and sell it at a profit, the tax on the increase will be at the capital gains rate in effect at that time. If you lose money on the sale of a home used personally and not for a profit-making purpose, however, you may not deduct the loss.

The capital gains tax on the sale of a residence is based on the difference between the sales price and your cost, a figure that includes not only your purchase price, but also your expenses in buying, improving, and selling the home. In addition, this tax may be deferred when you buy or build another home, if you meet three requirements: (1) both your old and your new home are your principal residence; (2) the new home costs at least as much as you received for the old one; and (3) your new home is bought, built, and occupied within two years before or after the sale of the old one.

Furthermore, if you are fifty-five years old or over and sell your home at a profit, you can claim a tax exclusion on profits up to $125,000. But to do so, you must have owned and occupied the home as your principal residence for at least three of the five years preceding the sale. This tax-free benefit is available to an individual only once in a lifetime and cannot be used piecemeal.

Then there are the ordinary income tax advantages of ownership. Mortgage interest and property tax payments are deductible from federal income taxes, so the effective monthly payment of a homeowner is cut. The higher your taxable income, the greater your tax saving on owning property. Renters do not obtain this benefit, although their landlords do and usually will not pass it along, except in the rare situations where competitive conditions in an area force a lowering of rents.

Other differences between owners and renters include the tendency of owners to have a stronger commitment to the community where they live, since they have an investment in its success. Owners also have more flexibility in making alterations to the home because of the awareness that they can retain this property indefinitely if they so desire.

Advantages of Renting

A corollary, of course, is that owners are tied to a home because of their financial involvement, while renters can easily move away at the expiration of a lease without worrying about a sale. And many renters can call the superintendent or handyman when something breaks in the house or apartment, but an owner is responsible for the maintenance and repairs in, on, or around the home, doing the work himself or hiring someone else to do it.

There is the additional cost and hassle of commuting long distances to and from work, plus the expense of operating a second car, which an owner is more likely to need than a renter. For some families, there is also a terrifying psychological block to undertaking such a large investment as the purchase of a home and to borrowing such a large amount of money for such a long time.

In working out the costs of owning versus renting, remember to include the annual interest lost on the funds applied as a down payment on the purchase. Even if the money were invested in a money market deposit account at a bank, a money market fund, or elsewhere, its earnings could be used for other purposes that are unavailable to the person who utilizes this asset to buy a house.

SHOPPING FOR A HOUSE

When buying property, as the old saw goes, the three most important things are location, location, and location. Before starting to look for the home that you like—and can afford—first decide on the neighborhoods in which you might want to live.

Driving around the areas, talking to residents there, asking friends and acquaintances about their experiences, and consulting real estate agents are all useful techniques for helping you concentrate your search. Whether in a city or a suburb, you will probably be concerned with schools, real estate taxes, houses of worship, shopping facilities, public transportation, and the other nitty-gritty aspects of daily living. By checking out these factors, you won't be buying a pig in a poke.

As for the house itself, an examination of the local newspaper advertisements will give you an idea of values in the neighborhoods you have selected. The selling price may be cheaper if you buy directly from an owner since there will be no real estate agent's commission. This commission, typically 6 or 7 percent of the purchase price and paid by the seller, is likely to be added to the cost of a home when an agent is used.

However, most sellers need, and use, real estate agents because of their sales ability, their knowledge of the community, their contacts with buyers, and their assistance in placing a realistic value on the property. Agents often seek an exclusive listing, but most sellers prefer multiple-listing services that bring many brokers into the picture for a chance at a shared commission. Some agents, moreover, are willing to reduce their commissions under certain circumstances to make a sale.

A relatively recent development has been an idea called buyer's brokerage, whereby the real estate agent is paid by, and is working for, the buyer, not the seller. Different payment schedules are used, including an hourly wage or a fixed amount if a home is found. With buyer's brokerage, the agent may make valuable suggestions that benefit the buyer, such as a particular negotiating stance or a lower bid for the property. If you decide to use a buyer's broker, make sure that he will not steer you to properties whose seller he also represents—in which case he is really not working for you at all.

CONDOMINIUMS AND COOPERATIVES

Condominiums and cooperatives are among the most rapidly growing categories of residential real estate ownership in the United States. Millions of these apartment units have been sold in recent years in cities, suburbs, and resort areas, particularly in such states as California, Florida, Illinois, and New York.

Both condominiums and cooperatives are forms of common ownership, although there are many distinctions between the two categories. They both allow an individual owner to have exclusive use of a specific unit in a group of housing units, such as a high-rise apartment house, garden apartments, or town houses. And they both permit individuals to share the use of common areas like the grounds, elevators, parking lots, hallways, and recreation facilities.

The concept of common ownership dates back more than 2,000 years to the old Roman civil law when desirable locations in the heart of the city were scarce and dwellings had to be stacked on top of each other to accommodate more people. All of these residents had common ownership and use of the land. The Latin word *condominium* was created, meaning "with others in residence."

In its modern American reincarnation, common ownership had antecedents in the 1920s, but really erupted in the 1970s when the high cost of housing, coupled with high interest rates, pushed traditional one-family housing beyond the means of many families. Condominiums and cooperatives are not only smaller, and therefore usually cheaper to purchase and maintain than houses of similar quality, but also likely to be in more convenient locations. Many of them offer recreational and social facilities not found in a single house and provide owners with a staff to care for the outside areas that an individual homeowner would be responsible for on his own.

What is the difference between the two classifications?

Under condominium ownership, you are the sole possessor of your inner living space and the joint holder with other owners of the grounds and exterior facilities. The maintenance of these common elements, toward which each owner contributes a proportionate monthly fee, is the responsibility of a nonprofit automatic-membership organization generally known as a condominium owners' association.

When you buy a condominium, you own real property just as when you buy a house. You have an individual deed to an apartment, arrange for your own mortgage financing, and pay your real estate taxes directly to the local taxing authority. You also become a voting member of the condominium owners' association and share with the other owners the right to use the association's common property.

Under a cooperative plan, you own stock in a corporation formed to take and hold title to all of the land, buildings, and other facilities in a single transaction. This ownership, evidenced by a stock certificate, entitles you to an apartment, with the amount of stock per apartment in proportion to the apartment's size and location. You also get a proprietary lease detailing your right to occupy your apartment and use the common areas. Monthly payments are made to cover your share of mortgage interest and principal, taxes, insurance, and maintenance and operating expenses.

Thus with a cooperative, you are participating in a syndication. If any owner in the cooperative corporation becomes delinquent in his monthly payments, he can be evicted and the other owners are obligated to make up this delinquency.

Maintenance charges for a condominium are likely to be substantially less, perhaps by 50 percent, than a cooperative's charges for an equivalent building. The reason is that condominium maintenance covers only the common-area upkeep—including repairs, labor, heating, and air-conditioning—whereas co-op maintenance fees cover all these items plus mortgage payments, taxes, and insurance.

Because a cooperative apartment is considered personal property instead of real property, prospective tenant-cooperators can usually be rejected by the co-op's board of directors for any but a discriminatory reason. A co-op owner may also have difficulty subletting his apartment if the board of directors of the cooperative does not approve of his choice. In contrast, a condominium owner has the right to sell or sublet to anyone he wants, generally subject only to the condo's right of first refusal.

Potential buyers of a condominium or cooperative should inquire whether the owners are required to lease certain facilities at the complex from the developer or a related company. At some developments, the developer continues to own the land under the buildings or the recreational facilities—such as the pool, meeting rooms, and auditorium—long after all the units have been sold and the condominium owners have elected a board of directors. These facilities, in turn, may be leased on a long-term basis, perhaps as long as ninety-nine years, to the owners by the developer, imposing an additional financial burden on them.

Conversions

Much of the recent growth in the condo and co-op market has been in converted rental apartments. Owners of apartment houses frequently can make more money by converting the building than by renting apartments, so tenants in these buildings are allowed to purchase their apartments for prices below the current market level. In that way, the tenants who buy get an immediate capital gain, at least on paper, and are not forced to find another apartment, possibly at a higher rental.

For tenants, there can be many pitfalls in a building converted to a condominium or cooperative. If the previous owner did not provide sufficient funds in a reserve account for repairs or rehabilitation, the new owners may be faced with a large assessment to do so shortly after taking over the building. During the conversion period, difficulties often arise between the landlord, the tenants planning to buy their apartments, and the tenants not planning to buy, who may also be legally protected from eviction. Even those who decide to purchase their apartments may find themselves spending more than they expected for either the purchase price or the monthly maintenance, or both.

If the demand for compact housing continues to rise, investments in condominiums and cooperatives will probably increase substantially. As with any real estate investment, careful analysis of all the available facts and study of the principal legal documents connected with the purchase are necessary to make the wisest choice.

VACATION HOMES

Many families buy a vacation, or second, home not only for the pleasure it brings, but also with an eye toward the additional income and tax benefits they hope to receive by renting it out for part of the year. The tax laws governing such matters, however, are sometimes difficult to follow.

Most homeowners cannot deduct on their federal income tax returns the losses—expenses that exceed income—derived from renting a personal vacation home. A series of tests based on the number of days of personal and rental usage governs whether deductions for such losses can be taken.

If you rent a vacation home for less than fifteen days, you are not permitted to write off any of the expenses attributed to the rental. But at the same time, you do not have to declare the income received and no taxes are due from renting the home for this short a period.

If you rent the home for fifteen days or more, however, and you use it personally for more than fourteen days—or more than 10 percent of the rented period, whichever is greater—you cannot deduct more than you receive in rental income. In other words, you cannot take off more in maintenance expenses than you receive in gross rental income to carry over to other income. But if you rent the home for fifteen days or more and the days of your personal use are less than those fixed by the fourteen-day/10 percent test, expenses in excess of rental income, such as depreciation, maintenance, and utilities, may be deductible.

The Tax Reform Act provides that mortgage interest on a principal and second residence is deductible only to the extent that borrowing does not exceed the original cost and improvements, along with medical and educational expenses. Thus you may not be able to deduct as much interest on a vacation home mortgage as you did before passage of this law.

Specific formulas must be used in determining which portion of the maintenance expenses, property taxes, and mortgage interest can be charged against rental income. In the case of maintenance expenses—all deductible costs of renting except for taxes and interest—you divide the number of days that the house is rented by the total number of days that the house is used during the year for both rental and personal use. If you rent the house for 75 days and use it personally for 75 days, you divide 75 by 150 and arrive at a deduction of 50 percent of your maintenance expenses.

As for allocating other expenses, you first subtract the mortgage interest and property taxes allocated to rental activity from rental income. The next step is to deduct operating expenses other than depreciation up to the remaining rental income. If any rental income is left, depreciation can be deducted up to the balance of this income.

HOME IMPROVEMENTS

Beyond the actual purchase of a home, physical improvements to the house are likely to be the largest single expense for many families. Yet the same families that insist on putting everything in writing when buying or selling a home may handle their home improvements in an extremely casual manner.

Because so many fraudulent schemes exist in this field, the

first step in planning a house improvement should be to find a reliable, honest contractor. If you haven't used such a contractor before, ask friends, relatives, or neighbors if they can recommend an experienced and competent person. Contact your local Better Business Bureau to check on complaints registered against the companies or individuals you plan to call. If a local or state agency licenses contractors, inquire about their background and record. Talk to a few contractors, especially for major jobs, and ask if you can get in touch with some of their previous customers. Request estimates or bids in writing with specifics of products and materials, even if a small preparation fee is involved. Prices or estimates can vary by 100 percent or more.

After you have selected a contractor, sign a clear, detailed contract that states the full price and includes dimensions, materials, finishes, brand names, model numbers, and other specifications. The contract should state the dates for commencement and completion of the work. Try to get a time-penalty clause included, even when it has to be balanced by a bonus clause for early completion. Insist on written guarantees from the contractor and, if available, from the manufacturer of the material used. Be prepared for many weeks of discomfort while construction is under way. Finally, don't sign a certificate of completion until everything, including the cleanup, is finished to your satisfaction.

An important part of the contract is the schedule of payment. The contractor will try to obtain as much money as soon as possible, but it is to your advantage to delay payment until you see how the work is progressing. A fair procedure would be to have staggered payments, perhaps in three equal installments: one-third at the time of signing, one-third after sufficient progress is evident, and one-third on completion. You should also attempt to insert a clause in the contract stating that you will retain a percentage of the final payment for, say, thirty days until you are certain that the job has been completed and the new installation is functioning well.

Another reason for delaying the final payment is to make sure that the contractor has no disputes with a subcontractor who may have worked on a portion of the job. A subcontractor not

paid in full for labor and materials could file a mechanic's lien—
the right to have his debt paid—against your home for his outstanding payment or even sue you, even though you are not a
direct party to the dispute. Not only may you be unaware that
such a lien has been filed, but you may also be unable to sell or
refinance your home until it is wiped off the books.

Most standard home improvement contracts are prepared for
contractors and written with their interests in mind. For a major
project like a renovation of the kitchen or an additional room
built on the house, you might do well to consult a lawyer before
signing on the dotted line.

As for financing your home improvement, there are many
possibilities. You can prepay your existing mortgage and obtain
a new one, thereby winding up with a large chunk of cash, especially if the value of the house rose over the years. You can
take out a second mortgage for the required amount. You can
apply for a personal loan, although the interest rates are normally
higher and the term is usually shorter than with mortgage loans.
You can have the contractor arrange the loan, but that will probably be more costly. And some banks may give you a mortgage
at the time of purchase that is large enough to include the cost
of planned renovations, with funds for the improvements ad-
vanced in stages as the work is done.

INVESTMENT REAL ESTATE

Investing in real estate, like purchasing a home, entails risk.
But the former is strictly a business risk and should not have
any of the emotional involvement that usually applies to the purchase of the property where you intend to live.

There are dozens of investments for individuals who are bitten
by the real estate bug, ranging from raw land to single- and multi-
family houses and from shopping centers to commercial properties. In most of these situations, the owner collects rent from
a tenant who pays for the temporary use of the property. Nevertheless, the major lure of any such investment is the possibility
of appreciation in value and the tax benefits accruing to holders
of real estate.

Capital appreciation is uncertain, of course, but real estate prices in general have gone up for decades, some categories at a more rapid pace than others. When short-term leases are involved and the owner thereby has the right to increase the rentals on his property periodically, the value of the real estate tends to grow faster than when there are long-term leases.

As for tax shelters, frequently the major appeal of investment real estate, there are first the deductions for mortgage interest and property taxes that homeowners receive. But rental buildings are also allowed a deduction from taxable income for depreciation, which often works out to be a big bonus to real estate investors.

Depreciation is the theoretical decline in value of a physical asset that results from normal usage and from age. In an accounting sense, depreciation is a means of returning to you part of the capital invested in a property through tax deductions. A building's useful life varies according to factors such as size, location, type of construction, and components. At the end of that useful life, the building has been depreciated from its purchase price to zero. In short, the bigger the depreciation, the lower your income tax from income-producing property.

Buildings placed in service after 1986 are affected by the provisions in the Tax Reform Act that increase the period of depreciation and change the rate at which properties can be written off. Instead of the previous uniform nineteen-year depreciation period, residential rental property is now depreciable over twenty-seven-and-a-half years and commercial property is now depreciable over thirty-one-and-a-half years. In both cases, depreciation has to be handled by using the straight-line method, with equal amounts written off each year over the life of the asset.

Whichever formula is used, depreciation is a theoretical expense on paper that does not involve any cash outlay. You are entitled to this deduction whether or not the building actually depreciates and even when the value of the property increases. The result is a reduction in the net rental income from your real estate and a corresponding reduction in income taxes due.

Taxpayers in higher income tax brackets frequently seek real estate investments in which the depreciation is large enough for

them to show a loss on the property—a loss that may be subtracted from certain other income in determining their overall
tax liability. But if the property is held long enough, at some
point rental income may exceed the deductions, and taxes will
be due even if no cash flow is generated from the property. That's
why many real estate investors sell a property when tax benefits
have been fully exhausted or refinance a building when the tax
shelter is no longer working to their advantage.

Real Estate Investment Trusts

Since there are relatively few investments in income-producing
property or other real estate that most people can afford to buy
on their own, programs have developed whereby individuals pool
their funds for this purpose. This pooling can be in such forms
as a corporation, a syndication, or a public or private limited
partnership. But the type of investment that has attracted the
broadest interest from the public has been real estate investment
trusts.

Real estate investment trusts—known as REITs and pro-
nounced "reets"—are publicly held companies set up like closed-
end investment companies for stocks and bonds. Basically they
sell shares to investors and put the proceeds in real estate. Despite
the name, REITs can be organized as corporations as well as
trusts. Their mission is to provide the advantages of collective
financing of large projects and professional management of real
estate portfolios.

As long as they follow the tax regulations by distributing at
least 95 percent of their earnings to stockholders, REITs pay no
federal taxes on income or capital gains. Another condition to
this tax break is that three quarters of total assets be in such
investments as real estate, mortgages, and shares in other REITs.

During the 1960s, REITs expanded enormously as the public
bought millions of such shares on securities exchanges and on
the over-the-counter market. But in the mid-1970s, foreclosures
were a common occurrence in commercial and industrial real
estate, and REIT earnings and share prices dropped precipi-

tously. Since then, the field has recovered somewhat and is again attracting large numbers of investors.

REITs generally fall into one of two categories: equity trusts, the more popular group, which invest in income-producing properties like stores, office buildings, industrial plants, and apartment houses; and mortgage trusts, which provide permanent mortgages and short-term construction loans. There are also hybrid REITs that have less than 75 percent of their funds in either properties or mortgages.

Mortgage REITs will sometimes hold property on which they have foreclosed, whereas equity trusts will sometimes make loans if financing cannot be obtained elsewhere. In general, mortgage trusts pay higher dividends than equity trusts, because there is greater risk in making loans than owning property—and often more return on the investment as well.

Some REITs self-liquidate, while others exist indefinitely. Whichever you choose, be alert for such danger signs as inflated predictions of rent increases, and heavy investments in obsolescent shopping centers, aging apartment houses, and one-industry towns. Your best bet is to choose a REIT with a good geographic mix, relationships with AAA-rated tenants, a powerful position in local areas, and investments in recession-resistant industries. The quality of the properties is one of the most important considerations in picking a REIT or any other real estate investment.

Part Five

Planning for the Future

Chapter Nineteen

Retirement

WILL YOU BE FINANCIALLY INDEPENDENT at retirement? Millions of Americans look forward to retirement with their health intact and the financial resources to enjoy their post-employment years. But unless one has a long-range plan for doing so, it has become increasingly difficult to accumulate a nest egg that will assure the funds necessary to make ends meet after retirement.

Retirement planning involves an analysis of the money that will be available to you from all sources when you retire, such as Social Security, a private pension, a personal retirement program such as an individual retirement account or Keogh plan, savings, and investments. According to mortality studies, most people will need retirement income for more than fifteen years and therefore would do well to develop a program for spreading the available funds to meet their needs during this period, taking into account inflation and the reduced purchasing power of their dollars.

The best time for retirement planning and saving is not at, or shortly prior to, retirement, but long before that time arrives. Assuming that you earn on your savings a compounded annual interest rate of 8 percent, if you are age thirty-five, you can accumulate $100,000 at sixty-five by saving $67 a month and $200,000 by saving $134 a month. If you are forty-five, you would have to save $170 a month to get $100,000 and $340 a month to reach $200,000. And if you start later in life, of course, the monthly savings requirement would be larger still.

A key point to remember is that you probably will not need the same pre-tax income after retirement to maintain a comparable living standard to your working years. Financial planners believe that the typical middle-income family can maintain its standard of living in retirement if it receives between 60 to 75 percent of gross pre-retirement income. But even achieving that level could be difficult and many individuals may have a cash gap. A Presidential Commission on Pension Policy reported that just one extra source of income in addition to Social Security can often make the difference between a life of relative comfort and one of near-poverty.

An important consideration for those not anxious to retire is that the mandatory retirement age for most employees is not age sixty-five, as it had been for generations, but seventy. The major exceptions to this rule are the two categories of tenured college professors and senior corporate executives. But individuals still can retire and collect Social Security payments beginning at age sixty-two. Moreover, an employee can continue to work past the mandatory age if his employer permits.

SOCIAL SECURITY

Social Security is the nation's basic method of providing continuing income when earnings are reduced or ended because of retirement, disability, or death. During your working years, you pay Social Security taxes based on your income; when you retire, become disabled, or die, you or your survivors receive monthly payments from Social Security based on what you and your employers have contributed. There is also Medicare, which helps to pay the cost of medical and hospital care for eligible men and women who are over sixty-five or who are disabled.

The American work force is taxed to pay for Social Security benefits according to a formula provided by law, involving earnings up to a specified maximum each year. The percentage of covered earnings taxed during these years for employees and employers on the one hand, and self-employed people on the other is:

SOCIAL SECURITY

Tax Rate for Employees and Employers (each)

Years	Percent of covered earnings		
	For cash benefits	For hospital insurance	Total
1983	5.40	1.30	6.70
1984	5.70	1.30	7.00
1985	5.70	1.35	7.05
1986–87	5.70	1.45	7.15
1988–89	6.06	1.45	7.51
1990 and after	6.20	1.45	7.65

Employees received a one-time tax credit of 0.3 percent of covered earnings for 1984.

Tax Rate for Self-Employed People

Years	Percent of covered earnings		
	For cash benefits	For hospital insurance	Total
1983	8.05	1.30	9.35
1984	11.40	2.60	14.00
1985	11.40	2.70	14.10
1986–87	11.40	2.90	14.30
1988–89	12.12	2.90	15.02
1990 and after	12.40	2.90	15.30

Source: Social Security Administration

Self-employed people receive a credit of 2.7 percent for 1984, 2.3 percent for 1985, and 2.0 percent for 1986–89.

Monthly Social Security checks may go to workers or to their dependents when the worker retires, becomes severely disabled, or dies. Social Security considers you disabled if you have a severe physical or mental condition that prevents you from working and is expected either to last at least a year or to result in death.

Before you or your family can obtain monthly cash benefits from Social Security, you must have credit for a certain amount of work under the program. The particular amount of work credit depends on your age.

This credit is measured by what the Social Security Administration calls quarters of coverage. Both employees and the self-employed receive one quarter of coverage for a certain amount of covered earnings that changes periodically to keep pace with average wages. No more than four quarters of coverage can be credited for a year. If you stop working before you have earned enough credit, you won't get any Social Security benefits.

The amount of your monthly Social Security check depends on your earnings over a period of years. Payouts are based on retirement at sixty-five. You can retire as early as sixty-two, but your payments—and those of your wife, husband, widow, or widower—will be reduced permanently. If your spouse earned her own benefits, her payments will not be reduced.

For retirement benefits, the specific number of years of work credit depends on when you reach sixty-two—the earliest that payments can begin. For survivors and disability benefits, the specific number of years of work credit for those born after 1929 depends on your age when death or disablement occurs.

Social Security benefits increase automatically as the cost of living goes up. Every year living costs are compared with those of the previous year and benefits will rise by the same percentage as the advance in the Consumer Price index.

If you qualify for monthly checks based on the Social Security record of more than one worker, such as your own and your husband's work credits, you will receive the larger of the two amounts. And if you receive a federal, state, or local government pension not covered by Social Security, in addition to your Social Security benefits as a wife, husband, widow, or widower, your

SOCIAL SECURITY

Work Credit for Retirement Benefits

If you reach 62 in	Years you need
1981	7½
1982	7¾
1983	8
1987	9
1991 or later	10

Work Credit for Survivors and Disability Benefits

Born after 1929, die or become disabled at	Born before 1930, die or become disabled before 62 in	Years you need
28 or younger		1½
30		2
32		2½
34		3
36		3½
38		4
40		4½
42		5
44		5½
46		6
48		6½
50		7
52	1981	7½
54	1983	8
56	1985	8½
58	1987	9
60	1989	9½
62 or older	1991 or later	10

Source: Social Security Administration

283

benefits as a dependent or survivor may be reduced by the amount of that pension. But your government pension will not affect any Social Security benefits based on your own work record.

In determining benefits for workers who reach sixty-two, become disabled, or die after 1978, earnings for past years are adjusted to account for changes in average wages since 1951. These adjusted earnings are averaged and a formula is applied to obtain the benefit rate, in order to ensure that benefits will reflect changes in wage levels during your working life. Benefits for workers who reached sixty-two before 1979 are determined differently so that no one nearing retirement would be hurt by this formula.

If you return to work after receiving retirement checks, your added earnings could result in higher benefits. The Social Security Administration automatically refigures your benefit after the additional earnings are credited to your record.

Furthermore, since 1982 a special credit has been in effect that in 1983 added 3 percent to a worker's benefit for each year after age sixty-five that he did not get benefits because of work. This credit is being gradually increased until it reaches 8 percent for workers at age sixty-two in 2005. The additional credit for workers, moreover, also increases payments to widows and widowers.

There is also a special minimum benefit for people who had low earnings and who worked under Social Security over twenty years. Most individuals who have been employed for twenty years or more under Social Security already receive higher benefits than this special minimum. The automatic cost-of-living benefit increases also apply to the special minimum benefit.

If you go back to work, however, and are under seventy, your earnings could reduce your Social Security benefits, but you don't have to stop working completely to obtain them. You can still receive all of your checks as long as earnings do not exceed an exempt amount, which changes annually in keeping with the annual level of rates and which is higher for those sixty-five or over than for those under sixty-five.

When earnings exceed this exempt amount, Social Security withholds $1 in benefits for every $3 of earnings above the limit for the period after normal retirement age and $1 for each $2 earned prior to normal retirement age. Other income from such sources as savings, investments, or insurance, though, will not affect your monthly benefits.

To avoid mistakes on your Social Security record that cannot be rectified, check every three years on the earnings credited to your account. You can obtain a pre-addressed "Request for Statement of Earnings" postcard at any local Social Security Administration office. If there are errors in the computation of total wages attributed to your Social Security account—errors that could affect your retirement, disability, or death benefits— you have a three-year deadline for making corrections.

1983 Social Security Amendments

A far-ranging package of tax increases and benefit reductions, designed to assure the solvency of the Social Security System for the next seventy-five years, was enacted in 1983. It resulted in a number of changes that were among the most fundamental since the start of Social Security in 1935.

Perhaps the most significant measure in this law was the provision that subjected the Social Security benefits of some higher-income retired people to federal income taxes. Such a tax will generally be levied on those whose income—including half of their benefits—exceeded $25,000 for single taxpayers or $32,000 for married taxpayers filing jointly. Income from tax-exempt bonds is included in this formula, although that income continues to be exempt from direct taxation.

Only about 7 percent of the approximately 36 million beneficiaries of Social Security will be required to pay federal income tax on their benefits. Nevertheless, everyone who gets them also gets a once-a-year notice, similar to the W-2 forms received annually from employers, detailing the total benefits that were paid.

Another change extended in steps the normal retirement age from sixty-five to sixty-six for those born from 1943 through the end of 1959. For those born in 1960 and after, the normal retirement age at which full benefits become available is sixty-seven.

Three other changes dramatically affected Social Security coverage for government and nonprofit organization employees. Despite strong lobbying from noncovered groups, employees of government and nonprofit organizations were required in different ways to join the Social Security System. For example, all federal workers hired after 1983 are required to participate in Social Security. Employees of nonprofit organizations became automatically covered at the beginning of 1984. State and local governments that have elected to give their workers Social Security coverage are prohibited from withdrawing.

PRIVATE PENSIONS

For those retired Americans who are unable, or unwilling, to live entirely on their Social Security benefits, supplementary income from other sources is a virtual necessity. One of the most important sources, perhaps the most far-reaching, is an employer-sponsored retirement benefits plan.

The nation's private pension system covers tens of millions of people and has hundreds of billions of dollars in accumulated assets. Private pension plans were generally introduced to the United States in the late nineteenth century as the economy shifted from agriculture to manufacturing and as workers became more dependent on their own financial resources at retirement. But not until the middle of the twentieth century did the greatest growth occur throughout the economy.

Following reports in those years of abuses by some trustees of pension plans, Congress attempted to remedy these and other problems with the passage of the Employee Retirement Income Security Act of 1974, widely known as ERISA. That same year, the government erected a safety net under many pensions with the creation of the Pension Benefit Guaranty Corporation. Even so, millions of workers are not covered by a private pension plan and millions of others who belong to a plan will never collect any benefits from it because of vesting provisions.

Although the establishment of pension plans by employers or through collective bargaining is still voluntary, ERISA mandated certain standards on all plans that do exist. Furthermore, all of these standards have to fit the different characteristics of the private pension system and the groups involved in operating it.

Today many private pension plans are integrated with Social Security so that Social Security benefits are taken into account in establishing the level of pension payments. The concept of integration is that Social Security provides the basis of adequacy, while other initiatives, such as private pensions, help to meet the more individualized goals of maintaining a standard of living at or near that of your pre-retirement years. When plans are set up in this manner, though, there is the possibility of discrimination in favor of higher-paid employees who might receive sizable private pensions based on their salaries, and against lower-paid workers who might be covered wholly or largely by Social Security.

In contrast to Social Security benefits, most private pensions are not indexed to the cost of living. As a result, inflation often reduces the living standards of pensioners on a fixed income. Inflation is, in fact, the worst enemy of private pensions because its eroding effect on current wages is magnified when applied to future pension benefits as part of a fixed income.

Retirement Plan Vesting

Vesting is the right of an employee to receive his benefit under the terms of the plan. Although the benefit is vested, it does not have to be paid until some later period, as defined in the plan, such as termination of employment or retirement. Full, or 100 percent, vesting gives you the right to all benefits accrued on your behalf in such situations as retirement from the company plan, inability to work because of disability, abolishment of the plan by the employer, completion of service with the employer, or death prior to retirement.

On the other hand, fractional vesting means that some, but not all, of the employer's contribution to your pension account belongs to you. The amount of vesting you have under such an arrangement depends on the number of years that you have been covered by the employer's plan and the vesting schedule it uses. Many employers keep their workers' right to vest at a low level because the money you leave behind stays in the plan and is reallocated to the remaining participants, frequently reducing the employer's future costs. If, for example, you have $5,000 in your pension account and leave the company when vested at only 20 percent, you would receive $1,000 and $4,000 would be retained by the plan.

Vesting schedules are established by the employer and described in a document called a *Summary Plan Description Booklet* that must be given to you when joining a plan or at any time upon request. Notwithstanding other rules of the plan, you must be 100 percent vested at normal retirement age.

Recognizing that there are now many more mobile, shorter-service employees in the work force than there have been before, the vesting schedules that had formerly been in effect were replaced, under provisions of the Tax Reform Act of 1986, by accelerated vesting. The new minimum vesting schedules for all tax-qualified plans, which begin with retirement plan years that start in 1989, are:

Five-Year Cliff Vesting. Under this procedure, all benefits will be vested after five years of service. Thus participants who belong to a retirement plan using this schedule for just five years will have a nonforfeitable right to 100 percent of their accrued benefits derived from employer contributions.

Three-to-Seven-Year Vesting. With this schedule, participants become 20 percent vested in employer-derived benefits after three years of service. Then vesting increases at the rate of 20 percent annually, so that they are fully vested after a total of seven years.

A major exception to these two standard vesting schedules is for participants in multi-employer retirement plans who are covered by collective bargaining agreements. Such plans may also use 10-year cliff vesting, whereby employees are 100 percent vested no later than the end of the tenth year of service.

In addition, a plan may now require two years of service before employees become eligible to participate, if they then become 100 percent vested. Previously, three years of service was required.

And if a plan's vesting schedule is changed by a formal amendment, every participant with at least three years of service in the plan must be given the alternative of having the nonforfeitable percentage of his accrued benefit computed as though the amendment had not been made. Otherwise, the plan will not be considered tax-qualified.

To protect your vesting rights, learn how your company plan's schedule works and calculate your current vesting. Remember that the number of years you are in the plan is not necessarily the same number of years that you have been with the company, since employees frequently have to wait from one to three years before being eligible to join the plan. Another precaution is to determine the anniversary date of your retirement plan, because if you work beyond that date you might get credit for another year of vesting.

Pension Distribution

For a number of reasons, pensions are often taken as a lump-sum distribution, rather than distributed periodically as an annuity or rolled over into an I.R.A. Among them are economic necessity, poor health, or special business or investment purposes.

But if you take your pension as a lump-sum distribution at retirement, the tax bite is likely to be heavy, since it is generally treated as ordinary income. However, you can reduce this burden by having the funds taxed through five-year forward averaging.

With five-year averaging, the money is taxed at single individual rates as though you received only 20 percent of it each year for five years and no other income in those years. Prior to enactment of the Tax Reform Act of 1986, ten-year averaging for certain lump-sum withdrawals from retirement plans was permitted.

However, some of those who receive large lump-sum distributions may have a lower tax liability by using five-year averaging than ten-year averaging. For instance, a recipient of a $400,000 lump-sum distribution would owe taxes of $97,440 with five-year averaging and $102,260 with ten-year averaging.

The entire tax must be paid when you receive this lump sum, since the calculated five-year spreadout is a tax-saving technique rather than an actual extension of the time in which you get the money. Five-year averaging, moreover, is allowed only if an individual receives the lump sum on account of separation from employment, death, disability, or after age fifty-nine-and-a-half.

If you take some of the funds from your corporate retirement account as a lump-sum and roll over the remainder into an I.R.A., five-year averaging is not permitted. And if you take the entire amount as a lump-sum and were at least 50 years old on January 1, 1986, you can still use the now-abandoned capital gains treatment involving 20 percent taxation on a phased-out basis over a six-year period for amounts attributable to pre-1974 participation in a plan.

There is another exception to the general rule of five-year averaging affecting such employees in the 50-and-over category. These individuals may still use ten-year averaging by computing taxes on the basis of the tax rate in effect in 1986.

INDIVIDUAL RETIREMENT ACCOUNTS

For millions of Americans, an individual retirement account, or I.R.A., is the third component of a retirement program, also encompassing Social Security and an employer-sponsored plan. I.R.A.s were created to encourage reliance on individual savings as a source of retirement income by providing two tax incentives: tax-deductible contributions to the account and tax-deferred compounding until the funds are withdrawn. Although contributions are no longer tax-deductible for many people, the tax-deferment factor is nevertheless a powerful lure for retirement saving.

The advantage of tax-free compounding can be demonstrated by illustration. If you contribute $2,000 annually between ages thirty-five and sixty-five, your total investment will be $60,000. But assuming an 8 percent annual rate of return, your investment will grow to $244,700. Of course, these amounts will be taxed when distributed and—if inflation continues—the accumulated funds will not have the same purchasing power as today's dollars.

Any wage-earning person under age seventy-and-a-half can establish an I.R.A. and, for a non-wage-earning spouse, a spousal I.R.A., even if he participates in an employer-sponsored retirement plan or tax-sheltered annuity plan. Earned income includes wages, tips, commissions, and self-employment income. It does not include income from interest, dividends, or property.

The maximum allowable deduction each year is $2,000 for an individual I.R.A. and another $250 for a spousal I.R.A. for a nonworking spouse. This total of $2,250 can generally be divided between two I.R.A.s in any manner, as long as no more than $2,000 goes into one account. Deposits in either or both accounts can be made up to the time a federal income tax return is due for the previous year, which for most people means on or before April 15.

You may, of course, contribute less than the maximum amount, although some types of investments require a minimum payment. But if you earn less than $2,000 in a given year, your contribution to an I.R.A. and corresponding income tax deduction can be no larger than your earnings. Contributions are voluntary and therefore can be made in whichever years you desire.

You can deduct your I.R.A. contribution even if you do not itemize deductions on your return. Any contribution in excess of the allowable amount is subject to a nondeductible excise tax of 6 percent, but this penalty can be avoided by withdrawing the excess plus the interest it earned before the due date for filing the return.

Withdrawals from an I.R.A. may begin between the ages of fifty-nine-and-a-half and seventy-and-a-half. If you dip into your I.R.A. account prior to age fifty-nine-and-a-half, a penalty tax of 10 percent on the amount withdrawn will be imposed, except for disability or withdrawals as a life annuity. Your beneficiaries can, however, obtain the funds without penalty if you die. Distribution, according to a formula, must start no later than the end of the year in which you reach seventy-and-a-half.

An advantage to keeping as much as possible in your I.R.A. as long as possible is that the balance which has not been withdrawn continues to grow on a tax-deferred basis. Once payments start, they are taxed as ordinary income as they are received. Unless you need all the money immediately, you probably should stretch withdrawals out over a number of years, with the maximum number of years determined by your life expectancy, that of your spouse, or your joint life expectancies, according to tables provided by the Internal Revenue Service.

I.R.A.s are best for those in a relatively high tax bracket who expect this tax rate to fall significantly after retirement. But the conventional wisdom that tax rates for all employees will be lower after retirement is not always true. For some executives, professionals, and others, their taxable income from retirement plans, savings, investments, and other sources can keep them in the same, or even a higher, tax bracket than they were in before retirement.

Investment Options

Since a variety of choices exist for putting your I.R.A. dollars to work, you should select the one appropriate to your financial situation and attitude toward risk. Among the variables to consider are whether you want the funds to be professionally managed and what fees you are willing to pay for such management. The only collectibles permitted for I.R.A.'s are U.S. gold and silver coins. The kinds of institutions that offer I.R.A.s, and are legally considered trustees of your account, include:

Banks, Savings and Loan Associations, and Credit Unions. At these institutions, I.R.A. purchasers can obtain certificates of deposit with a wide range of maturities. In addition, regular money market deposit accounts and savings accounts are available for I.R.A.s. Accounts in all those categories are insured for up to $100,000 by an agency of the federal government.

Relatively few depository institutions charge annual maintenance or management fees on I.R.A. deposits. However, early withdrawal penalties may be imposed by the institution if your I.R.A. is in a CD that has not yet matured.

Brokerage Firms. Most brokerage firms provide two types of I.R.A.s, self-directed accounts or mutual fund plans. Self-directed accounts let you buy and sell securities or even make less well-known investments like zero-coupon bonds as you see fit or as recommended by the broker. There is likely to be an initial charge of $10 to $50 to open the account and an annual maintenance fee of $20 to more than $100, in addition to the regular brokerage commissions.

Brokerage concerns also sell mutual funds to their I.R.A. customers. Here, too, there are initial and annual fees for such accounts, as well as sales commissions for purchasing the mutual fund shares.

Insurance Companies. The version of I.R.A.s sold by insurance companies is called individual retirement annuities. Such annuity contracts are guaranteed by the insurer to provide you or your beneficiary with a fixed amount of retirement income annually. This income, per $1,000 invested, is based on average life expectancies, in addition to the value of the securities bought with the insurance premiums. A drawback, though, is that since annuities already enjoy a tax-deferred buildup, putting them in an I.R.A. may well be redundant.

The two kinds of individual retirement annuities are fixed-premium and variable-premium. Both normally have annual administrative and management fees, but the fixed-premium annuities typically have a "front-end" load or sales charge of 8 to 8¾ percent of the investment, deducted from the amount initially deposited, and no company penalty for early withdrawal of the funds. Variable-premium annuities usually are "back-end" loaded, with no initial charge to open the account, but with a penalty of, say, 7 percent for withdrawing money in the first year and a declining penalty scale that disappears entirely somewhere between the seventh to the eleventh year. The annual maintenance fee for a front-end vehicle may be as low as $8, while the annual fee for a back-end product might be $25 or $30.

Mutual Funds. Many mutual fund groups, or "families," offer different funds to I.R.A holders on a "no-load," or no-sales charge, basis. These families, which often encompass separate funds specializing in stocks, corporate bonds, municipal bonds, Treasury securities, and money market securities, often give participants the ability to switch by phone or mail from one fund to another without charge or at a minimum fee. With "load" funds, you pay a sales commission on the amount of the investment. There generally is an annual management fee for I.R.A.s at mutual fund organizations. At most funds, that charge will probably be no more than $10.

Transferring I.R.A.s

You are permitted by the Internal Revenue Service to change trustees of an I.R.A. as often as desired, as long as you do not receive the funds yourself and transmit them elsewhere. The money must be transferred directly from your account at one institution to your account at another. As a practical matter, though, the institution losing the business may drag its feet and not rush to complete the transaction without your prodding.

The one exception to the trustee-to-trustee transfer requirement is a once-a-year right to personally withdraw your I.R.A. funds and deliver them to another institution. You are also allowed to retain these funds for sixty days prior to rolling them over into a new I.R.A. account. If you keep part of this money and transmit the other part to an I.R.A., your penalty, if any, and the tax are imposed only on the portion that is not rolled over.

What this means is that nothing in an I.R.A. investment is forever. You have broad-scale flexibility, with the opportunity to reinvest in another I.R.A. if and when market conditions change. Each contribution to an I.R.A. is independent of any other, so that you can invest in many different plans if you choose, within the $2,000-a-year limitation.

KEOGH PLANS

Keogh plans are tax-deferred retirement plans for the self-employed. Although the formal name for this program is the Self-Employed Individuals Retirement Act, or H.R. 10, it is widely known by the name of Eugene J. Keogh, a former New York representative, who introduced legislation to create such

plans providing for withdrawals starting between ages fifty-nine-
and-a-half to seventy-and-a-half and finally saw them authorized
by Congress in 1962.

The initial Keogh plan concept was for a limited retirement
plan, but it has since grown to represent an important financial
planning tool. It applies not only to those fully self-employed,
but also to those with self-employment earnings on the side, such
as freelancers or moonlighters. Those who have Keogh plans,
moreover, can also maintain I.R.A.s if they can afford to contribute to both.

At first, the contribution to a Keogh was restricted to the lesser
of $2,500 or 10 percent of earned income. In addition, the fed-
eral income tax deduction was limited to half of the amount of
the contribution. But many changes have taken place since then
to make this program more attractive to the public.

Contributions were made fully deductible in 1966. In 1974
the contribution limit was raised to $7,500 or 15 percent of
earned income, and in 1981 the dollar limit was increased further
to $15,000. Starting in 1984, the limits were changed to the lesser
of 25 percent of earned income, or $30,000.

The 1984 changes, authorized by the Tax Equity and Fiscal
Responsibility Act of 1982, marked an attempt to eliminate for
the first time the distinctions in the tax law between self-employed
and corporate retirement plans. Parity has largely been achieved
by making the regulations for self-employed plans more liberal,
called "parity up," while the regulations for corporate plans have
been made more restrictive, or "parity down."

Another major change affecting Keogh plans in the 1982 law
altered the definition of earned income. Starting in 1984, the
amount of a self-employed person's earned income was reduced
by his deductible contributions to a Keogh or other qualified
retirement plan. For instance, if a person earns $10,000 from
freelance work, his contributions to a Keogh plan can total
$2,000, rather than $2,500, because $2,000 equals 25 percent of
earned income of $8,000, as defined by the law.

If you have a business, no matter how small, and use your

income from that business to fund a Keogh plan, all of your employees must also be in the plan. Thus you have to contribute to their accounts at the same rate you do for yourself.

Like I.R.A.'s, Keogh plans also limit distributions to a five-year income averaging calculation. A major difference between the two, however, is that an I.R.A. can be established at any time up until April 15 of the following year, when your return is due, but Keoghs must be set up by December 31 of the year in which the tax deduction is taken, even though your payments to the plan are not required until the following April.

Keogh plan funds can be invested in any institution where I.R.A. money can be deposited. The changes in 1984, however, permit individuals to become their own trustee or to use an independent trustee for these accounts, rather than requiring the trustee to be the institution where the funds are located.

Chapter Twenty

Wills, Trusts, and Estate Planning

JUSTICE OLIVER WENDELL HOLMES OF the United States Supreme Court bequeathed almost two-thirds of his $350,000 estate to the federal government. President Franklin Delano Roosevelt placed a stipulation in his will that Missy LeHand, his secretary and intimate, be reimbursed by his estate for all of her medical expenses. Mrs. Sylvia Ann Howland Green, a New York millionairess, named in her will ten distant relatives as recipients of $100,000 each, all of whom were unaware of this largesse.

Although the extraordinary provisions of wills like these often make headlines, most Americans are not faced with anything as complex or as glamorous. Yet tens of millions of individuals probably have wills, millions probably have established trusts in one form or another, and everyone should have some form of estate plan to provide for beneficiaries. Therefore the concept of these legal and extra-legal arrangements ought to be comprehended by every adult who is in a position to bequeath assets or to receive them.

In these matters, especially in the formal preparation of a will or trust, the services of a lawyer are usually required. Understanding by a lay person of the necessity of proper planning is

297

one thing, while the proper follow-through by a professional who knows the potential pitfalls is quite another.

WILLS

A will, or last will and testament, is an expression of a person's intention about the specific distribution of the property he controls at the time of his death. It describes, in greater or lesser detail, to whom this estate should go and what conditions, if any, should be placed on the bequests, or property given in a will. Because it is alterable during the lifetime of its maker, a will can be revoked or changed at any time. One way of changing it is by codicil—a supplement written later that adds to, modifies, or partially revokes sections of the will.

The disposition of a person's property after his death through a will is one of the oldest transactions on record. Wills were written and witnessed on papyrus and clay tablets as long ago as 2000 B.C., while the Code of Hammurabi, promulgated about two centuries later, permitted a father to leave the bulk of his property to his son. By A.D. 1200, England had both church courts that directed the disposition of individuals' personal property according to a written "testament" and king's courts that decided on the disposition of real property according to a written "will." This dual structure led to the development of the words "last will and testament" to describe the formal document.

Each will should be long enough, clear enough, and explicit enough to say what the particular maker, called the testator when it is a man and the testatrix when it is a woman, intends to say. Trust and estate lawyers sometimes refer to this concept with the maxim that "no will has a brother." The bottom line in cases involving an ambiguously worded will is that the intent of the maker serves as the governing factor in interpreting and carrying out its provisions, rather than any past court interpretations of other wills with superficially similar language.

A will is necessary to dispose of property that is not jointly owned or does not have a named beneficiary. Furthermore, a guardian for your children can be appointed in a will, while the possibility of unintended beneficiaries can be minimized, if not eliminated, with such a document.

A will is composed, of course, of many clauses, depending on the needs of the individual and the requirements of the state in which he lives. However, one clause should not be missing from any will of a married person who is the owner of most of the family wealth: a simultaneous death provision applying to an accident in which the husband and wife both die at the same time. Without such a provision specifying the presumption in a common disaster that the wealthier spouse was survived by the less wealthy spouse, the tax benefit of the marital deduction would be entirely lost.

Forgery is a threat to the integrity of a will, so it is important to take whatever steps are necessary to ensure that no substitutions are made by others. Among the basics are: have the will typed on just one typewriter, avoid erasures and corrections of names or figures, and do not leave too much room at the bottom or sides of a page where unauthorized material can be inserted. Although the chances of a forged will are remote in most cases, precautions like these make them even more so.

After a will has been prepared, it should be executed by the maker signing the papers in the presence of witnesses. The witnesses do not have to read the will, since they are certifying only that they saw the testator place his signature on a document which he stated to be his last will and testament. Most states require two witnesses, although some require three or more. When choosing witnesses, try to find men and women who are younger than you, since they probably will outlive you and therefore will be able to authenticate their signatures if necessary. As a general rule, don't use beneficiaries as witnesses, because they could lose their legacies.

Following a person's death, his estate must be probated. The word "probate" refers to the filing of a will in the appropriate local court for authentication. Probate is the necessary first step in the orderly passing of assets to heirs by the terms of a will.

Once a probate judge is convinced that the will had been drawn up and signed by the maker as required by law, he issues letters testamentary, which approve the executor named in the will and allow him to act on behalf of the estate. Essentially, the court must provide its imprimatur. After that action has been taken, the estate can be distributed to the beneficiaries, a process that is usually completed within a year, but sometimes may continue for as long as three years because of the time needed to determine the estate or inheritance taxes that are due.

A periodic review of your will should be undertaken at least every two to three years. When there are marriages, divorces, births, adoptions, deaths, substantial changes in personal wealth, important developments in state and federal laws, or special circumstances in your family, even more frequent reviews are in order.

Purpose of a Will

A will is a means of helping you dispose of your assets after death exactly as you desire, with the fewest possible taxes and other costs. If you die intestate—the legal term for dying without a valid will—your estate will be distributed by a court-appointed administrator or administratrix in accordance with the state law of succession. And this law may differ from your wishes in both substance and detail.

In addition to the danger of having your intentions thwarted by intestacy, your estate is also likely to have additional expenses. Every state has its own laws governing intestate succession in the event of death without a will, but there are two broad categories in this regard: common law states and community property states.

Forty-two states have intestate laws based on the historical background of British common law. Their common denominator is that they specifically note the financial obligations individuals have to their surviving spouse, children, parents, and others. A husband or wife who is bequeathed less than would have been received in intestacy can usually assert the right of election to request the higher amount.

For example, in New York—a common law state—the section of the Estates, Powers, and Trust Law dealing with intestacy grants a surviving husband or wife $4,000 plus one half of the remaining assets if the couple had one child and one third if there were more than one. The rest of the estate goes to the child or children. If there are no children but a parent or parents of the deceased still live, the surviving husband or wife could receive $25,000 and half of the residue, while the parent or parents would get the rest.

In the eight community property states—Arizona, California, Idaho, Louisiana, Nevada, New Mexico, Texas, and Washington—assets acquired by a couple during their marriage are generally deemed to be owned one-half by each spouse during their joint lives. The exceptions are real or personal property obtained through gifts, inheritance, or personal injury compensation.

California's Probate Code, for instance, provides that without a will, the surviving spouse gets all of this community property. Transient employees who are transferred to a community property state after living in a common law state may therefore be subject to the laws of different jurisdictions for different parts of their assets.

Death Taxes

Death taxes follow quickly after death, although a properly drawn will can minimize the bite. One of the basic types of death taxes are estate taxes, levied by the federal government and some states, which are based on the size of the total estate. Other states have inheritance taxes, whereby the different rates of tax that are levied depend on the relationship of the beneficiaries to the decedent.

The federal estate tax is a progressive tax; the larger the estate, the higher the tax rate. In 1984 the lowest effective tax rate was 34 percent of the estate and the highest was 55 percent. But by 1986, according to federal tax legislation, the lowest effective rate was 37 percent and the highest was 50 percent.

These rates, though, apply only to estates with a value that exceeds a specified amount. On the basis of a "unified credit" of $96,300 allowed for federal estate and gift tax purposes, the equivalent amount of estate assets exempt from federal estate tax in 1984 was $325,000. This exemption equivalent figure grew until the maximum amount of $600,000 was reached in 1987, based on a credit of $192,800.

In addition to this exempt amount, there is also a 100 percent marital deduction. This provision of the tax law allows a married person to pass an estate to a spouse without paying any federal estate tax at all. In most states, one spouse cannot disinherit the other unless they have provided otherwise through a prenuptial

Unified Credit for Estate and Gift Taxes

Year	Amount of Credit	Amount of Exemption Equivalent
1977	$ 30,000	$120,667
1978	34,000	134,000
1979	38,000	147,333
1980	42,500	161,563
1981	47,000	175,625
1982	62,800	225,000
1983	79,300	275,000
1984	96,300	325,000
1985	121,800	400,000
1986	155,800	500,000
1987 and thereafter	192,800	600,000

Source: Internal Revenue Code

agreement. Of course, whatever is left at the spouse's later death will be subject to taxes in her own estate.

State inheritance taxes vary widely, depending on the state, the size of the bequest, and the relationship between the deceased and the beneficiary. Typically, tax rates increase with the size of the inheritance and start at a higher percentage as the degree of kinship becomes more distant. Furthermore, some states exempt certain kinds of property from inheritance taxation, such as life insurance proceeds, joint bank accounts, and the family home.

As an example, in New Jersey a spouse can be left only $100,000 free from inheritance taxes and a child only $20,000. A New Jersey estate amounting to $300,000, even though it is too small to be affected by the federal estate tax, would nevertheless receive an inheritance tax bill from the state.

A combination of the federal and state levies is thus necessary to compute the total tax likely to be due on your estate. A sample of the formula used to calculate federal and New York State taxes on estates of American citizens dying after 1984 is:

Federal and New York Estate Taxes for Estates of U.S. Citizens Dying After 1984

Taxable Estate $	Federal Estate Tax and Rate on Next Block $	%	Maximum Credit for State Inheritance Tax and Rate on Next Block $	%	Federal Estate Tax Less Maximum Credit Before Unified Credit and Rate on Next Block $	%	New York Estate Tax and Rate on Next Block $	%
10,000	1,800	20			1,800	20.0	200	2
20,000	3,800	22			3,800	22.0	400	2
40,000	8,200	24			8,200	24.0	800	2
50,000	10,600	24			10,600	24.0	1,000	3
60,000	13,000	26			13,000	26.0	1,300	3
80,000	18,200	28			18,200	28.0	1,900	3
100,000	23,800	30		.8	23,800	29.2	2,500	3
150,000	38,800	32	400	1.6	38,400	30.4	4,000	4
200,000	54,800	32	1,200	2.4	53,600	29.6	6,000	4
250,000	70,800	34	2,400	2.4	68,400	31.6	8,000	4
300,000	87,800	34	3,600	3.2	84,200	30.8	10,000	5
500,000	155,800	37	10,000	4.0	145,800	33.0	20,000	6
700,000	229,800	37	18,000	4.8	211,800	32.2	32,000	7
750,000	248,300	39	20,400	4.8	227,900	34.2	35,500	7
900,000	306,800	39	27,600	5.6	279,200	33.4	46,000	8
1,000,000	345,800	41	33,200	5.6	312,600	35.4	54,000	8
1,100,000	386,800	41	38,800	6.4	348,000	34.6	62,000	9
1,250,000	448,300	43	48,400	6.4	399,900	36.6	75,500	9
1,500,000	555,800	45	64,400	6.4	491,400	38.6	98,000	9
1,600,000	600,800	45	70,800	7.2	530,000	37.8	107,000	10
2,000,000	780,800	49	99,600	7.2	681,200	41.8	147,000	10
2,100,000	829,800	49	106,800	8.0	723,000	41.0	157,000	11
2,500,000	1,025,800	50	138,800	8.0	887,000	42.0	201,000	11
2,600,000	1,075,800	50	146,800	8.8	929,000	41.2	212,000	12
3,000,000	1,275,800	50	182,000	8.8	1,093,800	41.2	260,000	12
3,100,000	1,325,800	50	190,800	9.6	1,135,000	40.4	272,000	13
3,500,000	1,525,800	50	229,200	9.6	1,296,600	40.4	324,000	13
3,600,000	1,575,800	50	238,800	10.4	1,337,000	39.6	337,000	14
4,000,000	1,775,800	50	280,400	10.4	1,495,400	39.6	393,000	14
4,100,000	1,825,800	50	290,800	11.2	1,535,000	38.8	407,000	15

304 PLANNING FOR THE FUTURE

Federal and New York Estate Taxes for Estates of U.S. Citizens Dying After 1984 *(cont'd)*

Taxable Estate $	Federal Estate Tax and Rate on Next Block $	%	Maximum Credit for State Inheritance Tax and Rate on Next Block $	%	Federal Estate Tax Less Maximum Credit Before Unified Credit and Rate on Next Block $	%	New York Estate Tax and Rate on Next Block $	%
4,500,000	2,025,800	50	335,600	11.2	1,690,200	38.8	467,000	15
5,000,000	2,275,800	50	391,600	11.2	1,884,200	38.8	542,000	15
5,100,000	2,325,800	50	402,800	12.0	1,923,000	38.0	557,000	16
6,100,000	2,825,800	50	522,800	12.8	2,303,000	37.2	717,000	17
7,100,000	3,325,800	50	650,800	13.6	2,675,000	36.4	887,000	18
8,100,000	3,825,800	50	786,800	14.4	3,039,000	35.6	1,067,000	19
9,100,000	4,325,800	50	930,800	15.2	3,395,000	34.8	1,257,000	20
10,100,000	4,825,800	50	1,082,800	16.0	3,743,000	34.0	1,457,000	21

Unified Credit in 1985 is $121,800.
Unified Credit in 1986 is $155,800.
Unified Credit in 1987 and thereafter is $192,800.
Source: Internal Revenue Code and New York State Tax Laws

Executors

A key consideration in the process of drafting a will is the appointment of an executor or executrix. The executor is responsible for gathering together the testator's assets, paying any outstanding bills, paying the death taxes and then distributing the assets according to the testator's wishes, in the process coping with all of the arrangements affecting estate management.

In naming an executor, you can select either an individual—such as a spouse, other family member, friend, or lawyer—or a corporation—such as a bank or trust company. Some people appoint one in each of these categories to obtain the advantage of a personal approach by a trusted individual, as well as the continuity and knowledge of a professional organization.

Family members, particularly if they are beneficiaries, often waive their executor fee, which are established by a commission schedule fixed—depending on the state—either by law or by the local probate court. Such fees are payable only once during the administration of an estate. For example, in New York, the statutory schedule calls for payments based on the gross value of the estate, including its income. The fee is 5 percent for $100,000 or less; 4 percent for the next $200,000; 3 percent for the next $700,000; 2½ percent for the next $4 million; and 2 percent on the excess over $5 million.

Coexecutors in New York are entitled to a full commission each on estates of at least $300,000, unless there are more than three executors. Only two full commissions are allowed on estates between $100,000 and $300,000, and only one full commission on estates below $100,000.

In California, the statutory fees for executors are different. Executors there are entitled to 4 percent of the first $15,000, 3 percent of the next $85,000, 2 percent of the next $900,000, and 1 percent of the excess over $1 million. However, executors in the state are permitted to apply for an additional allowance for extraordinary services.

TRUSTS

Although trusts are associated with wills in the minds of many people, there are other kinds of trusts as well. As more and more individuals amass larger funds, even though the money may not be worth what it was when first received, the use of trusts as a device to hold, invest, conserve, or bequeath their assets is likely to increase, too.

A trust is created when the owner of property transfers its legal title to a trustee—an individual, bank, or corporation—to manage for the benefit of another person. This concept dates back to antiquity and was part of the English common law in the Middle Ages.

There are basically two types of trusts, testamentary trusts and living trusts. Although the establishment of a trust sometimes has many tax advantages, saving on taxes is not the only reason for creating one.

Testamentary Trusts

Testamentary trusts are created in the will of the grantor and become effective only upon his death. They are useful in maximizing the assets of an estate, obtaining professional money management, and assisting heirs who lack the necessary financial acumen.

Trustees of such trusts are paid, depending upon the state in which the testator resides, either according to a schedule established by state law or by court allowance. For instance, the Hawaii trustee schedule has two parts, in keeping with the laws of the state. The trustee's fee on the income from the trust is 7 percent of the first $5,000 and 5 percent of the excess. His fee on the principal is 4 percent of the first $15,000, 3 percent of the next $85,000, 2 percent of the next $900,000, 1½ percent of the next $2 million, and 1 percent of the excess above $3 million. Trustees may also request an additional allowance for extraordinary services.

With property in a testamentary trust, by definition, passing through probate, more than a year could pass before the process is completed. Furthermore, legal fees during this period could also be substantial.

But on the plus side, assets in certain trusts will not be subject to federal estate taxes if a spouse is the beneficiary or if the total amount of the estate is worth less than a specified limit. The reason is that an unlimited amount can be left tax-free via the 100 percent marital deduction to a spouse, and a specific amount that has risen annually until reaching $600,000 in 1987 can be left tax-free to other persons. Through trusts, further taxes can be saved at the spouse's later death.

Take a situation in which a husband who died in 1984 had $650,000 in his estate. He could leave the entire amount to his wife tax-free, but if she also died that year, her estate would be taxed for the amount above her own $325,000 credit equivalent. If his will, however, provided that his wife receive a $325,000 bequest and that the other half be placed in trust for her lifetime benefit, there would be no taxes at the husband's death and the trust would not be part of the wife's taxable estate at her demise.

Since the $325,000 bequest would be offset by her own credit equivalent, the full $650,000 would thereby pass to their descendants without the payment of any estate taxes.

Until 1982, an individual was not permitted to leave assets in trust for a spouse while taking the marital deduction without granting the surviving spouse the absolute right to distribute these assets by her will in any way the surviving spouse desired. Since then, a new type of terminable interest property trust, popularly referred to as a "QTIP Trust," has been authorized to qualify for the marital deduction. With this kind of properly structured trust, your spouse can obtain the income for life, and at her death the assets will be distributed according to your wishes in your testamentary instructions.

Living Trusts

Trusts established and made effective during the grantor's lifetime are called living, or inter-vivos, trusts. Such trusts can either be irrevocable or revocable, depending on the needs of the creator or beneficiaries of the trust.

The best known and most widely used of the irrevocable trusts are Clifford Trusts, a classic income-shifting device whose name is derived from a case involving some of the legal principles concerning these transfer arrangements. The major function of a Clifford Trust, a short-term reversionary trust, is to divert income from the grantor, who is usually in a relatively high federal income tax bracket, to someone else in the family, who is usually in a relatively low bracket.

However, the use of Clifford trusts, as well as other similar grantor trusts, like spousal remainder trusts, was sharply restricted by a provision of the Tax Reform Act of 1986. All income from such trusts established after March 1, 1986, is now taxed to the grantor, or creator, not to the child or other beneficiary.

Clifford Trusts set up before that date, though, are still taxed as they were before passage of the 1986 law—in the tax bracket of the lower-income beneficiary. But if that beneficiary is a child of the grantor and under the age of 14, the income tax would again be based on the grantor's bracket.

That's because another provision of the law requires that un-earned income of a child under age 14 in excess of $1,000 be taxed at the top tax rate of the child's parents. Even if this investment income is derived from a gift from a grandparent or if the gift was made before enactment of the 1986 law, the parent's bracket is nevertheless used for determining the tax. In the past, taxes on that income was based on the child's rate.

This tax affects custodian accounts established under the Uniform Gift to Minors Act, along with other accounts established in the name of a young child. As for children over age 14, all investment income, along with wages, continues to be taxed at their tax rate.

Revocable trusts are not set up principally for tax reasons. In fact, any income earned by the trust is taxed to the grantor and the trust's assets are considered part of the grantor's estate for estate tax purposes. The justification of revocable trusts, therefore, arises from their useful functioning during the life of the grantor, as well as the situation arising after his death.

Thus with a revocable trust, your assets will be managed for your benefit while living and the trust will detail how you want to dispose of these assets at your death. Because it is revocable, it possesses all of the flexibility of a will, being amendable or cancelable by the grantor at any time. Some individuals who have an irrational fear of making a will, which refers to death, may be more willing to create a trust, which deals with both the present and the future.

A major advantage of revocable trusts when the beneficiary is not the trustee is the service these trusts provide in managing securities, real estate, cash, insurance, and other assets for individuals unable or unwilling to devote the time required for this matter. Another benefit is that these trusts can protect their creators against the improvidence of others.

In addition, revocable trusts escape probate, since the assets go directly to the beneficiaries after the death of the grantor. As a result, the delays of probate so common with testamentary trusts are avoided.

Like other trusts, revocable trusts are sometimes criticized for maintaining too extensive a control over the way of life of beneficiaries. But unlike the others, revocable trusts can be revoked by a grantor who determines at a certain point that such control is no longer necessary. Of course, a revocable trust becomes irrevocable after your death.

ESTATE PLANNING

Many people believe that estate planning ends at the death of the testator, but this is not necessarily true. Further planning can be undertaken by the executor and beneficiaries of the deceased, particularly in the area of taxes.

After-death planning involves all of the opportunities that the executor or beneficiaries can take advantage of after the testator dies. Despite the size of the tax savings that might otherwise be realized, the best interests of the heirs should be the primary motivation in the overall construction of such a plan.

Decedent's Final Income Tax Return

Regardless of the date of death, a decedent's final income tax return is due by April 15 of the following year. Among the decisions that the executor must make is whether it is most beneficial to file a joint return with the decedent's surviving spouse or whether to file a separate return.

If the decedent has a substantial capital loss or net operating loss, a joint return may prove to be useful because these carryforwards end at death and would be lost otherwise. Remember, though, that consenting to a joint return also makes both the estate of the decedent and the surviving spouse liable for the tax indicated on that return.

In most situations, income and deductions on the decedent's final income tax return are reported on a cash basis, just as was the case for prior returns. As a result, only funds actually received and deductions actually paid before death would be reported on the form.

But there may be some exceptions to this procedure. An executor can deduct medical expenses paid by the estate within a year of death on either the final income tax return or the estate tax return. The choice is usually based on where the deduction would be most meaningful—taking into account the 7½ percent of adjusted gross income floor for medical expenses on the income tax return and the charitable, marital, and other deductions on the estate tax return.

If there is little income to offset the available deductions when an executor files the decedent's final income tax return, the desired goal of accelerating income can be accomplished by including the accrued interest on Series E and EE savings bonds owned by the decedent.

Disclaimers

With the benefit of perfect hindsight, an executor can find improvements that should have been made in a will or faults in the document that were not previously apparent. If the heirs are willing, these problems may be remedied by a "qualified disclaimer," which provides an opportunity for property to pass to someone other than the one who had been designated by the decedent. Its purpose is normally to minimize income, gift, or estate taxes.

A qualified disclaimer is an irrevocable refusal by an individual to accept an inheritance. It must be made within nine months after death and before that individual has accepted any property from the estate. Moreover, the disclaimer must be written and the assets must go to another person without any direction from the person doing the disclaiming.

The effect of such a disclaimer is to treat the person disclaiming as though he had died prior to the decedent. Thus the assets would go to the next person or persons in line as listed in the will. If no such provision is in the will, then the property would pass according to the appropriate state law.

For instance, if a person leaves his entire estate to a spouse who is wealthy in her own right, that spouse might disclaim the assets—which would then pass to their children, who are likely to be in a lower tax bracket. Sometimes successive disclaimers are necessary to achieve the objective, such as when the children themselves are in a high tax bracket and disclaim the property so that it will be inherited by the grandchildren.

Index